Contents

"Programs must be written for people to read, and only incidentally for machines to execute."

— Harold Abelson

1. Unveiling the Mystique of Linux: A Prelude to Discoveries

In the ever-evolving realm of technology, few subjects gleam with the innovation and intrigue akin to the Linux operating system. A beguiling labyrinth that has enchanted, and at times confounded, minds of tech enthusiasts, researchers, and developers alike, Linux is more than just software—it's a legacy. Whether discovered through its sprawling servers, dazzling desktops, or innovative device infrastructure, Linux is a tapestry of code, culture, and curiosity. Despite the cloak of technical jargon, at its core, Linux embodies a philosophy of collaboration and freedom that beckons the inquisitive spirit to explore deeper.

Join me, Diane B. Brown, as we embark on an explosive journey through the hidden alleys of Linux trivia, where each fragment of myth and fact intertwines to tell the grand tale of an operating system that changed the course of technology. We'll delve into the historical roots sprouting from Linus Torvalds' ambitious vision, traverse the technological evolutions that revolutionized the industry, and bash through the myths clouding Linux's true essence.

With each page, expect to dissolve misconceptions and illuminate the lesser-known facets of Linux. Whether you're a seasoned system administrator or a curious newcomer, there's a treasure trove of knowledge awaiting within these covers. Buckle up for an enthralling expedition where insight meets intrigue, as we traverse the nuances of this remarkable technology.

2. The Roots of Revolution: Birth of Linux

2.1. Linus Torvalds' Vision

Linus Torvalds' vision for the future of computing began as a spark in a university setting, where a deep-seated frustration would soon manifest into one of the most significant developments in the history of technology. In the early 1990s, while pursuing his master's degree at the University of Helsinki, he was dissatisfied with the proprietary operating systems available at the time. He believed that software should be an open playground, where anyone could not only use but also modify it. This ethos formed the foundation of Linux, rooted in his understanding that collaboration would lead to greater advancements than any single entity could achieve.

The conception of the Linux kernel was driven by a simple yet profound desire: the pursuit of a truly free operating system that anyone could use, change, and share. At the time, Torvalds was an admirer of the MINIX operating system, which was used for educational purposes about UNIX, yet he found its restrictions limiting. Rather than conforming to what was available, he envisioned a system that transcended boundaries, fostering a collective experience among its users. It wasn't about creating an industry behemoth or a commercially viable product; it was about empowerment through technology. This motivated Torvalds to code Linux, initially as a project that might serve him personally, but soon it grew into much more.

With the release of the first version of the Linux kernel in 1991, he invited others to join him. He famously posted on the comp.os.minix newsgroup, announcing the kernel and encouraging developers to contribute. Torvalds' open invitation exemplified his belief that the best innovations come from diverse contributions rather than from isolated visionaries. This groundbreaking decision marked the dawn of a community-centric approach to building software, leading to rapid improvements and widespread adoption.

What truly set Torvalds' vision apart was his commitment to the tenets of open source software. He recognized that code should not be treated as a luxury, but rather as a shared asset that fuels collective creativity and collaboration. The defining moment for Linux was not merely the kernel itself but the robust community that grew around it, one in which individuals from different backgrounds and skill levels could connect, collaborate, and flourish. In nurturing this communal spirit, Torvalds inadvertently established a model for software development that would ripple outward, influencing countless projects and organizations.

Torvalds' approach to leadership also evolved in tandem with his vision. He adopted the mantra of maintaining a 'benevolent dictator' stance—a role that allowed him to guide the project while empowering others. By keeping the decision-making centralized but inclusive, he was able to balance contributions from a myriad of developers while ensuring the overall vision remained intact. Throughout the years, this governance model has proven effective in scaling the project without sacrificing its core ideals, allowing Linux to thrive and expand into countless distributions tailored for a vast array of needs and users.

Linus Torvalds also embraced transparency as a key factor in fostering the Linux community. He encouraged open discussions around code, design decisions, and project iterations. This resulted in a vibrant ecosystem where any developer could exchange ideas, propose changes, or critique existing features. Through mailing lists, such as linux-kernel, he engaged with fellow developers, welcoming feedback while simultaneously demanding high standards for code quality and performance. This iterative process mirrored the scientific method, where testing, analysis, and peer review contributed to refining the kernel and solidifying Linux's reputation as a robust operating system.

As Linux gained traction, it became a testament to the power of collective leadership and shared knowledge. The vision Torvalds set in motion emphasized that greatness was achievable when diverse perspectives converged toward a singular goal. Organizations began to take notice, understanding that Linux's flexibility and rapid iteration allowed for innovation in various fields—from web servers to supercomputers.

Furthermore, Torvalds' vision was not just about the technical aspects; it reflected a wider philosophy regarding user rights and software freedom. This was echoed in the ethos of the Free Software Foundation, which championed the belief that software should be free to use, modify, and distribute without restrictions. Linus Torvalds aligned closely with these ideals; however, he focused more narrowly on the practicality and functionality of software—an approach that allowed him to garner support from both technical and non-technical communities.

Linus Torvalds' vision transformed a personal project into a global movement that emphasized openness, collaboration, and innovation. While the world was watching him lead, what emerged was not just the Linux kernel but an entire culture that defied traditional software development. His philosophy has left an indelible mark on technology, one that continues to inspire future generations of developers and technologists in their quests for creating a more open and interconnected digital world.

Today, that vision continues to resonate on multiple fronts. Whether through the expansive growth of the Linux ecosystem or the movement towards other open source technologies, Linus Torvalds' belief in the power of community not only altered the landscape of computing but also emboldened individuals worldwide to contribute their knowledge and creativity, pushing the boundaries of what technology can achieve. The legacy of his vision serves as a reminder that in collaboration lies the potential for unprecedented innovation—one that transcends beyond the lines of code and into the very fabric of our technological society.

2.2. A Leap from Academia to Global Stages

The remarkable journey of Linux from a humble academic project to a global phenomenon stands as a testament to the power of open-source collaboration and innovation. At its inception, Linux was merely an idea sparked by Linus Torvalds during his time at the University of Helsinki, but it quickly transcended the boundaries of academia, captivating developers, enterprises, and tech enthusiasts around the world.

When Torvalds released the first version of the Linux kernel in 1991, he catalyzed a movement that would revolutionize the software landscape. His initial approach, characterized by an openness and invitation for collaboration, resonated with a growing discontent among technologists regarding proprietary systems that were seen as restrictive and stifling to innovation. This dissatisfaction, coupled with Torvalds' vision for a freely usable and modifiable operating system, planted the seeds for a grassroots revolution that would gain momentum and evolve at an unprecedented rate.

As the years progressed, Linux transitioned from being a university project to an extensive open-source ecosystem embraced by a multitude of contributors. The momentum was bolstered through online forums and newsgroups, where engineers, students, and hobbyists converged to share ideas, code, and support. The collaborative nature of these platforms made it possible for anyone with an interest and skill to participate, democratizing software development in a way that had previously been unheard of.

This collective engagement created a vibrant community that contributed not just to the kernel itself but also to the myriad of distributions that now dominate the Linux landscape. Each contributor brought unique perspectives and expertise, enhancing the overall development and innovation processes. The communal effort transformed Linux into a comprehensive and versatile operating system, able to cater to a diverse range of applications—from personal computing to enterprise solutions.

One can also argue that the distinct governance model employed by Linus Torvalds played a crucial role in steering Linux toward global relevance. By adopting a 'benevolent dictator' approach, Torvalds could facilitate growth while maintaining focus on the project's core principles. This balancing act ensured that the project benefited from widespread input without losing its original vision. Contributors could suggest changes or improvements, ultimately leading to a refined and robust system, while Torvalds stepped in to keep the project on track and aligned with its overarching ethos.

Furthermore, the expansion of Linux into the corporate domain underscored its transformative potential. Major companies like IBM, Google, and Red Hat recognized Linux's adaptability and cost-effectiveness, choosing to incorporate it into their infrastructure. This endorsement from industry giants bolstered Linux's credibility, further attracting developers and organizations eager to leverage its open-source nature for their own advancements. The collaboration between influential corporations and the community highlighted the practicality of using Linux beyond personal projects, signaling a pivotal shift where academia and industry intertwined.

The significance of Linux's ascent cannot be overstated. Transitioning from classrooms into corporate offices and leading technology initiatives worldwide, Linux exemplified the capacity of open-source projects to foster innovation across both academia and industry. Its application spans diverse sectors—cloud computing, web hosting, supercomputing, and even embedded systems—all anchored in a philosophy that champions freedom, access, and communal growth.

Moreover, the reach of Linux has continued to expand into diverse geographical locales, especially in developing nations. Here, Linux provided an affordable alternative to expensive proprietary systems, empowering communities with greater access to technology. In countries where resources might be limited, Linux creates a pathway for education and technological literacy, nurturing ingenuity and opening doors to global participation in the digital economy.

Perhaps one of the most profound impacts of this journey from academic whim to worldwide utility is the mindset shift it facilitated within the tech community. No longer should innovation be confined to a select group of elite developers or major corporations; instead, it could flourish from the grassroots—where an individual's contributions count just as much as those from well-established entities. The ethos of collaboration became a norm, inspiring countless projects and communities dedicated to similar principles.

Through educational institutions, Linux has carved out a space that not only nurtures the next generation of developers but also encourages them to think critically about technology and its potential for societal advancement. The integration of Linux into academic curricula goes beyond technical skills; it fosters an understanding of collaborative practices and the notion that software is not just a product but a community-driven ecosystem.

In conclusion, the leap from academia to global stages exemplifies the profound transformation that Linux has undergone, encapsulating a dynamic journey that reshaped the perceptions of software development. The transition captures the spirit of innovation, empowerment, and collaboration that lies at the heart of Linux. As we stand at the juncture of technological evolution, it is essential to recognize and celebrate the collective legacy that has been built—one that serves as a powerful reminder that the strength of technology is best realized when shared among many, crossing borders, boundaries, and industries. Thus, Linux remains not just an operating system but a robust movement, echoing the fundamental beliefs of openness, cooperation, and the right to access and shape technology.

2.3. Open Source: The Heart of Freedom

In the vast landscape of software development, the philosophy of open source stands as a remarkable testament to the transformative power of freedom and collaboration. At its essence, open source represents an ideology that embraces the principle that software should be accessible to all—not just as a product to use, but as a shared resource that anyone can modify, improve, and distribute. This belief system fundamentally reshapes the traditional notions of proprietary software and creates an environment where innovation thrives through collective effort.

The roots of open source can be traced back to the early computing days when software was often shared freely among programmers. Information was treated as a communal asset, reflecting a culture where collaboration and knowledge sharing were paramount. Software development was regarded as a craft rather than a commercial enterprise, fostering a sense of community among developers who viewed their work as a contribution to the greater good rather than just a product to sell.

When Linus Torvalds announced the Linux kernel in 1991, he tapped into this prevailing ethos. His vision was clear: create a free operating system that anyone could use and contribute to. What set Linux apart was the invitation embedded in its creation—he openly welcomed contributions from developers around the globe. This call to action established the groundwork for a dedicated community of users and contributors who would perpetually reshape and enhance the operating system in ways no single entity could fathom.

Open source flourished not through commercial competition, but rather through collaboration. This decentralized approach enabled diverse voices and perspectives to coalesce around shared goals. Whether a hobbyist tinkering in their garage or a seasoned professional at a multinational corporation, everyone could participate in the Linux evolution, contributing code, documentation, bug fixes, and support. This rich tapestry of contributions nurtured a dynamic ecosystem where solutions to complex problems emerged collaboratively rather than being dictated from the top down.

One of the defining characteristics of the open-source movement is its foundation on transparency. The availability of source code allows developers to inspect, scrutinize, and understand the underlying mechanisms of the software they use. This visibility breeds trust, as any potential vulnerabilities or flaws can be identified and rectified by the community promptly. It is this process of collective scrutiny that helps maintain and improve the quality of open-source projects, rendering them generally more secure than their proprietary counterparts which rely on closed-door development processes.

Moreover, the ideals of open source extend to the very fabric of community-building. Developers have formed bonds over common interests, coming together to work on projects, share knowledge, and support one another. This camaraderie is especially evident in events like Linux conferences, code sprints, and online forums, where individuals from diverse backgrounds unite to tackle challenges, foster innovation, and share breakthroughs. The friendships forged in these collaborative environments often last a lifetime, resulting in vibrant networks that further propel the open-source movement.

Freedom is the heart of this philosophy. Users take the reins of their computing experience, unshackled from vendor lock-in or restrictive licensing agreements. With open-source software like Linux, individuals can design their systems to meet unique needs—choosing and configuring components without any corporate gatekeepers dictating how or when they can utilize the software. This freedom transforms technology from a commodity to a tool of empowerment.

In many parts of the world, open source acts as a vehicle for technological equity. Developing nations, often faced with the prohibitive costs of proprietary software, embrace open-source solutions like Linux to gain access to powerful tools without the financial burdens that typically accompany such resources. This democratization of technology creates opportunities for education, innovation, and social progress, allowing communities to leverage technology for their development challenges without being limited by budget constraints.

Furthermore, the open-source ethos resonates deeply within communities dedicated to human rights and advocacy. Around the globe, there are countless stories of individuals leveraging open-source technology as a means of resistance against oppressive regimes or as a vehicle for activism. Whether through creating secure communication tools, advocating for digital privacy, or promoting access to information, the ideals of open source serve as a beacon of hope and collaborative spirit in the face of adversity.

In recent years, the impact of open-source software has burgeoned beyond the realm of individual projects into encompassing entire industries. Tech giants like Google, Facebook, and Amazon not only employ open-source technologies but also actively contribute to them, recognizing the intrinsic value of collaboration and community development. This shift represents a paradigm where businesses acknowledge that open-source can provide competitive advantages, allowing them to innovate more rapidly, reduce costs, and nurture better interpersonal relationships within the tech community.

However, the journey of open source is not without its challenges. As open-source projects grow in popularity, they occasionally attract attention from commercial entities looking to profit from community-driven innovation without giving back. This tension between open-source ideals and monetary gain can lead to ethical dilemmas, spurring debates on ownership, contributions, and sustainability. The open-source community must continually engage in conversations about how best to nurture a culture of sharing while also keeping the balance with sustainability in a commercially-driven world.

As we move further into the digital age, the significance of open source cannot be overstated. It empowers individuals with the knowledge that they can shape the tools they depend on, fuels innovation by enabling vast community contributions, and affirms the belief that technology should be an inclusive endeavor. The heart of freedom beats strongly within the open-source community, where the sharing of knowledge and ideas continues to carve pathways for tech advancements that are accessible to all.

In summary, open source stands as a transformative force in the tech industry, shaping the way software is developed, utilized, and understood. It inspires collaboration, fosters innovation, and cultivates a spirit of freedom that echoes far beyond the lines of code. The success of Linux is a prime example of how embracing open-source principles can not only revitalize individual projects but can also engender a global movement united by shared values of accessibility, equity, and community spirit. In this ongoing journey, the essence of open source remains unwavering – a heartbeat that embodies the potential for humanity's collective intelligence to flourish through technology.

2.4. The Penguin Unveiled

The penguin, affectionately known as Tux, stands as a vibrant emblem of the Linux operating system, but the story of how this character became the face of one of the most impactful technologies in history is both charming and illustrative of the quirky spirit that pervades the open-source community. The journey to Tux's unveiling intertwines whimsical origins with profound significance, bridging the gap between fun and functionality. Understanding this mascot sheds light on what Linux embodies—a passionate community driven by collaboration, creativity, and freedom.

The inception of Tux traces back to 1996, when Linux's creator, Linus Torvalds, was searching for a playful yet distinctive symbol to represent his groundbreaking OS. While there were many contenders for a mascot, Tux quickly rose to prominence, largely due to its delightful and visually striking design. The credit for Tux's design goes to Larry Ewing, a graphics artist who created the first illustration of the penguin for a logo competition hosted by the Linux community. Ewing's portrayal captured the essence of Linux's approachable nature—an image that was both cute and inviting, embodying a sense of accessibility that was crucial to Torvalds' vision.

Tux the penguin was chosen not only for its quirky appearance but also because of Linus Torvalds' own fondness for penguins. Legend has it that during a visit to Australia, Torvalds had a somewhat traumatic experience involving an ill-tempered penguin which left quite an impression on him. Drawing from this encounter, the penguin became a fitting mascot—a symbol of resilience and adaptability. Tux embodied the qualities of the Linux community: open, friendly, and approachable, while also exuding a sense of tenacity that has characterized the journey of Linux itself.

As Tux gained popularity, it became more than just a mascot; it evolved into a branding element that represented the spirit of Linux and the open-source movement. The whimsical character found its way into a wealth of merchandise, including plush toys, stickers, and even video games, showcasing the lighthearted nature of the community. But beyond the merchandise, Tux became a rallying point for developers and users alike, fostering a sense of belonging among those who engaged with Linux. The penguin served as a reminder that technology could not only be powerful but fun and accessible too.

Moreover, Tux symbolizes the philosophy of open-source software: the idea that community-driven efforts yield collective benefits. Just as the penguin is a creature of resilience in the harsh conditions of the Antarctic, so too is the Linux community built on a foundation of support and encouragement, thriving in the face of challenges posed by the proprietary software landscape. Tux's presence in conferences, local meetups, and online interactions emphasizes the camaraderie among users and developers—a visible representation of an environment where contributions are welcomed and celebrated.

In addition to his playful appearance, Tux has become synonymous with the values of freedom and collaboration—the core tenets of the Linux operating system itself. The open-source ethos prioritizes the sharing of knowledge and code, fostering a culture of innovation where anyone with an idea can make an impact. Tux, as the mascot of Linux, serves as the friendly face that invites individuals from all backgrounds to engage, learn, and contribute to this ever-growing ecosystem. The penguin's enduring image communicates that Linux is not just for a select few; rather, it is for everyone who has a passion for technology.

In the broader tech landscape, Tux has transcended being merely a mascot; he has become a cultural icon representing the spirit of Linux and its community. Today, Tux appears in various forms of media, appearing in cartoons, websites, and even as an Easter egg in numerous applications, a constant reminder that the world of Linux is inclusive, collaborative, and always evolving.

In summation, the unveiling of the penguin Tux heralds an important narrative within the Linux story, where playfulness meets purpose. Tux epitomizes the essence of Linux: a platform not just driven by coding, but by people's passion and their collective contributions. As a cheerful and approachable avatar, Tux continues to motivate both newcomers and seasoned veterans alike, exemplifying the community spirit that fuels one of the most remarkable revolutions in the history of technology. As we delve deeper into the realm of Linux, it is valuable to remember that at its heart lies a rich tapestry woven from the contributions, creativity, and collaboration of everyone who proudly carries the spirit of Tux forward.

2.5. Early Challenges and Triumphs

The genesis of Linux presented a captivating narrative filled with both challenges and triumphs that characterized its early years. In the initial phase of development, Linux faced numerous hurdles that could have stifled the project's growth. Linus Torvalds, a university student with a vision of creating a free operating system, encountered not just technical difficulties but also societal skepticism about the viability of open-source development amid a predominantly closed-source software market.

One of the early challenges was the lack of widespread recognition and support for open-source principles. In a landscape where commercial operating systems like Microsoft Windows and MacOS dominated, many viewed the concept of open-source software with skepticism. Doubting whether a group of volunteer developers could rival the resources and expertise of corporate giants, the world questioned whether Linux could offer a practical alternative. Some critics argued that the amalgamation of diverse contributions could lead to an uncoordinated and chaotic development process, undermining the quality of the resulting software.

In response to skepticism, Torvalds and a small but passionate group of contributors forged ahead, laboring tirelessly to demonstrate the potential of their collective effort. Their resolve laid the groundwork for an engaging community, where users and programmers gathered to exchange ideas and solutions. They held steadfast to the belief that collaboration fostered innovation, a philosophy that would ultimately redefine software development.

Another crucial challenge faced during Linux's early journey involved compatibility issues. At the outset, the Linux kernel struggled to support numerous hardware configurations, unlike established operating systems that boasted extensive compatibility with a wide variety of devices. To mitigate these limitations, Torvalds encouraged collaboration among hardware manufacturers and developers to ensure that the kernel could run seamlessly on multiple platforms. Consequently, community members began to tackle the challenge head-on; through diligent effort, they expanded Linux's compatibility with different hardware, resulting in increased usability for users across various settings.

The process of building a functional and stable operating system involved rigorous testing, which often resulted in setbacks. Early versions of the Linux kernel contained bugs and vulnerabilities, creating roadblocks to achieving the stability that users expected. Nonetheless, each hurdle served as an opportunity for growth. Contributors continually collaborated and shared techniques for debugging and resolving issues, propelling the kernel forward. The spirit of resilience that emerged from these challenges helped establish a strong foundation for community-driven support and collaboration, which would become a hallmark of the Linux ecosystem.

As development progressed, Linux began attracting more attention and contributors, each rallying under the flag of open-source ideals. The critical milestone came in 1992 when the first officially recognized Linux distribution, early versions of Slackware and Debian, were created. These distributions not only exemplified the collaborative spirit of the community but also paved the way for various iterations that would follow—each tailored to meet specific user needs. The availability of user-friendly distributions marked a significant turning point, enhancing the accessibility of Linux for novice users and expanding its adoption rate.

Despite its triumphs, the journey was not without contention. The early Linux community grappled with philosophical disagreements regarding the nature of open-source software's freedom. Debates arose over the definition of 'free software' and how to balance the ideals of sharing with practical considerations of software sustainability. These discussions not only solidified Linux's identity but also encouraged a broader dialogue about the ethical dimensions of technology. The resolution of these debates ultimately fostered a thriving culture imbued with a commitment to collaboration, where functionality and user rights remained paramount.

Moreover, the commitment to transparency became a crucial factor in Linux's success. The open-source model encouraged users to examine the code, report problems, and suggest enhancements. This iterative process led to continuous improvements over time. Through this culture of feedback, Linux garnered a reputation for stability and reliability, which, in turn, attracted businesses and developers eager to utilize its capabilities. By presenting a compelling alternative to traditional software constructs, Linux slowly earned its place within corporate infrastructures, further proving its potential as a viable operating system for commercial applications.

In 1996, the formal establishment of the Linux Foundation served to anchor the development of Linux even further. This institution emerged as a vital player in advocating for the adoption of Linux and facilitating collaboration among businesses, developers, and users. By providing resources for training, community building, and development initiatives, the Foundation paved the way for future advancements and inspired a new wave of innovation across industries.

Each challenge faced by Linux molded its narrative—reinforcing values of adaptability and perseverance within the community. As the early years unfolded, the milestones achieved not only validated Torvalds' vision but also underscored the profound impact of collaborative efforts in software development. By navigating through trials and tribulations, Linux blossomed into a formidable operating system characterized by principles of freedom and community empowerment.

Ultimately, the journey of Linux from mere concept to a global phenomenon reflects a poignant narrative marked by dedication, innovation, and ceaseless passion. Each triumph celebrated the resilience of a community invigorated by shared values, further inspiring future endeavors within the realm of tech. As we look back on these formative years, it becomes evident that the synergy between challenge and triumph propelled Linux toward becoming an enduring legacy —one that continues to inspire generations to explore the depths of technology and realize the power of open collaboration.

3. Debunking the Myths: Setting the Record Straight

3.1. Linux is Only for Experts

The assertion that "Linux is only for experts" is one of the more pervasive myths that has arisen within the narrative surrounding the operating system, deterring potential new users from exploring its vast possibilities. This misconception stems from historically complex user interfaces, command-line reliance, and the prevalent notion that navigating the Linux environment necessitates extensive technical knowledge. However, as we peel back the layers of this myth, we uncover a vibrant ecosystem that is not only user-friendly but also increasingly designed with accessibility in mind for individuals of diverse skill levels.

To begin with, we have to acknowledge that Linux distributions have evolved dramatically since the initial versions were launched in the early 1990s. While early adopters often engaged with a less polished experience, fraught with intricacies that could bewilder the uninitiated, modern distributions such as Ubuntu, Linux Mint, and Fedora have made significant strides towards usability. User interfaces in these environments are strikingly intuitive, offering graphical desktop environments reminiscent of Windows and macOS. Distributions come pre-packed with user-friendly software applications that allow individuals to perform tasks, install programs, and manage system settings without delving into the command line.

Importantly, community-supported tutorials and forums have burgeoned around these distributions, providing newcomers with essential resources to guide them through the initial learning curve. Websites like AskUbuntu, LinuxQuestions, and official documentation pages offer step-by-step instructions and troubleshooting advice, creating a supportive atmosphere where questions are welcomed and answered by seasoned users. This collaborative knowledge base empowers beginners to engage with Linux environments confidently, dismantling the myth of exclusivity for the tech-savvy.

Furthermore, the misconception that Linux is only the domain of experts perpetuates an oversight regarding the communities that have adapted the operating system for everyday tasks. For example, educational institutions, small businesses, and home users have increasingly adopted Linux for its security, cost-effectiveness, and reliability. Many school districts have integrated Linux systems into their libraries and computer labs to demonstrate the value of technology without the financial burdens associated with proprietary software. This grassroots approach underlines that Linux can meet everyday needs while fostering a deep understanding in learners about the importance of technology literacy.

The rise of user-friendliness doesn't merely end with configurations; it extends into the world of software as well. With the introduction of Software Centers in many distributions, users have access to a repository of applications that can be installed with a simple click, similar to what is seen on other operating systems. Whether it's a game, a productivity tool, or a multimedia application, users are greeted by a multitude of options without the need to compile code or manipulate system files, further inviting a larger audience to unwind any preconceived biases regarding the operational ethos of Linux.

In addition, the perception that Linux inherently requires command-line proficiency is misleading. While mastering the terminal can enhance one's control over the operating system and facilitate troubleshooting, it remains just one within a spectrum of usability options. Users can find themselves comfortable within graphical interfaces, effectively meeting their functional needs without venturing into command-line territory. In fact, many desktop environments today—like GNOME, KDE Plasma, and XFCE—offer an extensive suite of graphical tools that cover most tasks a typical user would want to accomplish.

Moreover, for those willing to engage more deeply with Linux, the command line becomes an asset rather than a barrier. It offers a more powerful avenue to achieve tasks swiftly—enacting commands that would take multiple clicks within a GUI can often be condensed into singular commands in the terminal. This provides an efficient path towards mastery, suggesting that fluency in the command line can yield significant advancements in productivity while simultaneously enriching the user's engagement with the system.

Importantly, the narrative of Linux being reserved for experts often overlooks the educational dimension it offers. Exposure to Linux can serve as a gateway for users to enhance their technical skills in ways that proprietary systems frequently do not. Many technology enthusiasts find Linux a suitable platform to experiment with coding, system administration, and software development, effectively nurturing a generation of budding engineers equipped with practical knowledge and hands-on experience.

With that being said, organizations and tech companies are increasingly gravitating towards Linux as a viable proficiency for their teams, recognizing the growing importance of open-source solutions in the lucrative tech sector. This shift solidifies Linux as not only a lifeline for technical expertise but also a foundational tool for future career paths across various fields, further showcasing its accessibility and relevance.

Furthermore, it is essential to highlight that the myth poses broader implications for diversity and inclusion within the tech community at large. As we combat the notion that Linux is only for experts, we create openings for individuals from various backgrounds to engage with technology on their terms, increasing representation and participation in the open-source movement. By dispelling such barriers, we foster environments that harness a diverse range of perspectives, inevitably leading to richer collaborations and innovations.

In essence, the assertion that Linux is exclusively for experts is fundamentally flawed and reflective of a bygone era. The landscape of Linux has undergone a radical transformation that invites anyone —regardless of technical background—to immerse themselves in the rich tapestry of collaboration, accessibility, and innovation. As we work to shatter this myth, it becomes clear that Linux is not merely a tool for the elite; it is an inclusive space where everyone is encouraged to learn, create, and contribute, paving the way for a more sustainable and diverse technological future.

3.2. Security Misconceptions

In the rapidly changing landscape of cybersecurity, misconceptions about Linux and its inherent security strengths can heavily influence user decisions and attitudes. Many individuals, especially those new to technology or with limited experience in operating systems, hold firmly to a range of myths regarding Linux's security. Addressing these misunderstandings is essential to clarify the reality of Linux security and to empower users to make informed choices regarding their systems.

One prevalent misconception is that Linux is inherently immune to security threats simply by virtue of being Linux. This belief often stems from the perception that Linux users are more technically knowledgeable than average users and that the open-source nature of Linux makes it less vulnerable. While it is true that Linux can offer enhanced security features, it is not invulnerable to attacks. Security vulnerabilities can emerge from various sources, including poorly configured systems, unpatched software, and user error. Moreover, as Linux continues to grow in popularity, particularly on servers and as the backbone of cloud infrastructure, it attracts more attention from malicious actors who seek to exploit any weaknesses within the system. Therefore, while Linux may present a lower risk profile than some other operating systems, it is not exempt from security challenges.

Another common myth involves the notion that Linux is too complex for typical users to secure properly. While many aspects of Linux do require a certain level of technical expertise, user-friendly distributions have emerged that simplify the security management process. Many contemporary Linux distributions come with built-in security features such as firewalls, regular updates, and user permissions, making it easier for users—regardless of their technical background—to maintain a secure system. Moreover, the community-driven nature of Linux ensures that extensive documentation and support are available for users seeking help in configuring security settings, further demystifying the perception of complexity.

Furthermore, there is a prevalent notion that Linux users need to be perpetually vigilant and technically adept due to the potential for security threats. While vigilance is indeed crucial in maintaining security, this is a responsibility shared by all users of any operating system. Whether using Windows, macOS, or any variant of Linux, best practices like regularly updating software, using strong passwords, and being cautious with external links and downloads apply universally. Understanding that security is a holistic responsibility rather than a task only for advanced users helps redistribute the perceived burden across all operating systems.

The idea that Linux is largely the domain of skilled hackers and professionals contributes to the myth that it is overly complex in terms of security management. In reality, while programming and system administration skills can indeed enhance a user's ability to address security issues, an increasing number of tutorials, guides, and user-friendly tools are transforming the landscape. Users can now effectively implement security measures while enjoying the flexibility and power that Linux provides, without the need for deep technical expertise.

Another aspect worth highlighting is the misconception that Linux is only suitable for servers and not for personal use. While it is true that Linux has carved a niche in server environments, its additional desktop distributions offer rich functionality and security for personal use as well. These distributions, such as Ubuntu, Fedora, and Manjaro, often include robust security features, proactive updates, and intuitive interfaces that cater to everyday users. Many organizations and individual users have adopted Linux for its inherent security benefits, which include lower susceptibility to certain malware strains commonly targeting other operating systems.

Additionally, a prominent misconception is the idea that using Linux completely negates the need for any additional security measures. Users may assume that simply switching to Linux will eliminate all threats to their systems. While Linux does offer a more secure foundation compared to some other systems, users should still take active steps to enhance their security posture. Utilizing firewalls, antivirus solutions, and intrusion detection systems, along with following established best practices, are all valuable strategies in ensuring a Linux system remains secure. The absence of threats should not breed complacency; on the contrary, security requires continuous effort and diligence.

In addressing these security misconceptions surrounding Linux, it is vital to promote a culture of awareness that emphasizes the importance of security as a shared effort. It is paramount for users to educate themselves about the security landscape of Linux in order to fully leverage its advantages while remaining vigilant against potential threats. Whether for casual users or system administrators, understanding the complexities and benefits of Linux security can empower individuals to enhance their systems effectively.

Ultimately, debunking these myths fosters a more balanced perspective on Linux security, creating a path for users to appreciate the robust security features of the operating system while recognizing their role in maintaining a secure environment. As we navigate the modern cybersecurity landscape, one guiding principle remains clear: security is an ongoing process that demands active engagement, awareness, and collaboration from all users, regardless of the operating system they choose.

3.3. The Cost Myth

The prevailing myth regarding the cost of Linux can often overshadow its transformative impact, creating a misconception that using this operating system is either prohibitively expensive or, conversely, that it is cost-free in a way that might undervalue the resources and efforts involved in its development and support. To understand the true cost of Linux, we must dissect this myth by examining the various dimensions, including acquisition, support, deployment, and the hidden costs associated with proprietary software alternatives.

First and foremost, it is essential to recognize that many Linux distributions are available for free. The open-source nature of Linux permits users to download, use, and modify the operating system without incurring licensing fees, a feature that is particularly appealing to individuals, educational institutions, small businesses, and startups. Distributions like Ubuntu, Fedora, and Debian offer robust platforms that do not require upfront payment. However, presenting Linux as merely "free" simplifies a more complex narrative about value and sustainability.

In the professional realm, there are factors to consider beyond initial acquisition costs. Enterprises often engage with Linux through commercial distributions, such as Red Hat Enterprise Linux or SUSE Linux Enterprise. These distributions are accompanied by subscription services that provide essential professional support, training, security updates, and enterprise-grade features. Adopting a commercial distribution may incur costs, but these expenses can be juxtaposed with the potential savings from avoiding vendor lock-in and manipulation associated with proprietary systems that require costly licenses and limited options for customization.

Moreover, the long-term savings associated with Linux should not be overlooked. Linux systems tend to require fewer resources, can run efficiently on older hardware, and often exhibit greater stability and security compared to their commercial counterparts. The reduced risk of system failures can directly translate to lower maintenance and operational costs, which benefits organizations striving to maximize their return on investment. While there may be initial costs in training personnel or transitioning systems, the potential for an organization to exploit Linux's flexibility and scalability often leads to stronger financial performance over time.

The notion that Linux is inherently low-cost also includes considerations surrounding community involvement and development efforts. Open-source software thrives on the contributions of its user base, which means that while users are not paying for licenses, their investment in time—whether through coding, testing, or community support—serves a pivotal role in refining the operating system. This spirit of collaboration emphasizes a different form of cost: the human capital dedicated to developing and sustaining the Linux ecosystem. Organizations adopting Linux often find that they are gaining access to a vast wealth of collective knowledge, which can enhance their own capabilities without the traditional costs associated with proprietary software development.

Another aspect of the cost myth emanates from the perception of ease with which Linux can be installed and maintained. The learning curve for many users transitioning from proprietary systems may involve labor estimates and support costs that need to be considered. Organizations may need to invest in training sessions, workshops, or even hire consultants to help navigate the shift. However, this investment should be viewed not merely as a cost but as a long-term strategy to empower teams with skills that will yield dividends in innovation and efficiency.

While cost savings frequently referenced in favor of Linux hold weight, it's important to consider potential hidden costs that can arise with open-source software. Technical challenges, community engagement, and documentation quality may contribute to downtime or inefficiencies if not addressed properly. Therefore, the total cost of ownership is not solely defined by upfront expenses but also incorporates factors such as the quality of support, the cost of human resources devoted to overcoming challenges, and the ongoing commitment required to maintain proficiency with the system.

Furthermore, there is a common misconception that embracing Linux equates to abandoning quality or not being able to access suitable software applications. In reality, many powerful enterprise applications now run natively on Linux, and various open-source alternatives frequently match or exceed the functionality of proprietary software. In many instances, organizations can realize significant cost savings by utilizing these robust open-source alternatives while maintaining or even enhancing operational capability.

Ultimately, the true cost of Linux lies along a continuum encompassing initial acquisition, support services, long-term efficiencies, human resources, operational sustainability, and overall value derived from community contributions. When approached thoughtfully, investing in Linux can be immensely beneficial for individuals and organizations alike, leading to reduced overhead and expanded possibilities for innovation.

In demystifying the cost myth surrounding Linux, it becomes clear that understanding its value transcends the surface-level perceptions of expense. Instead, the conversation about costs must also highlight the transformative capabilities of open-source software, challenge conventional understandings of "free," and inspire engagement within a community that thrives on collaboration and shared advancement. The spectrum of costs associated with Linux represents not merely an expense ledger, but an invitation to explore a broader landscape where technological freedom and community empowerment intersect in profound and practical ways.

3.4. Administrative Complexity Exposed

In the exploration of Linux as an operating system, one concept that frequently emerges is its perceived complexity around administration. This perception often stems from historical contexts as well as the learned behaviors of users conditioned to interact primarily with proprietary operating systems such as Windows and macOS. However, unraveling the myth that Linux is excessively complex reveals a more nuanced story that highlights both the challenges and opportunities in system management.

At first glance, one might encounter the command line interface (CLI), which has long been synonymous with Linux. The CLI can seem daunting to those unfamiliar with its syntax or utility, contributing to the belief that managing a Linux system requires extensive technical knowledge. However, this viewpoint overlooks significant advancements in user experience design within many Linux distributions. Modern distributions such as Ubuntu, Fedora, and Linux Mint have invested substantially in graphical user interfaces (GUIs) that prioritize user-friendliness. By integrating intuitive desktop environments, these distributions ease the transition for users who favor visual interaction over command-line inputs.

Indeed, many users find that they can accomplish the vast majority of their tasks through graphical tools without having to delve deeply into the command line. Activities such as installing software, managing system updates, configuring hardware settings, and networking can now be accomplished with just a few clicks. Consequently, while the command line still serves as an incredibly powerful tool for those willing to learn, it no longer remains a prerequisite for effective system management on a Linux machine.

The myth of administrative complexity often intertwines with concerns surrounding software and hardware compatibility. Historically, Linux faced challenges in this area—particularly when it came to ensuring that drivers and applications were readily available for widespread consumer hardware. However, the rise of community collaboration and support has resulted in an extensive ecosystem of distributions that cater to various use cases and environments. Today, many enterprise-grade applications, productivity software, and multimedia tools are built with Linux compatibility in mind, enabling users to seamlessly integrate Linux into their workflows.

Moreover, tutorials, forums, and a wealth of open-source documentation amplify the resources available to users on their journey in learning Linux administration. The collaborative spirit at the heart of the open-source community fosters an environment of support where individuals share knowledge and solutions. Online platforms, such as AskUbuntu or the Linux Mint forums, serve as hubs for seeking assistance on issues that administrators might face, allowing new and seasoned users alike to engage with a vibrant network of contributors seeking to enhance their understanding.

Addressing security and maintenance also plays a crucial role in reshaping perceptions around administrative complexity. A distinctive characteristic of Linux is its vibrant community of active developers and users dedicated to security. Regular updates and patch releases are driven by community reviews and testing, ensuring that users are protected against vulnerabilities. Additionally, built-in tools such as firewalls and user permission settings simplify the process of fortifying one's system against potential threats—allowing administrators to configure security settings quickly and intuitively.

In terms of managing Linux systems within organizations, the myth of complexity dissipates upon considering the advantages of standardization. As Linux distributions are regularly used in many enterprise-level environments, businesses can simplify their administrative tasks by providing comprehensive training for their employees or by hiring professionals who specialize in Linux system administration. This approach ultimately leads to increased efficiency and reduced operational costs in comparison to managing diverse, proprietary systems that often require distinct skill sets.

Despite these advancements, Linux is not devoid of challenges that administrators must navigate. Certain tasks still retain an inherent complexity, whether it involves configuring devices, optimizing performance, or performing intricate network setups. Nevertheless, the landscape continues to evolve, bringing forth utilities and scripts that help automate previously manual tasks, further reducing the burden on administrators.

It's also worth mentioning that the educational aspect of Linux plays a pivotal role in shaping future technologists. Many institutions now teach Linux-based curricula, ensuring that the next generation of IT professionals is well-versed in managing and deploying Linux systems. Students who gain hands-on experience in these environments cultivate the skills necessary to navigate administrative complexities, reassuring employers of their proficiency in open-source technologies.

Ultimately, the exaggerated myth of administrative complexity surrounding Linux can be dismantled through a combination of education, community support, and the incredible strides made by the Linux ecosystem to improve user experience. Reframing this narrative emphasizes that rather than being an insurmountable barrier, Linux administration opens pathways for individuals eager to learn, contribute, and innovate. With the right understanding and resources, users can confidently step into the world of Linux, embracing its potentials while finding excitement in the way technology can flourish within a communal framework.

3.5. Compatibility Concerns

As we delve into the intricacies of Linux, one of the critical aspects that bears discussion is the recurring narrative surrounding compatibility concerns. The notion that Linux lacks software and hardware compatibility has shaped the perceptions of users and potential adopters alike. This myth warrants scrutiny as we untangle the reality surrounding compatibility within the Linux ecosystem.

Historically, Linux faced significant challenges regarding compatibility, particularly in the early 1990s when it was still in its developmental stage. The operating system was often dismissed as being incompatible with mainstream hardware and popular software. This belief stemmed from the fact that, at that time, many proprietary software products were designed strictly for Windows or macOS environments, leaving Linux users with limited options. Additionally, device manufacturers frequently prioritized proprietary systems over Linux compatibility, contributing further to the narrative that Linux was an outsider in the software landscape.

However, the turning point for Linux came with its community-driven approach and the steady growth of both user bases and contributions. As Linux began to gain traction, the collaborative spirit embedded in its development philosophy became a powerful catalyst for change. Enthusiasts and developers rallied to create drivers and software solutions that could bridge the compatibility gap. The open-source nature of Linux enabled individuals to develop and share their innovations, thus bolstering the ecosystem with a wider selection of supported hardware and applications.

Manufacturers began to take note of Linux's rise, recognizing that there was a burgeoning market of users who sought alternatives to proprietary systems. As a result, many started releasing drivers for Linux alongside their products. This shift allowed users to success-fully leverage a variety of peripherals and devices, from printers to graphics cards, thus dispelling the myth that Linux is incompatible with consumer technology. Nonetheless, the transition wasn't instan-taneous, and some challenges persisted for certain niche hardware categories.

Today, the landscape is vastly different from that early period. Many popular hardware manufacturers actively provide Linux-compatible drivers, and major distributions ensure that these drivers are readily accessible and easy to install. The Linux Kernel has also seen contin-uous updates, allowing it to support an expanded array of hardware configurations, which is crucial for both desktop and server environ-ments. The rapid advancements in kernel development further led to enhanced compatibility across motherboard chipsets, networking components, and graphics cards, pushing Linux into a more compet-itive stance against other operating systems.

Moreover, the rise of the Linux community has resulted in a vast pool of collaborative projects dedicated to creating compatible soft-ware alternatives for applications frequently utilized on proprietary platforms. Popular software like LibreOffice and GIMP illustrate how robust productivity and creative tools have emerged to meet the demands of the user community. The availability of these open-source alternatives means that users can accomplish tasks without needing to resort to proprietary software, significantly diminishing compati-bility concerns in daily computing activities.

That said, it is essential to recognize that some niche applications and specialized tools still may not have readily available versions for Linux. This can pose challenges for professionals in certain fields who rely on proprietary software with no direct open-source counterparts. However, this has spurred innovative efforts within the community to encourage development through compatibility layers such as Wine (which allows Windows applications to run on Linux) or the increasingly popular virtualization techniques that host proprietary operating systems within a virtual environment. Such strategies provide viable solutions for users needing access to specific software tools while maintaining the core benefits of working on Linux.

Educationally, compatibility has become a focal point for many institutions that adopt Linux as part of their curriculum. By teaching students about the compatibility landscape of Linux, they learn not only to navigate the operating system but also to develop critical thinking skills in troubleshooting and problem-solving—skills fundamental for future technologists. This educational focus reinforces the importance of understanding and overcoming compatibility issues as they emerge, thereby creating a new generation of developers and users who are well-versed in the intricacies of open-source ecosystems.

The advancement of container technologies, such as Docker, also underscores the progress made in addressing compatibility concerns. These solutions allow applications to run in isolated environments, further decoupling software dependencies from the underlying operating system. By employing containerization, developers can ensure that their applications are portable and compatible across different environments, bridging gaps between Linux and other systems.

In conclusion, compatibility issues that once haunted the narrative of Linux are being progressively addressed through community collaboration, growth of supportive ecosystems, and advancements in hardware support. While challenges remain, the perception that Linux inherently lacks compatibility has become outdated. Linux now stands as a powerful contender in the operating system arena, equipped to navigate the complex landscape of hardware and software interactions. By focusing on continuous improvement, adoption, and community engagement, Linux positions itself as a versatile choice for a diverse range of users, from individual enthusiasts to enterprise-level implementations. As we venture forth, acknowledging progress while remaining aware of potential challenges will allow us to harness Linux's full capabilities in an ever-evolving technological landscape.

4. The Timeline of Transformations: Key Milestones

4.1. A Decade of Change: 1990s

The 1990s marked an incredibly transformative period for Linux, defining its trajectory as an open-source operating system and setting the stage for its future prominence in both academic and corporate environments. Initially perceived as a niche alternative sparked by Linus Torvalds' vision of a user-friendly, collaboratively developed operating system, Linux transcended its humble beginnings to galvanize a diverse community of developers, users, and businesses.

At the dawn of the decade, in 1991, Torvalds released the first version of the Linux kernel, version 0.01. This kernel was primarily built on ideas gleaned from MINIX, a Unix-like operating system, but it quickly evolved into something greater. Torvalds sought to provide a more open playground where programmers could collaborate freely. The invitation he extended to developers through a simple post on the MINIX newsgroup set a precedent for community-driven software development. This moment not only marked the release of the kernel itself but also ignited a movement that would alter the landscape of software and operating systems permanently.

The early 1990s also saw the establishment of pivotal structures within the burgeoning Linux community. Supportive groups began to form online, offering forums for collaboration and knowledge-sharing among users and developers. Mailing lists like linux-kernel became essential channels for discussing technical problems, sharing patches, and refining the code. This decentralized model empowered contributors from diverse backgrounds to join forces, establishing a democratic environment that set Linux apart from its proprietary counterparts. The participation from individuals around the world stimulated rapid growth and enhancement of the kernel—creating an innovative feedback loop that led to consistent improvements.

In 1992, the public learned about the first official Linux distributions, namely Slackware and Debian, which facilitated the installation and use of Linux across various hardware configurations. The introduction of these distributions played a significant role in making Linux more accessible to a broader audience, easing obstacles that initially hampered its adoption. Users could now install Linux alongside existing operating systems, gaining firsthand experience without entirely relinquishing their familiar environments. This dual-boot model proved instrumental in converting skeptics into advocates.

As Linux gained recognition, an influx of developers began contributing to its development. The community-driven approach brought together enthusiasts, coders, and students who clung to a utopian vision of a world where software would be free and accessible to all. The Free Software Foundation, founded by Richard Stallman in the 1980s, particularly influenced this guidance as it preached the moral imperative behind free software and the significance of transparency. This ideological alignment with the open-source movement validated the collective ambitions of developers while emphasizing the potential movements toward software freedom.

Interestingly, 1993 also heralded the advent of several important applications that would further solidify Linux's presence in both personal and enterprise environments. The development of the Apache web server, which significantly relied on open-source principles, coincided with growing internet adoption. As Linux established itself as a robust server platform, it quickly became the backbone of the web, laying the groundwork for the explosive growth of online resources. This synergy between Linux and the web demonstrated not only the versatility of the operating system but also its emerging dominance in environments requiring scalability and reliability.

Towards the latter part of the decade, the Linux kernel continued to evolve, introducing features that would enhance its maturity as an operating system. The transition to version 2.0 in 1996 represented a watershed moment, enabling Linux to genuinely support multiprocessor architecture and thereby improving performance and scalability. This progression did not go unnoticed in the corporate landscape; businesses began to explore Linux as a serious alternative to commercial operating systems. Companies like IBM and Red Hat started investing in Linux, recognizing the potential benefits of adopting high-performance, flexible solutions over traditional closed-source systems. Such corporate interest breathed life and legitimacy into the open-source software model, fostering a sense of confidence that Linux could meet rigorous industry standards.

As corporate entities began to embrace Linux, the 1990s also ushered in the age of Linux advocacy—spurring a series of events and conferences that attracted attention and investment. LinuxWorld Expo and other similar gatherings became vital arenas for networking and knowledge exchange, showcasing innovations and fostering dialogue around open-source principles. These events acted as breeding grounds for the next generation of Linux adopters, encouraging collaboration while amplifying the voices of influential advocates.

Moreover, the widespread availability of Linux distributions served to further challenge the established order of proprietary software. By the time the decade drew to a close, the perceptions surrounding the open-source movement had shifted dramatically. What was initially viewed as a hobbyist endeavor had emerged as a formidable contender against industry giants. As more users recognized the power of community-driven development and the cost-effectiveness of Linux, its adoption escalated across various sectors, from education to government and beyond.

The 1990s served as the crucible for Linux, molding it not only into a robust operating system but into a thriving ecosystem defined by collaboration and innovation. The decade laid essential groundwork that would influence both the technical and social dimensions of Linux for years to come. From newfound stability and expanded use cases to the fostering of a passionate community, the 1990s marked a tumultuous yet exhilarating decade of growth—one that captured the essence of collaboration and marked Linux's evolution into a powerful and resilient force in the technology world. As we continue to explore Linux's journey, the lessons learned from the 1990s resonate profoundly, emphasizing that the origins of innovation often germinate from the collective contributions of passionate individuals, dreaming of a more open and accessible digital future.

4.2. Y2K and Beyond: 2000s

The turn of the millennium represented both a pivotal moment and a challenge for the Linux operating system. With the world anxiously anticipating the repercussions of Y2K, the decade shifted into a new era filled with heightened connectivity, broadened horizons, and an increasing reliance on technology. Linux, originally conceived as a personal project by Linus Torvalds, began to assert itself as a credible alternative to proprietary operating systems and as a formidable player on the global technological stage.

In the immediate aftermath of Y2K, concerns over computer systems' vulnerabilities were at an all-time high. Despite the scare being vastly overstated in terms of impact, it did reveal the urgency for robust, reliable systems in an increasingly digitized world. As businesses wrestled with integrating newer technologies to circumvent potential failures, Linux emerged as a beacon of reliability and flexibility. Its open-source nature empowered institutions to tailor their operating environments, reduce dependence on costly proprietary licenses, and maintain full control over their system configurations. These advantages positioned Linux as an ideal solution during a transformative time in the tech industry.

The 2000s also saw Linux's migration from its niche market into more extensive corporate use, particularly for server applications. A significant catalyst for this shift was the burgeoning adoption of the internet and the need for robust server solutions. With the rise of web hosting and e-commerce, organizations sought reliable, cost-effective platforms that could support their online ventures. Linux rose to the occasion, as it provided a stable and secure operating system for web servers, allowing companies to deploy applications and services effectively without incurring prohibitive costs. The combination of performance, flexibility, and a supportive community led many businesses, from startups to large enterprises, to embrace Linux as their backbone.

One key development during this period was the formation of business models centered around Linux, giving rise to influential companies such as Red Hat and SUSE. These organizations began offering commercial support for Linux distributions, bridging the gap between community development and business needs. This symbiotic relationship was revolutionary; while the software remained free and open-source, organizations could ensure that they had access to professional-grade support, training, and security measures, thus alleviating concerns regarding deployment and maintenance.

In addition to server solutions, Linux began making inroads into the desktop market, albeit at a slower pace. Projects to create user-friendly distributions gained prominence, with the emergence of distros such as Ubuntu in 2004. By introducing a polished interface and intuitive installation processes, Ubuntu attracted users who had previously viewed Linux as a complex or inaccessible environment. The focus on usability and community engagement initiated a cycle of growth where feedback from users informed further developments. This community-driven approach showcased Linux's adaptability, reflecting the needs and desires of its users.

Throughout the 2000s, the open-source community expanded its collaborative frameworks, enhancing development processes and spurring innovation on multiple fronts. The continued popularity of the internet fueled the desire among developers to create and improve software collaboratively. Projects like GNOME and KDE, which pro-vided graphical interfaces for Linux, gained traction and contributed to the operating system's appeal. The establishment of Linux confer-ences and user groups facilitated networking, knowledge sharing, and mentorship, fostering a thriving ecosystem around Linux while actively nurturing the next generation of technicians and developers.

Additionally, the 2000s witnessed the increasing relevance of Linux in the embedded systems domain, where its lightweight nature and flex-ibility found practical applications in various devices. As the Internet of Things (IoT) began to take shape, Linux proved itself indispens-able across numerous platforms, from set-top boxes and networking equipment to smart appliances. This trend illustrated not only Linux's versatility but also its capacity to interface within rapidly evolving technological developments.

Moreover, as organizations and governments sought to avoid the issues and dependencies associated with proprietary software, Linux was increasingly viewed as a viable alternative. The decade saw the growth of governmental initiatives supporting open-source software adoption, driven by the desire for cost-effectiveness, transparency, and independence from vendor lock-in. Countries such as Brazil and Germany made significant strides in promoting the use of Linux within public institutions and schools, recognizing the long-term benefits of creating a more inclusive tech landscape.

As the 2000s drew to a close, Linux had firmly established itself as a multifaceted platform poised for mainstream acceptance. Its growth during this decade illustrated not only its evolutionary journey from a college project to a globally recognized operating system but also underscored the importance of community, collaboration, and the open-source ethos. While the new environments amplifying Linux's role presented unique challenges, they simultaneously ignited opportunities for further growth, innovation, and accessibility that would come to define the Linux experience for years to follow. The decade marked a foundational shift, paving the way for subsequent advancements in mobile computing, cloud infrastructure, and applications spanning diverse industries. As we embark on this exploration of Linux's trajectory through the 2000s and beyond, we witness the remarkable adaptability and resilience of a platform predicated on a vision of collaboration and freedom, one that continues to inspire generations of developers, users, and innovators across the globe.

4.3. The Mobile Revolution

The mobile revolution epitomizes one of the most transformative shifts in the technological landscape over the past two decades, fundamentally altering the way people interact with technology, communicate, and access information. Central to this revolution is the Linux operating system, which, despite being known primarily for its power on servers and desktops, has become a defining component of the mobile computing experience. By delving into how Linux has shaped the smartphone and mobile device ecosystem, we can appreciate its pivotal role in facilitating connectivity and driving innovation.

Beginning in the early 2000s, the landscape of mobile technology was dominated by proprietary operating systems—most notably by platforms such as Symbian, Blackberry OS, and later, Apple's iOS. These solutions largely adhered to closed environments, limiting user customization and the community participation that open-source systems like Linux championed. In stark contrast, the collaborative nature inherent within the Linux framework made it a fertile ground for creativity and adaptability—a quality that would be pivotal as smartphones began to gain traction and market presence.

The watershed moment for Linux in mobile computing came with the advent of Android OS in 2007. Google's bold decision to build Android on the Linux kernel unleashed a wave of possibilities, drawing on the robustness of Linux while layering it with a user-friendly interface that appealed to both consumers and developers. By employing a model of openness akin to that of traditional Linux distributions, Android quickly attracted a diverse community of developers willing to innovate, create, and contribute applications that pushed the boundaries of mobile functionality.

This symbiotic relationship between Linux and Android marked a seismic change—creating a platform where developers could freely create apps and integrate hardware without the stringent limitations associated with proprietary operating systems. The result was an explosion of applications available through the Google Play Store, transforming smartphones into versatile tools for communication, productivity, entertainment, and more. From social media platforms to productivity tools and gaming applications, the unrealized potential of mobile technology was unlocked, illustrating how Linux could catalyze innovation in a rapidly evolving market.

Moreover, the open-source philosophy of Android enabled a vast array of custom ROMs (read-only memory images) that allowed enthusiastic users to tailor the user experience to their preferences. Communities across the globe emerged, fostering a sense of camaraderie among developers and users alike—fueled by shared enhancements, challenges conquered, and the joy of collaborating on an evolving product. This culture cemented the notion that Linux was not merely a tool for developers but also the backbone of a thriving ecosystem where user contributions were as valuable as those from corporate developers.

As mobile devices became permeated with Linux's open-source ethos, the operating system found itself in a unique position to influence the hardware it powered. Device manufacturers began embracing Linux not only as an operating system for smartphones but also for embedded systems used in a range of Internet of Things (IoT) devices—an evolution from mobile phones to smart home devices, wearables, and automotive technologies. Linux played a crucial role in enabling seamless connectivity across devices, allowing smartphones to communicate effortlessly with home appliances, smart sensors, and personal gadgets.

Moreover, Linux's ability to run on a myriad of hardware architectures fueled the proliferation of diverse devices, from budget-friendly smartphones to high-performance tablets and wearables. As manufacturers leveraged the versatility of Linux, the barrier to entry decreased, leading to a democratization of technology. Users gained access to longer-lasting, cost-effective devices that retained powerful functionality, thus expanding the reach of mobile computing and creating opportunities for people previously excluded from the digital landscape.

Additionally, the evolution of mobile computing prompted advancements in mobile hardware capabilities, particularly in high-performance multicore processors and advanced graphics handling. Linux, being lightweight and modular, was instrumental in optimizing performance on these hardware advancements, allowing mobile devices to evolve at a rapid pace without sacrificing user experience.

The mobile revolution, driven by Linux-based systems, not only revolutionized personal computing but also spawned new industries and economic prospects. Mobile app development burgeoned into a multi-billion-dollar industry, drastically transforming how consumers interact with businesses and services. This change has had profound implications for sectors already entrenched in the digital age, including e-commerce, social services, education, and entertainment.

The impact of the mobile revolution, with Linux at its core, extends beyond technology—it has reshaped societal interactions and behaviors. Communication has been transformed, with people relying on mobile devices for real-time interactions, thus fostering a new era of connectivity that bridges geographical divides. The accessibility of information has skyrocketed, empowering users worldwide to learn, explore, and engage in a global discussion that was once limited by cost or availability.

As we reflect on the mobile revolution, it becomes apparent that the influence of Linux stretches beyond traditional confines of computing —it has become an integral part of our daily lives, shaping how we connect, learn, and thrive in a fast-paced world. The innovative spirit that pervades the Linux community not only catalyzed this revolution but continues to inspire future developments in mobile technologies.

The legacy of Linux in mobile computing serves as a testament to the power of open-source collaboration, adaptability, and community spirit. As we gaze into the future, it remains exhilarating to imagine how the foundations laid by Linux will continue to propel mobile technologies forward, fostering advancements that enrich lives and nurture inclusive growth across diverse societies. In acknowledging the mobile revolution, we celebrate Linux as a powerful engine of change—igniting creativity, pushing technological boundaries, and connecting humanity in ways previously unimaginable.

4.4. Cloud Computing and Virtualization

In the current technological landscape, cloud computing and virtualization stand as two of the most transformative innovations reshaping how businesses and individuals interact with IT infrastructure. At the heart of this revolution lies Linux, an operating system that not only underpins a vast array of cloud solutions but also offers robust frameworks for virtualization. Understanding the relationship between Linux, cloud computing, and virtualization reveals not only their individual benefits but also the synergistic effects they create within the broader ecosystem.

To begin, it is essential to define cloud computing and virtualization. Cloud computing refers to the delivery of various services—including computing power, storage, and software—over the internet rather than through traditional on-premises infrastructure. This model offers organizations unparalleled flexibility, scalability, and cost-effectiveness. Meanwhile, virtualization involves the creation of virtual versions of physical resources, such as servers, storage devices, and network components, allowing multiple separate environments to be run on a single physical machine. Both technologies enhance resource utilization, facilitate rapid deployment, and streamline management processes.

Linux has been an integral player in the expansion of cloud computing. Its open-source nature allows service providers to modify and optimize their cloud platforms without the constraints of proprietary software licenses. This flexibility enables a rich tapestry of distributions tailored for cloud-specific workloads, from Ubuntu and CentOS to Red Hat Enterprise Linux and SUSE Linux Enterprise Server. Each of these distributions provides different functionalities, performance optimizations, and user experiences for cloud service providers and their customers.

The strength of Linux in cloud environments is reflected in its ability to support various types of deployment models, including public clouds, private clouds, and hybrid clouds. Public cloud services, like those provided by Amazon Web Services (AWS), Microsoft Azure, and

Google Cloud Platform, often rely heavily on Linux as the foundation for their infrastructure. In these environments, Linux offers reliability, security, and stability, which are critical when managing multi-tenant cloud hosting with thousands or millions of applications simultaneously.

Linux's versatility further extends to private cloud deployments, where organizations leverage Linux-based solutions to set up their data centers. Private clouds enable businesses to maintain control over their infrastructure while still reaping the benefits of cloud computing efficiencies. The ability to tailor configurations specifically to an organization's needs is made possible through Linux distributions designed for robust infrastructure management, such as OpenStack and CloudStack. These solutions enable users to create, manage, and scale cloud environments with relative ease, thanks to the extensive documentation and community support surrounding them.

Hybrid clouds, which combine on-premises resources with public cloud services, benefit enormously from Linux's seamless integration capabilities. Organizations can deploy Linux-based applications across their hybrid environments, allowing developers to manage workloads effortlessly while utilizing both their existing infrastructure and external cloud resources. This versatility is fundamental for businesses seeking to optimize performance, reduce costs, and maintain flexibility in their IT strategies.

Transitioning to virtualization, Linux has long been at the forefront of this technology as well. Numerous virtualization solutions leverage Linux as a foundation, enabling the creation of virtual machines (VMs) that run multiple operating systems on a single physical host. Technologies such as KVM (Kernel-based Virtual Machine), Xen, and QEMU allow organizations to create, manage, and orchestrate VMs efficiently, streamlining their infrastructure while optimizing resource allocation.

KVM, in particular, stands out as a key player in Linux virtualization. As part of the Linux kernel, KVM enables users to turn their Linux installations into hypervisors, supporting multiple guests essentially and effectively. This tight integration ensures that virtualization capabilities perform exceptionally well, taking advantage of Linux's core strengths in stability, performance, and security. Organizations can quickly provision VMs, scale their environments, and adjust resources based on demand—all crucial factors in today's fast-paced business landscape.

Virtualization technologies powered by Linux also contribute to the growth of containerization, an innovative approach that allows applications to run securely within isolated environments. Docker, a popular containerization platform, has gained significant traction since its inception, largely due to its compatibility with Linux. Containers provide a lightweight alternative to full VMs, offering the ability to run multiple applications on a single OS instance, thus improving overall efficiency and resource utilization.

The rise of cloud computing and virtualization has not only transformed how organizations manage their IT infrastructure but has also changed the dynamics of software development and deployment. With Linux as the backbone of these innovations, developers now have the flexibility to build, test, and deploy applications rapidly. The principles of DevOps—collaboration between development and operations teams aimed at maximizing efficiency—have flourished in environments leveraging Linux and its cloud capabilities. Continuous Integration and Continuous Deployment (CI/CD) practices have become commonplace, with automated pipelines allowing Teams to deliver software updates faster and with improved reliability.

The benefits of Linux in the cloud and virtualization space extend beyond operational efficiencies. They also foster a culture of collaboration, innovation, and experimentation. With the open-source model guiding Linux development, organizations can contribute back to the community, further advancing cloud technologies and virtualization techniques. This ongoing cycle of collaboration perpetuates a vibrant ecosystem that champions shared knowledge and continuous improvement.

In conclusion, Linux's role in cloud computing and virtualization is both foundational and transformative. By providing a flexible, reliable, and secure platform for these technologies, Linux enables organizations to navigate the complexities of the digital landscape efficiently. As businesses increasingly adopt cloud solutions and embrace virtualization, the contributions of Linux will undoubtedly continue to propel innovation, foster collaboration, and shape the future of technology. The synergy between Linux, cloud computing, and virtualization represents not just a technological evolution but a paradigm shift that empowers organizations to harness the full potential of their IT infrastructure and resources.

4.5. The Current Era and Future Prospects

In the current era, Linux stands as a central pillar in the tech landscape, distinguished by its widespread adoption across various domains and its continuous innovation amidst rapid advancements in technology. As we analyze the contemporary advancements in Linux, it becomes apparent that its evolution is marked by a robust community, a commitment to open-source principles, and the resilience to adapt to emerging challenges.

The influence of Linux is especially prominent in cloud computing and virtualization. Over the past decade, organizations have increasingly turned to Linux-based solutions to create scalable and efficient cloud environments. Providers such as Amazon Web Services (AWS) and Google Cloud Platform have leveraged the flexibility of Linux to offer a diverse range of services, optimizing their infrastructures for innovation and customer service. As businesses migrate to the cloud, Linux's characteristics—its scalability, performance, and support of various architectures—position it as a preferred choice for organizations aiming to streamline operations and reduce costs.

Moreover, Linux has become foundational in the burgeoning field of the Internet of Things (IoT). With the proliferation of connected devices, Linux-based platforms have emerged as viable solutions for developers and manufacturers striving to create secure and efficient IoT ecosystems. Distributions such as Yocto, OpenEmbedded, and

Raspberry Pi OS empower developers to build tailored systems for various applications, from smart homes to industrial automation, thereby underscoring Linux's versatility in adapting to new trends in connectivity.

Educational institutions, too, have embraced Linux, highlighting its significance in nurturing the next generation of technologists. By integrating Linux into curriculums, schools and universities are equipping students with practical skills in operating systems, programming, and system administration. Furthermore, access to open-source tools fosters a culture of innovation and collaboration among students eager to contribute to ongoing projects and engage with the tech community. This cohesive educational movement prepares learners to tackle the challenges of a digital future propelled by open-source values.

As we peer into the future, the prospects for Linux seem promising. The continued growth of machine learning, artificial intelligence, and big data analytics points towards increased demand for reliable, open-source solutions capable of managing and processing large datasets efficiently. Linux's robustness and adaptability will be critical as organizations seek technologies that can sustain the immense data flows and computation demands of these advanced applications.

However, with these opportunities come inherent challenges. As adoption scales, the Linux community must remain vigilant against potential fragmentation, ensuring that various distributions maintain compatibility and coherence. The need for clear communication, effective governance, and collaboration across the ecosystem is paramount to sustaining Linux's legacy and mitigating risks related to diverging paths.

The open-source movement, while flourishing, must also contend with issues of sustainability and funding. As developers contribute their time and resources, it is vital to devise mechanisms that support ongoing development and incentivize contributions. Organizations that rely on Linux must adopt ethical practices that acknowledge and reward the efforts of community contributors, safeguarding the future of open-source innovation.

Moreover, diversity and inclusion within the Linux community must continue to improve as it represents the foundation of a healthy and rich ecosystem. Attracting diverse talent will ensure varied perspectives in problem-solving, innovation, and community engagement. This inclusivity is essential as Linux faces competition from proprietary systems that may promote homogeneous environments. Strengthening collaboration and removing barriers for underrepresented groups will position Linux favorably in the collective narrative of technology.

In the face of evolving technologies, Linux must continue to champion its core values: collaboration, transparency, and freedom. The essence of the Linux ethos can inspire various sectors—drawing parallels between open-source principles and societal advancements within areas such as healthcare, education, and civic engagement. The ongoing political and social discourse surrounding technology and data privacy necessitates that Linux remains a beacon of ethical software development, advocating rights and access for all.

Ultimately, the current era presents a unique confluence where Linux's history, its community-driven development, and its inherent adaptability align to encourage further exploration and innovation. Excavating potential avenues of growth—whether in sustainable technologies, pervasive IoT, or the realms of education—Linux is well-poised not merely as a tool, but as a foundational element in shaping the future of technology. As we venture into this new landscape, the legacy of Linux carries forth, accentuating the power of community and collaboration as it stands at the heart of an ever-evolving digital world.

5. The Faces Behind the Code: Community and Developers

5.1. Pioneers of Linux

The journey of Linux is closely intertwined with the pioneers who dedicated their time, talent, and vision to its development. These individuals not only laid the foundations of Linux but also fostered its growth and evolution into the powerful operating system it is today. From the humble beginnings initiated by Linus Torvalds to the collective efforts of countless developers, each pioneer has played a crucial role in shaping the trajectory of Linux, creating a rich tapestry of innovation and collaboration that continues to thrive.

At the heart of this narrative is Linus Torvalds, who, in 1991, unleashed the first version of the Linux kernel to the world. His initial motivation was rooted in frustration with existing operating systems and a vision for a truly open and collaborative platform. Torvalds' unique approach to development emphasized community involvement, inviting others to contribute to his project. This pioneering spirit established the precedent for an inclusive development model, showcasing how open-source collaboration could lead to significant advancements in technology. His leadership style, often characterized as a 'benevolent dictator', helped steer the direction of the kernel while encouraging a diverse range of contributions, ensuring the integrity of the project while enriching it with varied perspectives.

Following Torvalds, many key individuals emerged who helped forge the Linux landscape. Among them was Marc Ewing, who played a pivotal role in popularizing Linux through the creation of the Red Hat distribution. By providing a user-friendly installation process and a robust support structure, Ewing made Linux accessible to a broader audience. Under his leadership, Red Hat became one of the first commercial distributions to focus on enterprise solutions, thereby reinforcing Linux's viability in the corporate sector. This shift not only emphasized collaboration within the community but also highlighted the potential of open-source software to thrive in commercial settings.

Another notable figure is Bruce Perens, a co-founder of the Open Source Initiative and a staunch advocate for open-source software standards. Perens's work in promoting the principles of open source and the creation of the Open Source Definition helped clarify the ethos underlying collaborative development. His advocacy work not only broadened the appeal of Linux but also encouraged other developers to embrace open-source methodologies, transforming the way software was perceived and developed around the globe.

The contributions of individuals such as Alan Cox, who became known for his significant enhancements to the Linux kernel, cannot be overlooked. His involvement in kernel development and his commitment to addressing bugs exemplified the power of community-driven efforts in refining the operating system. Cox's work exemplified the collaborative spirit of Linux, where developers worked collectively to troubleshoot, enhance, and innovate, showcasing how shared knowledge led to rapid advancements in technology.

As Linux expanded, so too did the myriad of contributors dedicated to specific projects within the ecosystem. Developers like Linus Walleij and Greg Kroah-Hartman have taken on leadership roles within the kernel community, ensuring ongoing development and maintenance while fostering an environment that encourages new contributors. Walleij's work on various drivers and the ongoing integration of new technologies reflects the adaptable nature of Linux, while Hartman's role in guiding the stable kernel series reinforces the importance of collaboration across the community to ensure that the kernel remains a reliable foundation for countless distributions.

Moreover, the Linux community has seen the rise of influential grassroots movements that advocate for users' rights and promote accessibility. The founding of organizations such as the Free Software Foundation by Richard Stallman ideally represents not just advocacy for free software but also the larger philosophical framework on which Linux is built. His vision served to align values of community, freedom, and collaboration, enhancing Linux's identity as more than just an operating system—it embodies a movement committed to the empowerment of users.

As the years progressed, the importance of diverse voices within the Linux community became increasingly evident. Efforts to enhance gender representation and inclusivity gained traction, with women like Kathy Sierra, who contributed to the advancement of programming and educational tools, and others making their mark. The initiative to acknowledge and support female developers became a guiding principle for the community, with various organizations and meetups focused on amplifying the presence of women in technology.

The idea of mentorship and fostering the next generation of contributors has also taken root within the Linux ecosystem, thanks to pioneers who saw the value in nurturing new talent. Programs aimed at providing educational resources, projects for students, and collaborative experiences have taken shape, further broadening the community of contributors. These initiatives reflect a commitment to continuity and growth, ensuring that the spirit of collaboration remains strong while encouraging newcomers to embrace the values that propelled Linux into the limelight.

The legacy of these pioneers continues to resonate as Linux evolves to meet the needs of modern technology. The collective contributions of passionate developers, advocates, and community leaders have shaped not only the technical foundation of Linux but also its cultural significance. With a vibrant network of contributions from individuals across the globe, the history of Linux stands as a testament to the power of collaboration and the belief that anyone can impact the world of technology.

As we look to the future, the pioneers of Linux remind us of the importance of fostering a diverse and inclusive community that welcomes new ideas and approaches. Their stories inspire a new generation of developers, each eager to leave their mark on the ongoing saga of Linux. By celebrating the contributions of those who have come before us, we can embrace the spirit of collaboration, innovation, and resilience that defines Linux, ensuring its continued evolution for years to come. The journey of Linux is far from over, with endless possibilities awaiting those willing to embark on this shared adventure in technology and open-source development.

5.2. Collaborative Culture

Linux has been shaped and powered by a remarkable collaborative culture that distinguishes it from its proprietary counterparts. At the heart of this ethos lies the fundamental belief that shared knowledge and collective contributions can lead to extraordinary innovation and creativity. This section of our exploration delves into how this unique community-driven model not only fosters Linux's development but also creates an inclusive environment where diversity of thought flourishes, and individuals from all walks of life can contribute to the evolution of technology.

From its inception, Linux was characterized by collaboration. Linus Torvalds, the creator of the Linux kernel, famously initiated the project as a personal endeavor but recognized early on the potential of open collaboration. When he released the first version of the Linux kernel in 1991, Torvalds did not just share his creation; he actively encouraged others to participate, inviting developers worldwide to contribute their skills and knowledge. This inclusive spirit set the stage for a culture where anyone, regardless of their background or experience, could play a role in refining and enhancing the software.

The collaboration did not stop with coding. The Linux community has built a rich ecosystem of resources, platforms, and forums where developers share ideas, troubleshoot issues, and provide support to one another. From mailing lists and online discussion forums to social media channels and meetups, the channels of communication are diverse and robust. This interconnectedness ensures that information flows freely and that good ideas can be collectively nurtured and transformed into reality.

The nature of collaboration within the Linux environment is also defined by its transparency. The open-source model allows anyone to inspect, modify, and share the underlying code, fostering an environment of trust and accountability. When vulnerabilities or bugs are discovered, the community comes together to address these issues collectively, reinforcing the notion that everyone shares responsibility for maintaining quality and security. This culture of transparency not only enhances the reliability of the software but also builds a foundation of mutual respect and shared achievement among contributors.

Moreover, the collaborative culture of Linux has proven to be a breeding ground for innovation. Hackathons, coding sprints, and collaborative projects often yield rapid advancements that would be inconceivable in more hierarchical environments. The diverse backgrounds of the contributors—from students and educators to professionals and hobbyists—bring a wealth of perspectives that can lead to creative problem-solving and out-of-the-box thinking. Features and functionalities in Linux systems often stem from community suggestions and experiments, resulting in a more agile development process that emphasizes user needs and desires.

Inclusivity is a core tenet of the Linux collaborative culture. The open-source community actively seeks to include a diverse range of voices, believing that varying perspectives only enhance the technology we create. Initiatives have been launched to encourage the participation of underrepresented groups in technology, including women and minorities. Through mentorship programs, outreach efforts, and supportive networking opportunities, the Linux community is collectively working towards a more equitable space for everyone to participate, ensuring that different experiences and backgrounds help shape the future of Linux.

In the face of challenges such as fragmentation, scalability, and standardization, the collaborative culture serves as a unifying element that binds contributors to a shared vision. Projects such as the Linux Foundation have played a pivotal role in advocating for collaboration across diverse Linux distributions, aligning community efforts towards common goals while still respecting individual projects' unique identities. By creating frameworks for cooperation and engagement, the Linux community has been able to attract ongoing interest and participation, ensuring that the spirit of collaboration remains alive and well.

Furthermore, as technology evolves, the Linux culture adapts. New developers are encouraged to engage with the community through educational programs, code reviews, and documentation, allowing the next generation to inherit and build upon the legacy of collaboration. Each new contributor adds a layer of depth to the communal knowledge base, continually refreshing the perspectives and ideas that drive innovation. This commitment to education and mentorship embodies the essence of the Linux ethos—where knowledge is shared generously to benefit all.

In summary, the collaborative culture of Linux exemplifies how collective effort can yield greater innovation than any solitary endeavor. By fostering an inclusive, transparent, and supportive environment, the Linux community has created a dynamic ecosystem where creativity flourishes, diversity is celebrated, and contributions are valued. As we continue to see advancements within technology, the collaborative spirit of Linux serves as a model for other sectors—demonstrating that when individuals come together with a shared purpose, they can transcend boundaries and create something truly extraordinary. The journey of Linux is a testament to the power of collaboration, and its legacy will undoubtedly inspire future generations to harness the art of working together as a catalyst for change.

5.3. Women in Linux

In exploring the role of women in the Linux community, we uncover a vibrant tapestry of contributions that highlight not just their participation but also the profound impact that diverse voices have on the evolution of this influential operating system. For too long, the narrative surrounding software development has been dominated by a mythos that overlooks the significant achievements of women and fails to recognize their vital roles in fostering collaboration, innovation, and community in the open-source ecosystem.

Historically, the technology sector, including the realm of open source and Linux, has faced challenges in achieving gender equality. Evolving from an era where women's roles within technology were often minimized or rendered invisible, the Linux community has made strides toward recognizing and amplifying female contributions. Efforts by pioneering organizations, grassroots movements, and individual advocates have fed into a larger conversation about inclusivity and representation, enabling women to carve out essential spaces within the Linux landscape.

Prominent voices such as Dr. Leslie Hawthorn have contributed significantly to the community, serving as a mentor, advocate, and organizer. During her tenure at Google, Hawthorn was instrumental in efforts like Google Summer of Code, which encourages students to engage with open-source communities, providing vital incentives that created pathways for underrepresented groups. Her work reflects a commendable commitment to fostering diversity and highlighting the importance of mentorship—a fundamental tenet for cultivating future generations of developers and contributors.

Similarly, women like Janie G, a respected developer and advocate for open-source software in the educational sector, have demonstrated how their experiences can influence institutional approaches to technology. Her advocacy for integrating Linux into educational curricula highlights the transformative power of making technology accessible to students at an early age, inspiring a more diverse generation of innovators keen on venturing into the tech field.

The rise of initiatives targeting women in technology, such as the 'Women Who Code' and the 'Diversity in Open Source' movements, represents an acknowledgment of the unique perspectives women bring to software development. These initiatives foster environments that encourage networking, mentorship, and skill development, enabling women to not only participate in but lead within the Linux community. Workshops, hackathons, and conferences focused on amplifying women's contributions provide vital spaces for skill-sharing and foster an environment where collaboration thrives.

Recognizing the importance of intersectionality, the Linux community has increasingly emphasized that the contributions of women come from diverse backgrounds—each bringing their own unique experiences and insights. The inclusion of voices from various cultural, socioeconomic, and geographical contexts enriches conversations around technology, creating software and projects that are reflective of the global community. Women from different walks of life have consistently leveraged their experiences to build technologies that address broad societal challenges, ensuring that the development of software aligns with the needs of those typically marginalized in traditional tech conversations.

Prominent projects within the Linux ecosystem have benefitted from this inclusive approach. For example, the rise of accessibility-focused tools and applications, many driven by women stakeholders, demonstrates how addressing the specific needs of users with disabilities requires contributions shaped by diverse experiences and perspectives. The Linux accessibility community is a testament to how focused efforts can result in technologies that do not merely function but truly serve the community's varied users.

Highlighting individual stories brings to light intricate narratives that underscore the power of women in shaping Linux. Developers like Karen Sandler, who champions ethical software development and leads efforts to ensure that technology remains accessible and beneficial to all users, exemplify the role of women not only as contributors but as advocates for justice, ethics, and responsibility in tech. Her leadership encourages ongoing discourse about the need for transparency and the moral implications of software choices within the open-source community.

In tandem with female developers, the presence of women in leadership roles within prominent Linux distributions and organizations is indicative of progress. For instance, women holding positions in senior management, project leads, and boards of open-source foundations not only pave the way for sustainable initiatives but also inspire further participation from women interested in technology. Their visibility amplifies the message that leadership is inclusive—an important aspect of fostering lasting change.

As we continue to navigate these evolving dynamics in the Linux community, it is crucial to recognize that the fight for representation within technology is an ongoing journey. To further enrich the Linux ecosystem, collective efforts must prioritize mentorship, education, and opportunities that can serve to inspire women and girls worldwide. Whether through increased visibility, support programs, or grassroots initiatives, it is vital that the contributions of women in Linux are acknowledged, celebrated, and amplified.

In summary, the narrative of women in Linux is multifaceted and evolving, marked by significant contributions that enrich the community while illustrating the transformative power of diversity and collaboration. Recognizing and honoring these contributions not only strengthens the foundation of Linux but also ensures that its future is brightened by the myriad voices contributing to its ongoing legacy—a reminder that empowerment and inclusion are integral to the development of technology in pursuit of a more equitable digital future. As we champion the achievements of women in Linux, we embrace the ethos that innovation flourishes when no voice goes unheard, fostering a community where collaboration is both cherished and celebrated.

5.4. Diversity and Inclusion

In navigating the complex ecosystem of the open-source community, diversity and inclusion have emerged as pivotal themes, acting as catalysts for innovation and reflection within the realm of Linux. The principle of diversity transcends simplistic demographics; it encapsulates the richness derived from a multiplicity of backgrounds, experiences, and perspectives that collectively drive the evolution of technologies. An evaluation of diversity within Linux not only reveals the potential reservoirs of creativity but also highlights the challenges that persist in achieving a truly inclusive environment.

Historically, the open-source landscape, particularly in its early days, mirrored the broader tech industry, where representation was unevenly skewed. Access to technology and the development community tended to favor certain demographics, rendering the contributions of women, people of color, and other underrepresented groups frequently overshadowed or overlooked. Recognizing and addressing these disparities is crucial in reshaping the narrative surrounding Linux and ensuring that it embodies the collaborative spirit of its founding principles.

As the community has evolved, a concerted effort has emerged to dismantle these barriers and cultivate inclusivity. Initiatives aimed at fostering a welcoming environment have gained traction, emphasizing the need for representation across various levels of engagement —from grassroots projects to high-profile leadership roles. Organizations and community groups have been established with the express purpose of advocating for equal participation, drawing upon a vast pool of talent, perspectives, and expertise that can enrich the Linux ecosystem.

The fostering of diversity transcends mere participation; it strengthens the fabric of collaboration that defines Linux. Diverse teams are proven to solve problems more creatively and effectively, fueled by the myriad ideas and insights that stem from varied cultural and life experiences. In the context of Linux development, this creative leverage enhances the adaptability and resilience of technological solutions, enabling responses that resonate with a wider audience and meet multifaceted user needs.

Moreover, the imperative for diversity in Linux is closely tied to the ethos of open source itself. In many ways, the success of Linux hinges on its community's ability to draw from the collective intelligence of its members. This interconnectedness transforms the operating system into a living, breathing entity—one that adapts and evolves through collaboration, with each contributor providing insights that inform its trajectory. Recognizing and encouraging diversity within this structure is paramount, ensuring that contributions reflect the global nature of our digital society.

While strides have been made toward inclusive practices, challenges remain pervasive. The technology industry, including open-source communities, faces systemic issues that must be confronted head-on, including biases in hiring, the availability of mentorship opportunities, and the lack of visibility for underrepresented contributors. Prioritizing diversity means actively working to dismantle these barriers while instituting mechanisms that foster equitable participation —such as mentorship programs, outreach efforts, community building, and inclusive events.

Efforts to cultivate a more inclusive Linux community are often depicted through various initiatives designed to engage those who have historically been left out of tech conversations. Programs aimed at providing resources and networking opportunities for underrepresented groups play a vital role in building relationships and dismantling stereotypes. Additionally, educational projects focused on increasing awareness of diversity's importance in tech can substantially shift perceptions and behaviors within the community. As individuals recognize the value of diverse contributions, the collective effort to build an inclusive culture flourishes.

Furthermore, the success of diversity and inclusion initiatives within the Linux community has implications that extend beyond the realm of software development. A commitment to inclusivity serves as a model for other sectors facing similar challenges, showcasing that fostering diverse environments ultimately leads to transformative and sustainable innovation. By highlighting the achievements and contributions of diverse individuals in the Linux community, it becomes possible to challenge prevailing narratives that box technology into narrow archetypes, opening up pathways for broader engagement and participation in the future.

In reflection, the journey toward improved diversity and inclusion within the Linux community is just beginning. However, by acknowledging past shortcomings and committing to embedding inclusivity in every facet of development, the Linux community can pave the way for a brighter, more representative future. The ongoing pursuit of diverse participation not only reaffirms the core values of open-source collaboration but also signifies a determination to build a technology landscape that champions representation and inclusivity at every turn, ensuring that the Linux journey remains vibrant and accessible to all.

5.5. Famous Projects and Collaborations

The history of Linux is rich with notable projects and collaborations that have shaped its development, demonstrating the power of open-source software and the vibrant community that drives it. Among the most famous collaborations are those that have brought together diverse groups of developers, institutions, and organizations to create software that has revolutionized industries, transformed how we interact with technology, and made powerful tools accessible to a global audience.

One of the hallmark projects that exemplifies successful collaboration within the Linux ecosystem is the Apache HTTP Server. Originally released in 1995, Apache was developed by a group of programmers who were frustrated with existing web server software. They came together to build an open-source solution that would serve web content more efficiently and reliably. The success of Apache is a testament not only to the technical skills of its contributors but also to the collaborative spirit of the Linux community. Today, Apache remains one of the most popular web servers in the world, powering over a quarter of all websites. Its widespread adoption underscores the impact of collaborative projects that foster innovation while encouraging community input.

Another groundbreaking collaboration is the Linux Journal, which has chronicled the advancements of the Linux community since its inception in 1994. This publication serves as a platform for sharing knowledge and information among Linux enthusiasts, providing insight into emerging technologies, user experiences, and coding practices. By facilitating communication and collaboration, the Linux Journal has played an integral part in building a sense of community among developers and users, encouraging shared learning and the exchange of ideas.

The development of the GNOME desktop environment is another emblematic example of collaboration in the Linux ecosystem. Initiated in the late 1990s, GNOME aimed to create a free and user-friendly desktop interface for Linux users. Collaborative contributions poured in from developers across the globe, resulting in a powerful environment that prioritizes usability and accessibility. GNOME has since become the default desktop environment for many Linux distributions, reinforcing the importance of collaboration in creating software that meets diverse user needs and enhances the overall Linux experience.

The Debian Project is also a cornerstone of the collaborative spirit within the Linux community. Founded in 1993, Debian is known for its commitment to free software and its extensive package management system. The project has relied on thousands of contributors who contribute code, maintain packages, and support users—all in the spirit of collaboration. Debian's dedication to transparency and community involvement has allowed it to flourish, giving rise to numerous derivatives and distributions, such as Ubuntu, which have further broadened Linux's reach and usability.

The changes brought forth by the collaboration of corporations with the open-source community have significantly impacted Linux's trajectory. Red Hat, one of the leading open-source companies, exemplifies how corporate participation can enhance collaboration. Through its contributions to the Linux kernel and the establishment of the Fedora Project, which serves as a testing ground for new features in Red Hat Enterprise Linux, the company has established a framework for cooperative development that bridges the gap between commercial interests and community engagement. This model showcases how businesses can successfully contribute to and benefit from the open-source fabric while fostering collaboration among developers.

The Linux Foundation, founded in 2000, has taken collaborations to an even broader scale, acting as a central hub for various projects and initiatives within the Linux ecosystem. The foundation is committed to promoting, protecting, and advancing Linux through the support of developers and companies alike. With initiatives like the Linux Kernel Mentorship Program, which helps first-time contributors navigate kernel development, the foundation reinforces its dedication to collaboration while empowering future generations of developers.

Networking plays a pivotal role in these collaborations, as many conferences and events convene participants from around the world. Events such as LinuxCon and FOSDEM provide platforms for developers to come together to share ideas, showcase projects, and ultimately collaborate on initiatives that enhance Linux. These gatherings are crucial in fostering relationships that transcend geographical barriers, instilling a sense of camaraderie among participants while paving the way for innovative projects to emerge.

Moreover, the academic community has played a significant role in Linux's development through various collaborations. Research universities have frequently adopted Linux for research projects and teaching purposes, contributing code, developing new technologies, and providing valuable feedback to the community. Collaborations with academic institutions have yielded projects like the Linux Audio Developers (LAD) community, which focuses on creating tools and software for audio production, highlighting how academia can enhance Linux's capabilities in creative fields.

One cannot ignore the unique partnerships formed between Linux and other technologies; for instance, the integration of Linux in various Internet of Things (IoT) devices and platforms emphasizes the collaborative efforts of hardware manufacturers and developers. The growth of platforms like Arduino, Raspberry Pi, and other open-source hardware projects showcases the unifying power of Linux, sparking projects that combine software and hardware innovation. These collaborations lead to practical applications in various fields, inspiring hobbyists, educators, and professionals to develop creative solutions that utilize Linux's capabilities in novel ways.

In summary, the story of Linux is one of unparalleled collaboration, vibrant projects, and shared ambition. The collective efforts of developers, academics, organizations, and enthusiasts have transformed it into a tool that extends far beyond individual contributions. It is a testament to the power of working together, transcending boundaries to create software that serves millions of users around the globe. As we look to the future, the continued spirit of collaboration will undoubtedly fuel further innovations within the Linux ecosystem, paving the way for the next generation of technologies that promise to revolutionize how we engage with the digital world.

6. Linux in the Enterprise: Adaptation and Integration

6.1. Linux's Rise in Business

Linux's rise in business is a fascinating narrative that crystallizes the operating system's evolution from an academic experiment into a dominant force across multiple enterprise environments. This journey is underpinned by a blend of technological innovation, community collaboration, and the adaptation of businesses to meet the ever-evolving demands of the digital landscape.

The ascent of Linux in the corporate sphere prominently began during the late 1990s and early 2000s, a time when businesses were seeking alternatives to the increasingly costly licensing structures of proprietary systems like Microsoft Windows. As corporations grappled with escalating software costs and the desire for flexible, customizable software solutions, Linux emerged as a viable option. The open-source nature of Linux offered organizations the freedom to utilize the operating system without incurring hefty licensing fees —an appeal that was particularly enticing to startups and small-to-medium-sized enterprises.

This burgeoning interest laid the groundwork for large-scale adoption within the enterprise, and several factors influenced Linux's growing appeal. The introduction of robust distributions tailored for business use, coupled with the enhanced support networks established by companies like Red Hat and SUSE, played a vital role in fostering confidence among corporate IT departments. These companies not only provided reliable distributions but also tested and packaged essential enterprise applications that optimized Linux for business environments. This made it easier for organizations to make the leap from proprietary systems to Linux.

As companies began deploying Linux on their servers, they discovered significant advantages concerning performance, scalability, and stability. Linux's modular architecture allowed for the optimization of server configurations, enabling businesses to maximize resource utilization and reduce overhead costs. Many enterprises capitalized on Linux's exceptional performance in web servers, database management systems, and back-end processing tasks, leading to improved operational efficiency and a greater return on investment. For instance, web hosting services rapidly adopted Linux due to its reliability, security features, and the support of the Apache web server, which became the dominant choice for running web applications.

As Linux extended its reach, multi-billion-dollar tech giants like IBM and Google publicly lent their support, validating its presence in the enterprise. These companies contributed not only financially but also through development efforts, ensuring that Linux remained at the forefront of technological advancements. This corporate backing propelled Linux into new frontiers, including cloud computing, where its scalability and flexibility proved invaluable for organizations transitioning to cloud-based solutions.

The introduction and growth of cloud services further solidified Linux's foothold in the enterprise sector. As businesses increasingly adopted cloud strategies, Linux's compatibility with various hypervisors and virtualization technologies allowed for seamless integration into cloud environments. Moreover, Linux distributions specifically designed for cloud deployment emerged—cutting-edge solutions such as Ubuntu Cloud and Red Hat OpenShift facilitated the transition for many enterprises venturing into the cloud. Organizations could build and manage scalable cloud infrastructures without compromising on performance or flexibility, creating new growth opportunities.

Linux's impact on enterprise software development also cannot be overstated. Organizations started to leverage the open-source landscape to develop proprietary applications that integrated with Linux, laying the foundation for a thriving ecosystem of business-focused applications. Software vendors began offering solutions optimized for Linux, catering specifically to the needs of businesses that required reliable, enterprise-grade software accompanied by community-driven support.

The adaptability of Linux also became particularly relevant within the context of cybersecurity. As data breaches and cyber threats became increasingly prevalent, companies recognized the security advantages inherent in using open-source software. With Linux, organizations could engage with the community to audit code, quickly patch vulnerabilities, and tailor specific security measures to suit unique business needs. This degree of transparency and collaboration fostered a trust that some organizations found lacking in proprietary systems.

Despite its rapid rise, Linux's journey within enterprises has not been without hurdles. Some businesses initially struggled with compatibility issues, particularly when integrating Linux with legacy systems or specialized applications that were traditionally built for proprietary operating systems. Organizations needed to carefully navigate these challenges while making incremental adjustments to facilitate that integration. However, the resilience of the Linux community and the continued development of tools and frameworks have helped to mitigate those challenges over time.

As we look toward the future, Linux is poised for continued expansion within the business world. The evolution of emerging technologies such as artificial intelligence, machine learning, and the Internet of Things (IoT) promises to create exciting opportunities for Linux to enhance operational capabilities further. Enterprises increasingly recognize that Linux's adaptability and strong community support ensure they remain agile and innovative amid disruptive changes.

In conclusion, Linux's ascent within the business sector epitomizes a remarkable evolution marked by resilience, adaptation, and community-driven collaboration. Transitioning from a university project to a mainstream operating system, Linux has firmly established itself as an indispensable tool for enterprises of all sizes. Sustainability, flexibility, and security continue to characterize Linux's journey, as businesses embrace open-source solutions to navigate the complexities of the digital landscape. As the future unfolds, the enterprise landscape will undoubtedly benefit from the collective innovation that Linux fosters within its passionate community, ensuring that this powerful operating system remains at the forefront of technological advancement and business success.

6.2. Enterprise Solutions and Linux Distributions

In the vast landscape of enterprise solutions, Linux has surfaced as a transformative force that is reshaping how businesses operate. Its adaptability, performance, security, and cost-effectiveness have established it as the foundation for numerous enterprise applications across various industries. This subchapter delves deeply into the specific Linux distributions designed to cater to enterprise needs, showcasing their unique features, strengths, and the communities that sustain them.

Linux distributions specifically tailored for enterprise solutions provide organizations with a robust platform to build upon, ensuring that they can navigate the complexities of modern digital environments while prioritizing efficiency and security. Among the most popular distributions that enterprises have come to rely on are Red Hat Enterprise Linux (RHEL), SUSE Linux Enterprise Server (SLES), and Ubuntu Server. Each of these distributions has its distinct characteristics that make them appealing for enterprise deployment.

Red Hat Enterprise Linux has earned its reputation as a powerhouse in enterprise solutions. Originating from the community-driven Fedora project, RHEL provides an enterprise-grade operating system that is designed for stability, security, and support. One of the defining features of RHEL is its subscription model, which offers customers access to comprehensive support and certified software, ensuring that organizations can maintain a secure and performance-optimized environment. RHEL's extensive documentation, training programs, and community resources also enhance its value, empowering users to leverage the distribution effectively. The inclusion of advanced security features, such as SELinux (Security-Enhanced Linux), amplifies its appeal in sectors that prioritize data protection and compliance.

SUSE Linux Enterprise Server is another significant player in the enterprise arena. It is recognized for its flexibility, compatibility with various infrastructures, and strong support for mission-critical workloads. SLES emphasizes interoperability, allowing organizations to run their applications seamlessly across diverse IT environments, whether they are on-premises, in the cloud, or a hybrid model. With its focus on enterprise resource planning (ERP) solutions, SLES has been widely adopted in industries such as manufacturing, finance, and healthcare. The availability of a rich ecosystem of third-party applications and systems also makes SUSE a preferred choice for enterprises looking to integrate various software tools efficiently.

Ubuntu Server has carved a niche for itself as a go-to solution for many enterprises, particularly in the realm of cloud computing. As an accessible and user-friendly distribution, Ubuntu has gained traction due to its emphasis on simplicity and ease of use, enabling organizations to deploy Linux quickly and cost-effectively. Ubuntu Server is heavily utilized in cloud environments, with a strong integration path into platforms such as OpenStack, making it a popular choice for building private and public cloud architectures. Canonical, the company behind Ubuntu, provides commercial support and enhanced services, allowing businesses to engage with the community while having the option for professional assistance. The extensive package repository, along with the support for container technologies like Docker and Kubernetes, positions Ubuntu as a strong contender for organizations venturing into DevOps and microservices architectures.

In addition to these primary distributions, there are many specialized Linux variants tailored to meet specific enterprise requirements. For example, CentOS, built from RHEL's source code, serves as a free alternative to its commercial counterpart—providing organizations with a capable and community-supported distribution without the cost of a subscription. Similarly, Oracle Linux offers enterprise features and optimizations specifically designed for running Oracle products, appealing to businesses heavily invested in Oracle technologies.

These enterprise distributions thrive due to the passionate communities that support them. The open-source nature of Linux empowers users to contribute back to the distribution through code, documentation, and community support, leading to continuous improvements and innovations. Forums, online discussions, and collaboration tools allow system administrators, developers, and users to engage with one another, share knowledge, and solve challenges collectively. This sense of community significantly enhances the value proposition of Linux distributions—organizations not only gain access to an operating system but also become part of a vibrant ecosystem that fosters collaboration.

It's also essential to explore how these distributions enable enterprises to adapt and respond to emerging technological trends. For instance, as businesses increasingly migrate to cloud-centric models, Linux distributions have evolved to provide specialized features that facilitate cloud integration, containerization, and orchestration. The integration of tools like Ansible (for automation), OpenShift (for container orchestration), and Prometheus (for monitoring) reinforces the role of Linux as a dynamic platform that can accommodate modern enterprise needs.

Moreover, another key advantage of Linux distributions is their focus on security and compliance, particularly in industries such as finance and healthcare that face stringent regulations. Tools for system hardening, auditing, and compliance reporting are integral parts of distributions like RHEL and SUSE, allowing enterprises to ensure their environments meet industry standards. In light of growing cyber threats, organizations prioritize security, and the strong security posture of enterprise Linux distributions enhances their appeal as foundational components of IT architecture.

In conclusion, the landscape of enterprise solutions continues to evolve, with Linux distributions standing at the forefront of transformation. Their adaptability, community support, security features, and cost-effectiveness render them invaluable assets for organizations seeking to thrive in a fast-paced digital era. By leveraging the strengths of tailored distributions, enterprises can forge paths toward innovation, efficiency, and resilience while remaining rooted in the principles of collaboration and open-source development that have driven Linux's success from its inception. As we look forward, the ongoing evolution of enterprise solutions rooted in Linux will undoubtedly influence the future of technology and business.

6.3. Compatibility in Enterprise Systems

Linux's compatibility in enterprise systems is a multi-faceted concept that encompasses the integration of the operating system with both legacy and current infrastructure, ensuring that organizations can leverage their existing investments while benefiting from the adaptability and robustness that Linux offers. As businesses seek to navigate the complexities of modern IT environments, understanding how Linux interacts with diverse hardware, software, and deployment scenarios is crucial.

Historically, compatibility challenges have posed a considerable barrier to Linux's adoption in enterprise settings. In its earlier years, enterprises often operated within ecosystems dominated by proprietary operating systems, which raised concerns about whether Linux could integrate effectively with existing tools and applications. Many businesses were hesitant to transition to Linux, fearing potential disruptions in their operations or the need to overhaul their entire infrastructure.

In response to these challenges, significant efforts have been made within the Linux community to enhance compatibility and interoperability. One of the most notable approaches has been the development of various distributions tailored for enterprise use, including Red Hat Enterprise Linux, SUSE Linux Enterprise, and Ubuntu Server. These distributions provide comprehensive support for enterprise-grade applications, ensuring that essential software tools integrate smoothly with Linux environments.

Moreover, Linux boasts a strong capability to support virtualization technologies, which allows organizations to run multiple operating systems on a single physical server. This feature is particularly valuable for enterprises looking to maintain legacy systems while experimenting with newer technologies. Solutions like KVM (Kernel-based Virtual Machine), VMware, and VirtualBox enable administrators to create virtual machines that host Windows, BSD, or other operating systems seamlessly, facilitating a coexistence model that minimizes disruption and maximizes resource utilization.

Hardware compatibility has also been a focal point for Linux developers. By collaborating closely with hardware manufacturers, the Linux community has expanded the range of supported devices and platforms significantly. Many major hardware vendors now provide drivers for their products compatible with Linux, ranging from network adapters and storage solutions to advanced graphics cards. This increased hardware support has made it feasible for enterprises to deploy Linux on new hardware without facing significant compatibility issues.

The rise of cloud computing has further transformed the compatibility landscape for Linux. As organizations increasingly migrate to cloud-based infrastructures, Linux's open-source nature allows for easy integration with various cloud service providers. Platforms like Amazon Web Services, Google Cloud Platform, and Microsoft Azure have embraced Linux, allowing businesses to deploy and scale their services rapidly. The adaptability of Linux serves as a cornerstone for organizations wishing to leverage the cloud while ensuring compatibility across diverse infrastructure components.

Moreover, Linux's community-driven model encourages active feedback, enabling the prompt identification and resolution of compatibility issues. Organizations can benefit from this collaborative spirit, accessing a wealth of knowledge from forums, user groups, and community resources. Challenges encountered by one organization are often tackled collectively, providing innovative solutions and workarounds that can be applied across various systems and use cases.

In the case of specialized applications, enterprises utilizing Linux can often find open-source alternatives to proprietary software that seamlessly integrate with existing workflows. For example, businesses in sectors such as finance or healthcare frequently rely on specific software applications tailored for their industry requirements. The emergence of robust open-source tools—like GnuCash for accounting or OpenEMR for medical practices—provides organizations with the flexibility to meet their needs without relying solely on traditional proprietary solutions.

Furthermore, compatibility is not limited solely to software and hardware. It also encompasses aligning organizational policies and procedures with Linux solutions. Enterprises looking to adopt Linux must consider how their existing IT governance structures, compliance frameworks, and operational processes can evolve to accommodate the shift. Training and upskilling personnel to manage Linux environments effectively are essential steps in ensuring smooth transitions while simultaneously enhancing the company's technological capabilities.

As organizations continue to embrace digital transformation, the relevance of Linux's compatibility will only grow. Emerging technologies such as edge computing, machine learning, and the Internet of Things (IoT) demand flexible, resilient, and adaptable systems that can integrate seamlessly into existing infrastructures. Linux, with its culture of innovation and community support, is exceptionally positioned to meet these compatibility needs, enabling enterprises to future-proof their operations while benefiting from the cost-efficiency and agility that Linux solutions provide.

In conclusion, the compatibility of Linux in enterprise systems is a dynamic and evolving concept that focuses on the seamless integration of diverse technologies, applications, and infrastructure. As organizations navigate the ever-changing digital landscape, understanding the options and strategies for leveraging Linux compatibility will empower them to adapt effectively and optimize their operations. The collaboration between the Linux community, hardware vendors, software developers, and users ultimately emphasizes the adaptability and reliability of Linux, ensuring that it remains a cornerstone in the enterprise technology toolkit.

6.4. Linux and Cloud Enterprises

In a world increasingly driven by cloud computing, Linux has emerged as the operating system of choice for many enterprises seeking scalable, reliable, and open-source solutions. The interplay between Linux and the cloud represents not just a technological adoption but a transformational shift that has fundamentally altered how businesses manage their IT infrastructure. This shift is characterized by the convergence of several factors: the rise of cloud services, the efficiency of Linux as a server OS, and the collaborative nature of the open-source community fueling innovation.

The cloud revolution gained momentum in the early 2000s, providing businesses with unprecedented flexibility to scale resources up and down based on demand. Traditional infrastructure models often necessitated significant capital expenditures on hardware and software licenses, while cloud computing has introduced a pay-as-you-go model that optimizes costs. Linux, with its robust performance and adaptability, has become the linchpin of many cloud infrastructure strategies. Major providers, including Amazon Web Services (AWS), Google Cloud Platform (GCP), and Microsoft Azure, predominantly deploy Linux servers, capitalizing on its capabilities to support significant workloads and varied application environments.

One of the key advantages of using Linux in cloud environments is its exceptional performance and reliability. Linux distributions are known for their minimal resource footprints and efficiency in handling concurrent processes, which is crucial when running multiple virtual machines or applications on a single server. With Linux's lightweight architecture, enterprises can maximize their hardware utilization, ensuring that they derive the maximum value from their investments.

Moreover, the flexibility offered by Linux allows organizations to deploy tailored solutions that align specifically with their operational requirements. Whether it's utilizing Ubuntu for rapid cloud app deployment or leveraging Red Hat for enterprise-scale applications requiring more sophisticated support, the ability to customize Linux distributions means that organizations can optimize their cloud environments for specific workloads, applications, and scalability needs.

An essential aspect of cloud enterprises leveraging Linux is the significant emphasis on containers, which have revolutionized application deployment and management. With technologies such as Docker and Kubernetes, businesses can develop, ship, and run applications in isolated environments. Linux has proven to be the leading operating system for containerization, primarily due to its support for cgroups and namespaces, which facilitate the efficient management of resources and security. As enterprises increasingly adopt microservices architectures, containers powered by Linux allow for rapid development cycles, seamless updates, and efficient management of complex applications.

The support for Linux within the cloud infrastructure also stems from the vibrant ecosystem fostered by the open-source community. The collaborative nature of Linux development means that enhancements and features are continuously refined and made available to users. This ecosystem encourages innovation where new tools, libraries, and frameworks are developed alongside Linux, providing enterprises with a plethora of options to enhance operational efficiencies. The rapid evolution of open-source tools such as OpenStack, which enables users to create private and public clouds, showcases how community contributions have reshaped enterprise cloud strategies.

Furthermore, security remains a paramount concern within cloud environments, and Linux's inherent security features fortify enterprises against potential threats. Access controls, SELinux (Security-

Enhanced Linux), and active community audits of software through the open-source model enable organizations to adopt stringent security measures without incurring significant costs traditionally associated with proprietary solutions. The transparency that comes with open-source software means that vulnerabilities can often be identified and resolved more swiftly, leading to a more secure enterprise environment.

The integration of Linux into cloud enterprises has also opened new avenues for organizations transitioning to DevOps practices— methodologies that emphasize collaboration between development and operations teams. With Linux as the backbone of cloud applications and infrastructure, teams can benefit from streamlined workflows, automated processes, and improved communication channels. The synergy between Linux, cloud services, and DevOps culturally aligns with principles of open-source collaboration, allowing teams to innovate faster and respond more effectively to market demands.

As enterprises continue to navigate the complexities of digital transformation, the intersection of Linux and cloud computing will remain a focal point. Companies that embrace Linux in their cloud strategies not only stand to benefit from cost efficiencies and enhanced performance but also position themselves to thrive in a rapidly changing technological landscape. The fusion of these two powerful forces exemplifies how open-source solutions can empower organizations to adapt, innovate, and excel in a world driven by cloud technology.

Looking forward, we can anticipate ongoing advancements as the technologies surrounding Linux and cloud computing continue to mature. As enterprises seek to harness emerging technologies such as artificial intelligence, machine learning, and the Internet of Things (IoT), the flexibility and reliability of Linux will be essential in providing the infrastructure necessary to support these innovations. Thus, the interplay between Linux and cloud enterprises is poised to define the future of business technology, offering exciting opportunities for growth, collaboration, and transformation across diverse industries.

6.5. Open Source Business Models

The phenomenon of open source business models represents a paradigm shift in how technology companies create value and sustain themselves financially. Unlike traditional proprietary models that typically hinge on licensing fees and tightly controlled distribution, open-source business models embrace transparency, community collaboration, and user engagement as core components of their strategies. This subchapter aims to dissect the intricate relationship between open source and business frameworks while exploring successful examples, emerging practices, and the challenges inherent in this innovative approach.

Open-source business models can be categorized into several distinct strategies, each tailored to leverage the benefits of community-driven development and collaborative engagement. A prevalent approach involves adopting a dual-licensing strategy, where the software is offered under both an open-source license and a proprietary license. Companies that employ this model often provide a free version of their software to attract a user base while simultaneously offering a commercial, feature-rich version for enterprises willing to pay for additional services, dedicated support, or advanced functionalities. Examples of successful dual-licensing models can be observed in companies such as MySQL (now owned by Oracle), which has commercialized its database effectively through this hybrid approach, and MongoDB, which similarly leverages the community edition alongside premium offerings.

Another strategy thriving within the open-source ecosystem is the subscription model that focuses on providing value-added services. Companies offer their open-source products for free while charging customers for professional support, consulting services, training, or managed hosting. This model has gained considerable traction among enterprises seeking reliable support for critical applications without the hefty price tag of proprietary software. Red Hat epitomizes this strategy with Red Hat Enterprise Linux (RHEL), which allows businesses to utilize the Linux operating system at no cost while offering subscription-based support and updates that are essential for maintaining enterprise-level environments. By positioning itself as a dependable partner in open-source, Red Hat has emerged as a billion-dollar company that capitalizes on services rather than traditional software sales.

The freemium model, a prevalent approach in consumer tech, has also found its footing in open source. Under this strategy, companies offer a basic version of their software for free, enticing users to adopt the platform. Users may then opt to pay for premium features, advanced functionalities, or enhanced performance. This model is particularly effective for projects with widespread appeal, as it garners a large user base quickly, fostering community engagement and advocacy. Firms like GitLab and Atlassian have effectively utilized this approach, providing fundamental tools for software development and management while monetizing premium offerings such as additional storage, advanced collaboration features, and priority support.

Service and consulting-based business models also represent a viable avenue for open-source firms. Companies may choose to build their entire operation around providing consulting services, implementation support, and custom development for open-source projects. This approach capitalizes on the knowledge and expertise derived from deep familiarity with open-source technologies while allowing flexibility for adaptation to client-specific needs. For smaller firms, this model can be especially effective, as it establishes credibility and encourages brand loyalty among clients seeking to incorporate open-source solutions into their business strategies.

Furthermore, open-source business models have moved beyond traditional software, expanding into hardware, data, and various emerging fields. For example, organizations like Arduino have developed open-source hardware platforms that allow users to create, modify, and share electronic designs. By promoting a vibrant community of creators and hobbyists, Arduino has not only succeeded commercially but has also inspired a dedicated group of designers and engineers who contribute to its ecosystem. Similarly, open-source data platforms, such as Apache Hadoop, have emerged in response to the growing demand for big data solutions, allowing companies to leverage open-source tools while providing opportunities for consulting and support services.

However, while open-source business models offer remarkable advantages, they also pose several challenges. One major hurdle is the tension between maintaining a thriving, collaborative community and sustaining financial viability. Companies must strike a delicate balance between participating openly and protecting their business interests. They must also navigate potential concerns surrounding the perception of commercialization within the open-source community, which can lead to backlash from users who feel that their contributions are being exploited for profit.

Additionally, companies operating under open-source models must ensure that they are not solely dependent on services revenue to sustain innovation. As the open-source landscape matures and competitors emerge, organizations need to innovate constantly, seeking new avenues for revenue generation while keeping their offerings robust and engaged with the community.

Despite the potential pitfalls, the opportunities presented by open-source business models remain compelling. Companies that cultivate strong relationships with their user bases, leverage community contributions, and provide ongoing support can tap into significant sources of revenue while continuing to drive innovation. As the technology landscape continues to evolve and businesses increasingly recognize the value of open-source solutions, we can expect to see more organizations adopting open-source models as a catalyst for growth and sustainability.

In conclusion, the exploration of open-source business models reveals a landscape rich with possibilities and challenges. By embracing principles of collaboration, transparency, and community engagement, companies can not only thrive but also foster innovation that transcends traditional boundaries. As organizations forge new paths within the realms of software and technology, navigating the interplay between open source and business strategies will remain a pivotal journey, shaping the future of both the Linux ecosystem and the broader tech landscape.

7. Linux in Education: Brewing the Next Generation

7.1. Linux in Schools

In the ever-evolving educational landscape, Linux has established a notable presence in schools and academic institutions worldwide, providing both students and educators with powerful tools that not only enhance the learning experience but also foster a sense of collaboration, innovation, and empowerment in technology. This subchapter delves into the multitude of ways Linux is integrated into educational curricula, its benefits for both students and teachers, and the broader implications for technological literacy and engagement in learning environments.

As educational institutions strive to provide students with the skills necessary for the modern workforce, integrating Linux into the curriculum serves as a gateway to understanding both the fundamentals of computing and the intricacies of software development. Linux, being an open-source operating system, allows students to explore the underlying mechanics of software without the constraints posed by proprietary systems. This transparency encourages a deeper comprehension of programming, system administration, and technological problem-solving, equipping students with valuable skills that are highly sought after in today's job market.

Many schools and universities recognize the flexibility and affordability of Linux as an operating system, particularly in comparison to the licensing fees associated with proprietary software. This financial model allows institutions to allocate limited resources more effectively while providing students with access to powerful applications. As a result, various educational institutions have transitioned to Linux-based systems, utilizing distributions like Ubuntu, Fedora, and Debian, which come packaged with essential educational tools and software suites.

Linux's adaptability makes it an ideal fit for computer labs, where students can engage with programming languages such as Python,

C++, and Java, all of which are natively supported on Linux systems. Moreover, the existence of vast repositories of free, open-source educational software—ranging from programming environments to graphics and design tools—offers students opportunities to experiment and innovate without facing financial constraints. Programs like GIMP, LibreOffice, and Scratch illustrate how educational resources can flourish within the Linux ecosystem, enhancing creativity and collaboration among peers.

The collaborative spirit imbued in Linux naturally extends to educational settings, where students can work together on group projects, share knowledge, and contribute to open-source initiatives. Many educators leverage the community-driven nature of Linux to teach students about the importance of collaboration in software development, leading to hands-on experiences where they contribute code, create documentation, or engage with community forums. This exposure not only fosters technical skills but also social skills, encouraging teamwork, communication, and peer-driven problem-solving.

Interestingly, the role of Linux in education extends beyond the classroom. Numerous community-oriented projects and initiatives aim to teach underprivileged or underserved populations about technology through open-source platforms. Programs such as "Linux in Schools" and "Raspberry Pi educational initiatives" are designed to democratize access to technology, equipping students with computational thinking skills that drive innovation and creativity. These endeavors emphasize inclusivity and access, directly addressing the digital divide often present in modern society.

Educators also find value in the educational resources that come with Linux, including extensive documentation and a plethora of online tutorials dedicated to teaching various aspects of operating systems and programming. This wealth of knowledge empowers teachers to integrate technology meaningfully into their lessons without requiring extensive training or expertise in proprietary systems. Additionally, engaging with open-source communities can lead to networking opportunities with other educators, fostering the sharing of best practices and resources across schools and universities.

As students learn to navigate the Linux environment, they cultivate a sense of ownership over their learning experience. Linux encourages exploration and experimentation—students can customize their operating systems, install applications, and even contribute to the development of software that meets their specific needs. This spirit of innovation is invigorating for young minds, fostering an entrepreneurial approach to technology where students envision, create, and implement solutions to real-world problems.

However, it's essential to recognize that the transition to adopting Linux in education is not without its challenges. Some educators may initially face resistance when introducing new systems, stemming from a lack of familiarity among students and staff. To combat this, successful implementations often require thorough planning, extensive training, and ongoing institutional support. Schools that have thrived in adopting Linux typically foster a culture of collaboration among educators, guiding them in integrating Linux seamlessly into their classrooms.

Furthermore, as technology continues to advance, Linux presents an opportunity for educators to prepare students for emerging trends in the tech industry, such as cloud computing, artificial intelligence, and cybersecurity. By incorporating Linux into educational frameworks, institutions can nurture a generation of technologists equipped to contribute meaningfully to the evolving landscape of technology.

In summary, the integration of Linux in schools represents a compelling narrative of innovation, collaboration, and inclusivity in education. By promoting acccss to technology, fueling creativity, and fostering a culture of collaboration, Linux empowers students and educators alike to explore the realms of computing while leaving behind the constraints of proprietary systems. The ripple effects of adopting Linux in educational settings extend beyond the classroom, as they cultivate technological literacy and inspire future generations of learners to embark on paths that lead to empowerment and innovation in the digital age. As we continue to witness alterations in the educational landscape, the potential for Linux to bridge gaps in technology education remains a vital pursuit for institutions seeking to empower students in today's interconnected world.

7.2. Academic Contributions

In the realm of academia, the contributions to the development of Linux have been profound and transformational, melding theoretical research with practical application. Academic institutions, researchers, and students have played a crucial role in not only enhancing Linux's functionality but also in promoting its adoption and understanding within educational frameworks.

One of the most significant avenues through which academic contributions impact Linux is through collaborative research initiatives. Universities often engage in research projects that focus on optimizing the Linux kernel or developing new features that cater to specific academic interests. For instance, projects in fields such as high-performance computing often leverage Linux to conduct experiments, simulate complex systems, and analyze vast datasets. Academics contribute code, conduct reviews, and publish findings that can lead to improved efficiencies and new functionalities, with the collective goal of advancing Linux as a formidable operating system at the intersection of cutting-edge technology and research.

Additionally, many academic fields utilize Linux to support specialized applications. In bioinformatics, for example, researchers develop software tools to analyze genetic data and evolutionary patterns. The ease of customization and the ability to control the code in an open-source environment make Linux a preferred platform for such endeavors. Furthermore, the academic community benefits from Linux's high-performance capabilities, which are essential for handling the substantial workloads associated with genomics or proteomics research.

Academic collaborations have also inspired the creation of diverse distributions specifically tailored for educational purposes. Distributions like Edubuntu and DoudouLinux embody the spirit of teaching and learning in a Linux environment, providing user-friendly interfaces and educational software that introduce students to computing concepts in an engaging manner. These tailored distributions emerge from joint efforts between educators, developers, and the open-source community, ensuring that the next generation of users gains early exposure to Linux's strengths.

Moreover, the engagement of academic institutions with Linux is bolstered through initiatives such as summer coding programs or workshops that invite students to contribute to Linux development. These programs instill a sense of ownership and empowerment among students, who gain hands-on experience while honing their skills in software development, systems administration, and project management. By partnering with organizations like the Linux Foundation and participating in events such as the Google Summer of Code, students can bridge the gap between theory and practice, applying their learning in real-world contexts.

The academic contributions extend beyond code, encompassing research in fields such as computer science and information technology aimed at enhancing user experience on Linux. Scholars have published extensive literature addressing topics like usability studies, user interface design, accessibility, and software engineering practices related to Linux, contributing to a deeper understanding of how users interact with technology. The findings from such research inform not only the development of distributions but also the broader strategies that Linux projects might employ to enhance user engagement.

Additionally, the community-centric nature of Linux resonates well with academic values, inspiring a culture of sharing knowledge, findings, and innovations. Academic conferences, workshops, and online forums dedicated to Linux provide platforms for researchers and practitioners to collaborate, sparking new ideas and initiatives.

Such environments foster cross-disciplinary engagement, allowing academics in various fields—ranging from artificial intelligence to network security—to converge and contribute to honing the capabilities of Linux.

Another critical aspect to consider is the educational role Linux plays in preparing the next generation of developers, researchers, and IT professionals. Institutions widely employ Linux in their curricula, teaching students not only how to use the operating system but also how to contribute meaningfully to its development. This educational approach ensures that graduates exit their programs equipped with not just theoretical knowledge but practical skills—ranging from programming to system administration—that are directly applicable to real-world technological environments.

Moreover, specialized grants and funding opportunities aimed at open-source initiatives have also emerged within the academic sector, empowering researchers to pursue ambitious projects that extend Linux's capabilities. Grants often support the exploration of emerging technologies—like machine learning, cloud computing, and security enhancements—within the Linux context, enabling researchers to contribute to the operating system's evolution while advancing their own academic pursuits.

In summary, the symbiotic relationship between academic contributions and Linux's development showcases the powerful influence of research and education on the open-source landscape. Academic institutions serve as incubators for innovation, providing a fertile ground for collaboration that enriches Linux through code, research, and education. As Linux continues to evolve, the ongoing engagement of academic contributors will undoubtedly shape its future, reaffirming the pivotal role of education and research in technology's advancement. Emphasizing the integration of Linux within academic curricula and collaborative projects not only nurtures talent but also lays the groundwork for sustained innovation in the world of open-source software, echoing the fundamental principles of collaboration, community, and shared progress that lie at Linux's core.

7.3. Online Learning and Linux

In recent years, the integration of Linux into online learning platforms has gained momentum, revealing a potential for immense growth in the educational space. As learning systems evolve to meet the demands of a tech-savvy population, the flexibility and power of Linux enable institutions to provide innovative educational experiences tailored to diverse learning needs. This subchapter explores how cloud-based education platforms utilize Linux technology, examining both its benefits and the future prospects of this relationship.

The advent of cloud-based education platforms has transformed how learning materials and experiences are delivered. Traditional classrooms, often limited by physical resources and logistical challenges, are increasingly supplemented by online resources that offer accessibility, scalability, and an interactive learning environment. Linux, known for its stability and open-source nature, serves as the backbone for many of these platforms. Its ability to support a wide range of applications enhances the functionality and performance of educational tools, creating an effective environment for students and instructors alike.

One of the most notable advantages of utilizing Linux in online learning platforms is its cost-effectiveness. Many educational institutions operate on tight budgets, and choosing Linux-based solutions allows them to eliminate significant software license fees traditionally associated with proprietary systems. By adopting Linux, schools and universities can allocate resources toward educational materials and mentorship opportunities instead of monopolizing funds for licensing. This financial relief is particularly crucial for developing countries, where access to quality education can be limited by economic constraints.

Another significant benefit of integrating Linux into cloud-based education tools is its open-source flexibility. Educational programmers and institutions can customize Linux applications to meet specific needs without seeking permission from a proprietary software vendor. This adaptability fosters innovation, enabling educators to design tools that suit their teaching style or curriculum requirements. Moreover, as Linux thrives on community contributions, educators and students can collaborate on improving and building upon existing software, ensuring that the educational resources evolve in tandem with the needs of learners.

Security is also a priority for online learning platforms, particularly when sensitive student data is involved. Linux's reputation for robust security features, along with its proactive community approach to identifying vulnerabilities, makes it an attractive option for institutions handling private data. With proper configurations and security practices, Linux can provide a secure environment that protects users from potential cyber threats while maintaining the integrity of educational institutions and their online offerings.

Additionally, the introduction of virtual learning environments (VLEs) enhances the learning experience and expands access. VLEs built on Linux provide students with online collaborative spaces for discussions, project management, and peer-to-peer learning, thus fostering a sense of community distinct from the physical classroom. These platforms utilize the power of Linux-based servers to handle significant volumes of data and user interactions simultaneously, ensuring a smooth, interactive experience for participants.

Linux's contributions to cloud-based education extend to its compatibility with various programming languages, development tools, and software frameworks. For instance, educators can introduce students to coding and software development using popular tools such as Python, Ruby, and JavaScript—commonly supported by Linux distributions. This exposure equips learners with essential skills and knowledge for succeeding in the rapidly evolving tech landscape.

Furthermore, as institutions increasingly adopt online learning models, Linux enables the development of Massive Open Online Courses (MOOCs), which democratize education on a global scale. Platforms like Coursera and edX utilize Linux servers to deliver courses to hundreds of thousands of participants worldwide, showcasing the scalability and reliability of Linux-based solutions within prominent educational frameworks.

The future of online learning intertwined with Linux technology appears promising. As educational institutions continue to embrace the transformative nature of online learning, the role of Linux will likely expand. Enhanced contributions from educators, students, and developers could lead to the creation of specialized Linux tools and applications that redefine educational engagement and interactivity.

In conclusion, the integration of cloud-based education platforms leveraging Linux technology signifies a turning point in educational practices. The cost-effectiveness, flexibility, security, and collaborative capabilities offered by Linux allow institutions to provide enriched learning experiences that cater to current and future technological advancements. By continuing to develop and promote Linux solutions in educational settings, we can anticipate a future where accessibility and innovation empower learners globally, ultimately transforming the educational landscape for generations to come.

7.4. The Education of Developers

The education of developers in the context of the Linux operating system offers a unique glimpse into how the principles of open-source software can cultivate a new generation of technical talent equipped with essential skills for the future. As technology continues to advance and permeate various aspects of society, understanding the mechanisms and philosophies inherent in Linux not only prepares developers for careers in the tech industry but also empowers them to become active contributors to a widespread movement advocating for collaboration, accessibility, and innovation.

At its core, Linux represents more than just an operating system; it symbolizes a way of thinking about software development and community engagement. As developers immerse themselves in the world of Linux, they gain insights into how open-source systems function, the collaborative nature of project development, and the importance of clear documentation and user feedback. This foundational knowledge serves as an essential launching pad for understanding broader software development practices.

The ethos of collaboration present in Linux projects encourages developers to work collectively, share their knowledge and experiences, and contribute to a larger goal. This immersive atmosphere helps break down traditional hierarchies found in corporate environments, fostering an understanding that innovation often arises from the diverse insights and perspectives brought together by a community. Developers engaged with Linux ecosystems learn the value of mutual support—co-founding mentoring relationships that can lead to greater skill advancement and knowledge sharing.

Educational institutions have increasingly recognized the importance of incorporating Linux into curricula aimed at producing well-rounded developers equipped for the demands of modern technology. Many computer science and software engineering programs offer courses centered around Linux, covering essential topics such as system architecture, programming languages, and open-source software principles. Through a combination of theoretical and hands-on learning experiences, students become adept at navigating Linux environments, using programming languages such as Python, C, and Java, and collaborating on real-world projects.

Furthermore, competitions and collaborative initiatives often foster Linux skills among students. Programs like Google Summer of Code and various hackathons challenge developers to contribute to existing open-source projects or create new solutions using Linux. These opportunities provide a unique platform for students to showcase their capabilities, engage with experienced mentors, and collaborate with peers from around the globe. The sense of accomplishment derived from contributing to popular projects fuels motivation and confidence, propelling students to further explore their passions within the tech sphere.

The widespread availability of resources and learning platforms has made learning Linux even more accessible. The online community surrounding Linux thrives, offering extensive documentation, tutorials, and forums designed to support both beginners and advanced developers. Platforms like Codecademy, Coursera, and edX host courses focused on Linux, enabling individuals to learn at their own pace. This democratization of knowledge fosters an environment where anyone, regardless of background or geographical location, can gain proficiency in Linux and contribute meaningfully to the community.

Moreover, the alignment of Linux with emerging technologies ensures that developers educated in this environment are well-prepared for the jobs of the future. As industries increasingly adopt cloud computing, artificial intelligence, and machine learning, proficiency in Linux becomes a valuable asset. Many of the tools—such as TensorFlow or Keras—designed for these applications have robust support in Linux environments. By educating developers in these tools on Linux, educational institutions foster a pipeline of talent ready to innovate in rapidly evolving sectors.

Beyond technical skills, Linux education emphasizes attributes like problem-solving, critical thinking, and adaptability. Developers working with Linux often encounter various challenges, whether it be adapting to a particular network configuration or debugging code. Overcoming these hurdles not only sharpens their analytical abilities but also instills a growth mindset—an invaluable quality as they embark on their careers in technology where change is constant.

In conclusion, the education of developers within the Linux ecosystem is a multifaceted endeavor that equips them with essential technical skills while fostering a mindset fostered in collaboration and innovative thinking. By engaging with Linux, learners are not only introduced to the technical intricacies and best practices of software development but also nurture their commitment to open-source principles, empowering them to contribute positively to the technology landscape. As we continue to confront new challenges in the digital age, it is clear that the foundation built through Linux education will play a pivotal role in shaping the developers of tomorrow, inspiring them to leverage their skills for the betterment of society and the broader world of technology.

7.5. Educational Projects and Competitions

In the dynamic landscape of education, hands-on projects and competitions have emerged as powerful tools for fostering engagement and skill development among students interested in Linux and open-source technologies. Recognizing the need to cultivate technical aptitude and creative problem-solving skills, educational institutions, organizations, and communities have initiated various initiatives designed to provide meaningful experiences for learners. This sub-chapter explores notable educational projects and competitions that have successfully promoted Linux skillsets among students, illustrating how these opportunities not only enhance technical knowledge but also encourage collaboration and community building.

One of the most well-known educational programs that leverage Linux technology is the Google Summer of Code (GSoC). Launched in 2005, GSoC has provided countless students from around the world with the opportunity to work on open-source projects during the summer months. Participants are paired with mentoring organizations, allowing them to collaboratively develop code and contribute to existing projects. Many of these projects are Linux-centric, making GSoC an invaluable opportunity for students to gain practical experience in software development while honing their skills in Linux environments. The initiative not only empowers students to engage with real-world software development challenges but also fosters connections within the global open-source community.

In addition to GSoC, various local and regional hackathons have sprung up as exciting competitions focused on Linux. These events bring together students and developers for a specified time, where they collaborate in teams to create innovative projects or solutions using Linux-based tools and technologies. Hackathons promote creativity, critical thinking, and teamwork, enabling students to apply their knowledge in a practical setting while also learning from peers. Moreover, language barriers and geographical distances are minimized as participants often represent diverse backgrounds, fostering enriching exchanges of ideas and perspectives.

Organizations such as the Linux Foundation and regional Linux User Groups (LUGs) often host coding competitions that target both high school and college students. These competitions allow participants to tackle specific challenges, such as developing applications or contributing to open-source projects within a limited timeframe. The competitive environment encourages students to think critically and creatively while experiencing the collaborative nature of open-source development firsthand. Additionally, participants can engage with experienced mentors who provide guidance and feedback, thereby enhancing the overall learning experience.

The outreach initiatives by educational institutions also play a significant role in increasing student engagement with Linux. Many universities have adopted programs where students can participate in supervised projects or internships centered around Linux. These projects are designed to help students tackle real-world problems while contributing to ongoing community efforts. Such experiences bridge the gap between theoretical knowledge and practical skills, ensuring that students graduate with industry-ready competencies.

Moreover, initiatives like "Linux in Schools"—a global effort aimed at introducing Linux into educational settings—demonstrate how collaborations with schools foster knowledge-sharing and technology literacy among students. By providing training sessions and resources, volunteers work closely with educators to implement Linux-based solutions in classrooms. These efforts highlight the importance of integrating open-source technologies into educational curricula, preparing students for future careers in technology.

Additionally, competitions focused on cybersecurity and ethical hacking utilize Linux as a core component in training participants. Events like "Capture the Flag" (CTF) competitions challenge students to solve security-related puzzles or work on real-world scenarios involving penetration testing, system vulnerabilities, and data protection—all conducted in Linux environments. These competitions emphasize the practical applications of Linux skills and equip participants with critical cybersecurity knowledge necessary for today's digital landscape.

The significance of community involvement in educational projects is also worth noting. Volunteer-led initiatives and collaborations between educational institutions and industry partners provide students with opportunities to engage with professionals already working in the Linux space. Workshops, guest lectures, and mentorship programs create dynamic learning environments while also inspiring students to pursue careers in open-source development and related fields.

Furthermore, online platforms dedicated to teaching Linux fundamentals and technical skills, such as The Linux Foundation's training programs or the "Linux Essentials" certification, are often integrated into educational curricula. These resources not only equip students with vital skills for the workforce but also encourage a culture of lifelong learning—an essential quality as technology continues to evolve rapidly.

In summary, educational projects and competitions centered around Linux play a critical role in promoting technical skills, collaboration, and community engagement among students. Through initiatives like Google Summer of Code, hackathons, coding competitions, and outreach programs, learners gain practical experience, deepen their understanding of Linux, and build connections within the open-source community. As these opportunities continue to expand, they will serve as foundational experiences that inspire and empower the next generation of innovators, equipping them with the skills necessary to navigate the ever-changing landscape of technology. By nurturing a passion for open-source solutions and collaborative development, educational projects pave the way for a more inclusive, engaged, and knowledgeable population prepared to tackle the challenges of the digital age.

8. Ecology of a Distribution: The Linux Kernel and Ecosystem

8.1. Understanding Distributions

Understanding distributions within the Linux ecosystem is a vital aspect of harnessing the power of this versatile operating system. At the very foundation of Linux's strength lies its extensive variety of distributions, each with its unique characteristics, target audiences, and intended uses. This diversity ensures that Linux can cater to a broad spectrum of users—from hobbyists and developers to enterprises and specialized industries—while embodying the principles of open-source, community collaboration, and adaptability that define its ethos.

At its core, a Linux distribution comprises the Linux kernel, the essential core of the operating system, amalgamated with a collection of software packages, applications, and system utilities that create a functional computing environment. These distributions, often referred to simply as "distros," can be broadly categorized into various types based on their focus, user experience, and package management systems. Understanding these categories is crucial for individuals seeking to utilize Linux effectively in their endeavors.

One of the most significant classifications of Linux distributions includes general-purpose distributions, designed to be versatile and customizable for a wide range of use cases. Popular examples include Ubuntu, Fedora, and Debian. Ubuntu, widely recognized for its user-friendliness and extensive community support, targets both newcomers to Linux and seasoned users. It offers comprehensive documentation and a vast software repository, making it accessible to individuals looking to transition from proprietary operating systems. Fedora, in contrast, emphasizes cutting-edge technology and innovation, providing users with access to the latest software and features while maintaining a strong connection to the upstream development of Red Hat Enterprise Linux. Debian, known for its stability and robustness, serves as a foundation for many other distributions, focusing on reliability and adherence to open-source principles.

On the contrary, specialized distributions concentrate on niche markets or particular tasks, ensuring optimal performance in specific environments. For example, Ubuntu Studio caters to multimedia professionals, incorporating an extensive suite of creative software tailored for audio, video, and graphic design. Likewise, Kali Linux serves the cybersecurity community by providing tools for penetration testing, vulnerability assessment, and ethical hacking. These specialized distributions frequently adopt customized configurations, pre-installed applications, and tailored user interfaces to meet the unique demands of their target users, enabling heightened efficiency and effectiveness in their respective fields.

Moreover, enterprise-focused distributions have gained traction within the business sector, offering stability, support, and additional features that cater to organizational environments. Red Hat Enterprise Linux (RHEL) and SUSE Linux Enterprise Server (SLES) exemplify this category, providing commercial support, certification, security updates, and advanced systems management tools. These distributions are designed to integrate seamlessly with enterprise infrastructure while addressing the performance and operational needs of businesses.

Additionally, the choice of package management systems marks a pivotal differentiator between distributions. Package managers are essential tools that enable users to install, update, and remove software packages efficiently. Different distributions often utilize distinct package management systems—such as APT for Debian-based distributions (including Ubuntu), RPM for Red Hat-based distributions, and Pacman for Arch Linux—each presenting unique commands and functionalities for managing software. Understanding how to navigate these package systems is critical for users seeking to customize their Linux environment effectively and leverage the vast array of applications available across the various distributions.

The inclusivity of Linux distributions allows diverse user communities to develop and share their customizations, tools, and resources. This collaborative aspect epitomizes the open-source philosophy, where individuals contribute to the collective knowledge base and enhance the functionality and usability of their chosen distributions. Engaging with forums, mailing lists, and online communities further aids users in finding solutions to challenges, discovering new tools, and collaborating on joint projects.

Importantly, distribution selection is a nuanced and personal decision. Users ought to consider factors such as hardware compatibility, software needs, skill levels, and intended applications. Newcomers to Linux may prefer beginner-friendly distributions characterized by graphical interfaces and comprehensive documentation, while experienced users might gravitate toward distributions that offer greater control, customizability, or experimentation opportunities.

In conclusion, understanding the various distributions of Linux is paramount for fully realizing the potential of this powerful operating system. The diversity of distros ensures a tailored experience for every user, allowing individuals and organizations to select precisely what fits their needs while upholding the principles of openness, community collaboration, and innovation. With thousands of Linux distributions available, each engaging a global community of developers and users, the landscape remains dynamic and continuously evolving—empowering users to delve into an expansive ecosystem that can adapt to their unique requirements and aspirations.

8.2. The Kernel's Role and Development

The Linux kernel is the very heart of the operating system, forming the backbone upon which various distributions are built. Its role and development are not just about leading technical improvements but also about fostering a collaborative environment that supports continuous evolution. Understanding the kernel's function aids in comprehending how Linux, as an open-source project, adapts to users' needs and the broader technological landscape.

At its core, the Linux kernel serves as a bridge between the hardware of a computer and the applications that run on it. It manages hardware resources, such as memory, processor time, and device input/output, ensuring that software applications can interact with the underlying hardware efficiently. The kernel acts as a mediator, processing requests from programs and allocating resources appropriately while ensuring system stability and security. With its modular architecture, the kernel can support a vast array of hardware and perform tasks such as process scheduling, memory management, file system operations, and device management.

The development of the Linux kernel is a dynamic and community-driven process that exemplifies the open-source ethos. Since Linus Torvalds first released version 0.01 in 1991, the kernel has undergone numerous iterations, each aimed at enhancing performance, security, and compatibility. The open-source nature of the kernel means that anyone can contribute to its development—this has led to contributions from individuals, corporations, and research institutions around the globe. The inclusivity of the development community is integral, fostering collaboration that drives innovation and addresses the evolving needs of users.

Maintaining a stable release cycle is another important aspect of kernel development, wherein major versions introduce new features while ensuring backward compatibility. The kernel's development is organized into several branches, with long-term support (LTS) releases designed for stability over extended periods. These LTS versions are critical for enterprises and infrastructures that depend on reliability, allowing them to enjoy the benefits of community support and security updates for years without having to frequently upgrade to the latest versions.

The kernel has continuously adapted to emerging technologies, embracing advancements in fields such as virtualization, cloud computing, and Internet of Things (IoT) applications. With the rise of cloud environments, the kernel has evolved to support features that enhance resource sharing and isolation, allowing multiple virtual machines or containers to run efficiently on a single physical host. Innovations like cgroups (control groups) and namespaces provide essential capabilities for managing resources and ensuring security in multi-tenant environments, making Linux a preferred choice for cloud deployments.

The development process of the Linux kernel also includes rigorous quality control practices, where patches and submissions undergo thorough review before integration. This peer review mechanism enhances code quality, as contributors test and critique one another's work, ensuring that only the most effective solutions become part of the kernel. Additionally, regression testing ensures that new features do not introduce unexpected issues to existing functionality, thereby maintaining the reputation of Linux as a stable platform.

One of the notable strengths of the Linux kernel development process is its vibrant mailing list culture. The linux-kernel mailing list serves as the primary forum for discussions about kernel development, where contributors can present ideas, propose changes, and provide feedback. This open dialogue ensures transparency in the development process while allowing individuals to influence decisions that shape the future of the kernel.

Furthermore, the kernel's growth has been paralleled by an expanding ecosystem of tools and projects that aim to enhance its capabilities. Projects that provide graphical interfaces for kernel configuration, tools for monitoring kernel performance, and extensive documentation empower users and developers to interact with the kernel more effectively. This ecosystem fosters educational endeavors as well, enabling new contributors to learn about kernel internals and actively participate in the community.

As we look to the future, the development of the Linux kernel will continue to reflect both the needs of users and advancements in hardware and software technologies. With the growing emphasis on security, performance, and adaptability in today's fast-changing tech landscape, the kernel's evolution will remain a focal point for innovation within Linux. It will also play a crucial role in helping Linux retain its position as a frontrunner in various domains, from server environments to mobile devices and beyond.

In summary, the kernel's role as the core of Linux extends far beyond simply managing hardware resources. Its continuous development, driven by a collaborative community centered around open-source principles, empowers Linux to adapt, innovate, and thrive in an ever-evolving technological landscape. The dynamics of kernel development pave the way for broader engagement with Linux, fostering a culture of contribution and shared knowledge that will undoubtedly inspire future generations of developers and users alike. This ongoing journey of collaboration, innovation, and technological advancement will ensure that Linux remains not just an operating system but a robust ecosystem that evolves to meet the ever-changing demands of its users.

8.3. Popular Linux Distributions

The world of Linux is a treasure trove of diverse distributions, each uniquely tailored to meet the specific needs of different user groups and scenarios. These distributions, or "distros," are the manifestation of the collaborative spirit that underpins the entire Linux ecosystem, allowing users from all walks of life to leverage open-source technology for personal, academic, or commercial purposes. Each distribution comes with its own features, strengths, and characteristics, reflecting the multitude of goals and philosophies that drive its development.

One of the most prominent distributions is Ubuntu, known for its user-friendly interface and strong community support. Ubuntu is designed to make the transition to Linux seamless for newcomers, offering a polished desktop experience and easy access to software through its Software Center. Its regular release cycle, extensive documentation, and robust community forums have earned it a devoted following, particularly among first-time Linux users. Ubuntu's commitment to usability and accessibility ensures that users can easily find help and resources as they embark on their Linux journey.

Fedora serves as a platform for those looking to experience the latest innovations in the world of open-source software. Backed by Red Hat, Fedora is often at the forefront of incorporating new technologies, making it a favorite among developers and tech enthusiasts looking for cutting-edge features. Fedora's commitment to free software principles, along with its focus on stability and efficiency, make it a powerful tool for developers who thrive on experimentation and exploration.

Debian, the foundation for many popular distributions, is renowned for its stability and reliability. It embraces a commitment to free software and emphasizes a thorough testing process before releasing updates or new versions. This commitment to stability makes Debian the go-to choice for many servers and production environments, where uptime and reliability are paramount. Its rich repository of software packages ensures that users can find the tools they need while also promoting collaboration among contributors to maintain a diverse suite of applications.

For those who prioritize ease of installation, Linux Mint provides a familiar interface akin to Windows, making it an excellent choice for users migrating from proprietary systems. With a focus on providing a complete out-of-the-box experience, Linux Mint comes pre-installed with necessary applications, codecs for multimedia playback, and intuitive features designed to simplify everyday tasks. This emphasis on user experience has made Linux Mint one of the most popular alternatives among new users.

Specialized distributions cater to niche markets, exhibiting the incredible versatility of Linux. For instance, Kali Linux is widely known among cybersecurity professionals for its suite of penetration testing tools. With hundreds of hacking tools pre-installed, Kali allows security professionals to assess systems for vulnerabilities and improve security measures. This specialized focus demonstrates how Linux can serve highly specific needs while maintaining the foundational principles of open source software.

Another example is Raspberry Pi OS (formerly Raspbian), tailored for use on the Raspberry Pi hardware platform. Raspberry Pi OS is particularly popular in educational settings and for DIY projects, providing a lightweight foundation that enables users to create a variety of personal and professional applications ranging from home automation to robotics. By empowering hobbyists, educators, and innovators, Raspberry Pi OS embodies the democratization of computing that Linux represents.

From enterprise-focused distributions, such as Red Hat Enterprise Linux (RHEL) and SUSE Linux Enterprise Server (SLES), to community-driven projects like Arch Linux—favored by experienced users for its design philosophy that grants complete control over system architecture—there is a distribution for every user, task, or scenario. The emergence of these diverse variations underscores the adaptability and strength of the Linux community, which continues to thrive on the contributions and collaborative efforts of individuals and organizations around the world.

In summary, the array of popular Linux distributions forms a rich tapestry of functionality and purpose, providing users with a custom-fit operating system that aligns with their specific needs and objectives. This diversity fosters innovation through collaboration, ensuring that Linux remains a powerful tool while reflecting the collective desires and aspirations of its user community. As new technologies and use cases continue to emerge, the landscape of Linux distributions will expand further, continuing the tradition of transformation and adaptability that has defined Linux from its inception. Each distribution is a testament to the power of community-driven development, ensuring that users can forever customize their experience within the vibrant world of Linux.

8.4. Niche and Specialized Distributions

Niche and Specialized Distributions provide a fascinating lens through which to view the vast ecosystem of Linux. While many users may gravitate toward popular distributions like Ubuntu, Fedora, or Debian, a myriad of niche and specialized distributions exist, tailored to meet the unique needs of specific user groups, industries, or purposes. The beauty of Linux lies in its flexibility and the ability to cater to diverse environments, ensuring that every user can find a distribution suited to their requirements.

One prominent example of a niche distribution is Kali Linux, widely recognized in the cybersecurity community for its powerful set of tools designed for penetration testing and security assessments. Kali is built on Debian and comes preloaded with numerous tools for tasks such as network monitoring, digital forensics, and vulnerability assessments. It's an ideal choice for ethical hackers and security professionals who require an environment tailored specifically for testing and securing systems. By focusing on the specific demands of cybersecurity, Kali Linux has carved out a reputation as a go-to platform for security experts and enthusiasts alike.

Another notable mention is OpenSUSE, which offers two distinct versions: Leap and Tumbleweed. Leap is a stable release, suitable for users seeking a reliable operating system for production environments, while Tumbleweed operates on a rolling-release model, providing the latest software and updates. This dual offering allows users to choose a version that aligns with their needs—navigating the line between stability and cutting-edge technology. OpenSUSE's YaST (Yet another Setup Tool) simplifies system configuration, making it an excellent choice for system administrators and developers.

For those interested in multimedia production, distributions like Ubuntu Studio are specifically designed to offer a robust environment for audio, video, and graphic design. With a comprehensive suite of creative software pre-installed, users can dive right into artistic endeavors without the hassle of sourcing and configuring individual applications. Ubuntu Studio embodies the idea of a specialized distribution, providing tools and resources specifically curated for media professionals.

Similarly, in the realm of education, Edubuntu serves as a dedicated distribution tailored for educational institutions. Built on the foundation of Ubuntu, it comes pre-loaded with a variety of educational applications aimed at students and teachers, fostering an engaging learning environment. With features designed for ease of use in a classroom setting, Edubuntu embodies the commitment to making Linux accessible and useful in academia.

Gaming has also seen a surge of specialized Linux distributions. SteamOS, developed by Valve Corporation, is a Debian-based distribution designed for living-room gaming. It provides an optimized environment for running games and integrates seamlessly with Steam, the leading gaming platform. This focus on gaming positions SteamOS uniquely within the broader Linux ecosystem, appealing to gamers wishing to leverage the power of Linux for their entertainment needs.

Moreover, there are distributions aimed at specific hardware, such as Raspberry Pi OS (formerly known as Raspbian), tailored for the Raspberry Pi single-board computer. This lightweight distribution maximizes the limited resources of the Pi while offering a user-friendly environment, making it a favorite among hobbyists and educators alike for projects ranging from home automation to programming exercises. The specialization of Raspberry Pi OS highlights the adaptability of Linux, making it viable for low-cost hardware solutions.

A prominent example within the realm of scientific computing is BioLinux, a Linux distribution specifically geared toward bioinformatics applications and tools. It provides researchers in the life sciences with a pre-configured environment equipped with essential software packages for genomic research, data analysis, and scientific computing. By attending to the unique requirements of the scientific community, BioLinux showcases the diverse use cases that specialized distributions can serve.

The extensive array of niche and specialized distributions extends to fields such as health care with distributions like OpenMRS, which focus on healthcare management solutions, or to server environments with distributions like CentOS, specifically tailored for enterprise-grade solutions. These distributions come equipped with tools and configurations that cater to the specific operational contexts and regulatory requirements of their respective fields.

Furthermore, specialized distributions foster community-driven innovation by encouraging users to collaborate and contribute to their specific areas of interest. Users of niche distributions often form dedicated communities, sharing best practices, troubleshooting advice, and modifications that are relevant to their specific use cases. This communal effort aligns with the underlying philosophy of Linux itself, creating a vibrant ecosystem characterized by collaboration, knowledge-sharing, and inclusivity.

In conclusion, niche and specialized distributions play a crucial role in the Linux ecosystem, exemplifying the operating system's adaptability and community-driven nature. By addressing the unique needs of various user groups and industries—ranging from cybersecurity and education to multimedia and scientific research—these distributions extend the reach of Linux and enrich its legacy. As the demand for tailored solutions continues to grow, we can expect further innovations and specialized distributions to emerge, underscoring Linux's commitment to serving diverse communities while maintaining its fundamental ethos of collaboration and open-source development.

8.5. The Role of Package Managers

In the digital world of software management, the role of package managers cannot be overstated. They serve as vital tools that dramatically simplify the process of installing, updating, and removing software on Linux distributions. Whether you are a casual user or a seasoned system administrator, understanding how package managers function is key to mastering your Linux experience.

At its core, a package manager automates the process of managing software packages on your system. A software package is essentially an archive file containing the executables, libraries, documentation, and metadata required for software to function correctly. With countless software options available for Linux, package managers streamline the installation process by locating, downloading, configuring, and installing these packages while managing their dependencies—other packages required for the software to run effectively.

One of the primary advantages of using package managers is the inherent organization they provide. Instead of manually searching the web for software, often dealing with conflicting versions or dependencies, users can access vast repositories of vetted, stable software through a package manager. Each Linux distribution typically maintains its own repository, which is curated by the community or maintainers.

For example, in Debian-based distributions like Ubuntu, users can rely on the Advanced Package Tool (APT). APT simplifies the installation process with commands that allow users to search for, install, and update software. Commands such as `apt install`, `apt update`, and `apt upgrade` are intuitive, letting users manage software with minimal effort. When a user installs a software package via APT, it automatically resolves dependencies by searching the repository for necessary packages and installs them concurrently.

Similarly, Red Hat-based distributions utilize the Yellowdog Updater, Modified (YUM) or DNF (Dandified YUM) package managers. These tools emphasize efficiency, providing users with commands like `yum install` or `dnf install` to manage software. They also connect to repositories, checking for the latest versions of programs and their dependencies, facilitating a smooth updating process. Notably, YUM has become synonymous with the management of RPM (Red Hat Package Manager) files, another fundamental software package format within the Linux ecosystem.

The community-driven nature of many Linux distributions encourages developers to contribute to their respective package management systems. As a result, users often benefit from the collective expertise embedded in the repositories. Software is not merely listed by name; it includes detailed descriptions, version information, and documentation about its dependencies and usage. This information streamlines decision-making when users seek software solutions tailored specifically to their needs.

Yet, package managers do not just stop at installation and updates; they also prioritize security. Most package managers use cryptographic signatures to validate the integrity of packages before installation, ensuring that users download only software from trusted sources. This security feature is particularly beneficial in an era where cyber threats and malicious software are omnipresent. Administrators can rest assured that the applications they install are legitimate and unaltered through package managers' validating processes.

In addition, package managers are essential for keeping systems up-to-date. With the command for upgrades, users can update both software and the system with a single command, ensuring all packages are current. This not only mitigates security vulnerabilities but also enhances the overall performance and functionality of the system.

Furthermore, package management systems encompass software repositories that can vary in levels of stability. Typically, distributions maintain several repositories, such as stable, testing, and unstable, enabling users to select the degree of reliability they prefer based on their needs. Users interested in cutting-edge software might opt for rolling release repositories, while those seeking reliability could choose stable repositories.

As we consider the future, the role of package managers is likely to continue evolving alongside new technologies and practices. The rise of containerization, exemplified by platforms like Docker, presents opportunities for integration with traditional package management systems. Containers encapsulate applications and their dependencies, providing a minimal environment that can be deployed across various systems. As developers adopt these technologies, package managers may adapt to include container-based solutions, facilitating new pathways for software distribution and management.

Moreover, the advent of universal package managers, such as Snap and Flatpak, aims to simplify software distribution across different Linux distributions. These systems encapsulate applications, enabling developers to create packages that work across various environments without worrying about dependency conflicts or distribution-specific issues. This versatility emphasizes the ongoing need for package managers as a crucial component of software management, offering solutions that transcend individual distribution boundaries.

In conclusion, the role of package managers in the Linux ecosystem is foundational to the efficiency and functionality of managing software. They simplify processes that would otherwise be cumbersome and overwhelming, acting as a bridge between users and the vast array of software available in the Linux ecosystem. By facilitating installation, updates, security, and organization, package managers empower users and contribute substantially to the comprehensive and collaborative nature of Linux as an open-source operating system. As technology continues to evolve, package managers will adapt alongside, demonstrating their enduring importance in shaping users' experiences within the Linux landscape.

9. Software Technologies: Developing on Linux

9.1. Development Environments on Linux

In the realm of software development on Linux, various environments cater to the diverse needs of developers across different disciplines. The Linux operating system's flexibility and robust community support enable the creation of development environments that not only promote coding efficiency but also foster innovation and collaboration. Understanding these environments is crucial for developers seeking to leverage the full potential of Linux.

One of the primary features of development environments on Linux is their adaptability to different programming languages and frameworks. Various IDEs (Integrated Development Environments) and code editors are available, catering to distinct programming languages while providing code completion, debugging, and project management features. For instance, Visual Studio Code, a popular open-source code editor, supports numerous programming languages and extensions specifically designed for web development, Python programming, and more. Its cross-platform capabilities enable developers to work seamlessly on different operating systems while utilizing the same development tools.

Python developers, in particular, benefit from a rich ecosystem of tools available on Linux. Anaconda, a distribution for data science and machine learning, comes preloaded with numerous packages and libraries, allowing users to manage dependencies effortlessly. Integrated tools like Jupyter Notebook offer interactive capabilities, enabling developers to create engaging educational materials or conduct data analyses directly within their browsers.

Furthermore, Linux has established itself as the primary operating system for server-side development, with environments such as LAMP (Linux, Apache, MySQL, and PHP) becoming industry standards for web applications. The simplicity of deploying and maintaining LAMP stacks on Linux servers makes it a preferred choice for developers creating dynamic websites and web applications. Many developers opt for containerized solutions like Docker, which allows them to create lightweight, reproducible environments for application development. Docker provides the ability to package applications with all their dependencies in a single container, ensuring consistency across various deployment environments.

For those engaged in mobile app development, Linux provides numerous tools tailored specifically to that domain. The Android development environment, for instance, allows developers to create, test, and deploy Android applications efficiently. The Android Studio IDE, based on IntelliJ IDEA, empowers Linux users to utilize features like an emulator, code analysis, and a visual layout editor—all seamlessly integrated into the Linux environment. As the importance of mobile technology grows, Linux-based solutions are pivotal for developers aiming to build versatile applications across platforms.

Another key aspect of the Linux development environment is its command-line interface (CLI), which is particularly valued by experienced developers. The CLI provides unparalleled control over system functions and allows for automation of repetitive tasks through shell scripting. Command-line utilities, such as Git for version control or Make for managing build processes, empower developers to tailor their workflows to be more efficient and streamlined. Mastering the command line enhances productivity and fosters a deeper understanding of how the Linux operating system operates under the hood.

While managing dependencies and software updates are common pain points in development, Linux package managers simplify these processes. Tools such as APT, YUM, and Pacman manage the installation and updating of software repositories, ensuring that developers have access to the latest libraries and tools required for their projects. This infrastructure allows quick adaptation to evolving technologies in the development landscape.

Collaboration and open-source contributions further enrich the development environment on Linux. Platforms such as GitHub and

GitLab enable collaborative workflows among developers, fostering an ecosystem of shared knowledge and innovation. Contributions to open-source projects not only enhance individual skills and experiences but also build a strong sense of community within the Linux development sphere.

Educational institutions have also recognized the importance of Linux in software development. Many universities leverage Linux-based platforms to teach essential skills for coding, system administration, and open-source contributions. Online learning platforms provide tutorials and resources for learners to explore various aspects of Linux development. As a result, students graduate with proficient skills in operating systems and their accompanying tools, ready to enter a technology landscape that continues to emphasize the significance of open-source software.

In conclusion, the development environments on Linux exemplify adaptability, collaboration, and innovation within the software development landscape. With an extensive array of tools and frameworks at their disposal, developers are empowered to create efficient, high-quality applications while contributing to the broader community. The thriving ecosystem surrounding Linux ensures that developers are well-equipped to adapt to evolving technologies, reinforcing the operating system's position as a cornerstone in the world of software development. As we advance further into a technology-driven future, Linux's contribution to the way we think about development continues to reshape the possibilities for innovation and creativity.

9.2. Programming Languages and Tools

Programming languages are the lifeblood of software development, and their compatibility with Linux significantly enhances the creativity and productivity of developers. Linux offers remarkable support for an extensive array of programming languages, from established favorites to emerging options, bridging the gap between theory and practical application. This environment fosters innovation through flexibility, performance, and the rich ecosystem of tools available to developers, making Linux an ideal platform for programming across various disciplines.

One of the most vital programming languages in the Linux environment is C, as it directly interfaces with the operating system's kernel. Many system-level tools, applications, and libraries are written in C, reflecting the language's efficiency and direct hardware manipulation ability. Students and developers who embrace C within the Linux ecosystem gain valuable insights into how operating systems are built, leading to a deeper comprehension of software architecture and performance optimization.

C++ builds upon the foundation laid by C and introduces object-oriented principles. Many applications and software solutions leverage C++ within Linux for its powerful features, providing programmers with the tools to develop high-performance applications. This language is widely used in game development, simulation, and graphical applications, enabling developers to harness Linux's capabilities to create visually engaging and resource-intensive software.

For web developers, the presence of languages like Python, PHP, and Ruby on Linux provides many opportunities for building dynamic and interactive applications. Python's simplicity and versatility have made it a favorite among both beginners and experienced developers. Its extensive libraries and frameworks, such as Django and Flask, are readily accessible in Linux environments, making rapid web application development and prototyping a smooth process.

PHP, a server-side scripting language, thrives on Linux as the foundation for many popular web frameworks and content management systems like WordPress and Drupal. With its extensive support for databases like MySQL, it enables developers to create powerful web applications that can handle large volumes of data and traffic efficiently.

Ruby—which gained popularity through the Ruby on Rails framework—showcases how Linux can serve as an excellent development platform for modern web applications. This language emphasizes convention over configuration, allowing developers to build complex applications quickly. The Ruby community is vibrant and collaborative, often working within Linux environments to enhance and broaden the capabilities of Rails.

Java, despite being cross-platform due to the Java Virtual Machine (JVM), continues to be widely utilized on Linux systems, especially in enterprise applications. The robustness and portability of Java applications have made Linux an attractive environment for companies deploying large-scale solutions. Development environments, such as Eclipse or IntelliJ IDEA, provide a comprehensive toolset for Java developers working on Linux, allowing them to leverage the full power and flexibility of both the language and the operating system.

The emergence of languages catering to specific modern paradigms has also influenced the Linux ecosystem. For instance, JavaScript, once primarily confined to web development on the client side, now finds application in server-side programming through Node.js, utilizing Linux servers to create scalable web solutions. Developers embracing JavaScript can integrate it easily within various Linux distributions, ensuring a cohesive environment conducive to rapid development cycles.

Emerging languages such as Go and Rust are gaining traction within the Linux community due to their focus on performance, memory safety, and concurrency. Go, developed by Google, is renowned for its simplicity and efficiency, often used for building cloud-native applications and microservices. Rust emphasizes safety and performance, making it attractive for system programming and application development where low-level memory access is required. Both languages benefit from the supportive nature of Linux's development tools and collaborative community efforts, promoting innovation across diverse fields.

Linux also supports scripting languages like Bash, which is integral for system administration and automation. Mastery of scripting enables developers to streamline workflows, automate repetitive tasks, and manage systems more effectively. The Linux command line provides a powerful interface for these languages, allowing users to integrate programming into their daily operations easily.

Development tools tailored for Linux enhance the overall experience for programmers. The availability of integrated development environments (IDEs) and text editors—for example, Visual Studio Code, Atom, and Vim—offers developers various options to customize their workflows. These tools typically support multiple languages, plugins, and integrations, facilitating efficient coding, debugging, and project management.

Version control systems, such as Git, are seamless on Linux, empowering developers to manage source code and collaborate with others effectively. Whether on personal or team projects, the integration of Git within Linux makes it a valuable tool for tracking changes and maintaining project consistency.

In conclusion, the diverse programming languages and tools available on Linux create a vibrant ecosystem where developers can collaborate and innovate. The flexibility, performance, and rich set of development tools make Linux an attractive platform for programming across various disciplines. Moreover, as technology evolves, the integration of emerging languages and paradigms ensures that Linux remains at the forefront of software development, empowering developers to explore new frontiers and push the boundaries of what is possible in the world of technology. Linux not only serves as a platform for traditional development but also inspires the next wave of innovation in an increasingly connected and complex digital landscape.

9.3. Linux for Application Developers

The Linux operating system has become increasingly relevant for application developers, offering a robust platform characterized by flexibility, efficiency, and a rich pool of development tools. As the software landscape evolves, Linux continues to adapt, ensuring developers have access to the capabilities they need to build high-quality, innovative applications.

Developing applications on Linux provides numerous advantages, notably its open-source nature, which allows developers to view and modify the underlying code. This transparency fosters a deeper understanding of how the operating system functions, enabling developers to identify bottlenecks or inefficiencies and optimize their applications accordingly. For those new to development or those seeking to deepen their understanding of systems programming, Linux serves as an excellent educational resource, providing opportunities for hands-on experience that are often not available in proprietary environments.

Linux supports a wide range of programming languages and frameworks, making it suitable for various development tasks. Application developers working with popular languages such as Python, C, C++, Java, Ruby, and PHP will find seamless support within Linux environments. The availability of integrated development environments (IDEs) and code editors, such as Visual Studio Code, Eclipse, and PyCharm, allows developers to choose tools that align with their workflows, thus enhancing productivity.

Moreover, the flexibility of Linux distributions means that developers can select environments tailored to their project needs. For example, developers focusing on web applications may prefer using Ubuntu or Fedora, while those building enterprise-level solutions may gravitate toward Red Hat Enterprise Linux or SUSE Linux Enterprise Server. Each distribution comes equipped with different tools, package managers, and default configurations that align with distinct use cases.

The package management systems inherent to Linux simplify the process of acquiring and maintaining libraries essential for application development. Tools such as APT for Debian-based distributions and YUM or DNF for Red Hat-based distributions allow developers to easily install, update, and manage software dependencies. This streamlining not only saves time but also ensures the stability and security of the development environment.

Additionally, Linux serves as a preferred platform for developing software that spans various deployment environments. Its compatibility with cloud services and containerization technologies, such as Docker and Kubernetes, allows developers to build and test applications in environments that mirror production settings. The containerized nature of applications streamline the deployment process, enabling developers to run their software consistently across different stages and platforms.

Another significant component of application development on Linux is the vibrancy of community involvement. The open-source nature of Linux invites collaboration among developers worldwide, fostering an environment where knowledge-sharing and mentorship flourish. Online forums, mailing lists, and community-driven platforms enable developers to seek guidance, exchange idea, and troubleshoot issues collectively. This communal approach not only enriches the learning experience but also results in contributions that continuously enhance the broader Linux ecosystem.

For mobile applications, Linux has carved a niche through platforms such as Android, which is built upon the Linux kernel. This offers developers the unique opportunity to create applications that run on millions of devices globally, expanding the reach of their work. Tools like Android Studio provide integrated development experiences tailored for mobile app development, allowing developers to leverage Linux environments while targeting the Android platform.

Moreover, application security remains a critical focus for developers using Linux. The operating system's architecture offers features allowing deeper control over system permissions and user access. Tools and libraries designed for monitoring and securing applications are readily available, ensuring developers can maintain high security standards throughout the development lifecycle. The ongoing community scrutiny inherent in the open-source model perpetuates an environment where security vulnerabilities can be quickly identified and addressed, safeguarding applications against potential threats.

As we consider the developments on the horizon, the potential for innovation within the Linux environment remains vast. Initiatives focused on machine learning, artificial intelligence, and data analysis continue to bolster Linux's relevance for application developers. With the rise in demand for solutions leveraging these cutting-edge technologies, developers engaged with Linux will find numerous opportunities to explore and capitalize on this growth.

In summary, Linux stands as a dynamic, open-source platform that significantly enhances the capabilities and opportunities for application developers. Its support for a multitude of programming languages, robust package management systems, strong community involvement, and adaptability to modern technologies create an environment conducive to innovative software development. As we move forward, the ongoing exploration and development of tools, frameworks, and best practices within the Linux ecosystem ensure its position as a vital resource for aspiring and established developers alike, paving the way for new applications that embody creativity and technical excellence.

9.4. Open Source Software Innovation

Open source software innovation is a cornerstone of the Linux operating system and its expansive community. This sector of Linux development showcases the incredible power of collaboration, transparency, and community engagement to drive significant advancements in technology. Rather than relying on centralization or proprietary controls over software, open source embodies a philosophy that invites any developer to contribute, modify, and share their creations. The result is an ecosystem teeming with innovative tools and applications that reflect the diverse needs and aspirations of users worldwide.

One of the most compelling examples of open source innovation within Linux is the rapid evolution of software projects that leverage the kernel's capabilities. For instance, the cloud computing space has witnessed immense growth, with tools like OpenStack representing a remarkable communal effort to create an open-source cloud framework. Initially sparked by growing demand for flexible cloud solutions, OpenStack emerged through the collaboration of various contributors who sought to provide users with a comprehensive platform for building and managing cloud infrastructures. Its modularity allows organizations to customize their cloud environments while avoiding vendor lock-in, thereby amplifying opportunities for innovation across numerous sectors.

Another notable area of open source innovation lies in the realm of artificial intelligence and machine learning. Projects such as Tensor-Flow, initially developed by Google, are designed to run seamlessly on Linux. By embracing open-source frameworks, developers and researchers can share their findings, resources, and tools, leading to rapid advancements in the field. The ability to leverage community-driven improvements forms the backbone of AI innovation on Linux, where contributors worldwide test algorithms, enhance functionality, and validate methodologies that push the boundaries of machine learning capabilities.

The software development process has also been transformed by the waves of innovation driven by open source principles. Development practices such as continuous integration and continuous deployment (CI/CD) have gained traction within the Linux community. Tools such as Jenkins and GitLab automate the deployment pipelines, enabling developers to maintain rapid iteration cycles, test frequently, and ensure quality assurance. These tools, built around collaborative principles, reflect the community's commitment to continuous improvement and innovation.

The concept of containerization has revolutionized the development and deployment landscape. Technologies such as Docker and Kubernetes extend the capabilities of Linux, allowing developers to build scalable applications that can be easily deployed across different environments. As organizations increasingly favor microservices architectures, the adaptability and efficiency offered by Linux, combined with containerization tools, foster rapid innovation in application development.

Open source innovation transcends technical developments and permeates the very culture surrounding software development. Communities of practice have emerged around specific projects, where developers collectively engage in discussions, code reviews, and brainstorming sessions. This collaborative culture spurs creativity, nurtures mentorship, and provides new developers with valuable guidance that heightens their skills. The inclusion of diverse voices leads to a richer tapestry of ideas and solutions, enabling faster resolution of challenges and the refinement of tools.

Furthermore, the educational impact of open-source innovation is profound, as institutions increasingly embrace Linux and open-source technologies within their curricula. Students not only gain technical skills but also learn the values of collaboration, transparency, and ethical considerations in software development. Engaging students in projects that contribute to real-world open-source initiatives fosters a sense of ownership in the development process and inspires them to pursue careers that embody their passion for technology and community engagement.

Additionally, governments and organizations worldwide have recognized the merits of open-source innovation, driving adoption strategies that promote economic development and technological equity. Open-source solutions allow regions with limited resources to access advanced technologies without incurring prohibitive costs. This accessibility empowers underserved communities and students, equipping them with the tools necessary to participate in and shape a digital future.

As we explore the impact of open-source software innovation, we must also acknowledge the challenges that accompany it. Issues such as sustainability, funding models, and continued engagement within communities can pose hurdles to sustained progress. However, many organizations, including the Linux Foundation, actively work to address these challenges by creating initiatives that encourage continued contributions and investment in open-source projects.

In conclusion, open-source software innovation represents a dynamic tapestry of collaboration, creativity, and technical advancement within the Linux ecosystem. By fostering an inclusive and participatory culture, Linux thrives on the collective energy of its contributors, enabling ground-breaking projects, transformative development practices, and advancements across diverse fields. As we look ahead to the future of open-source development, its potential to inspire creativity, drive technological progress, and empower communities remains limitless, ensuring that Linux continues to solidify its role as a beacon of innovation in the digital landscape.

9.5. The Future of Linux Software Architecture

In the rapidly evolving world of technology, Linux has established itself not only as a robust operating system but as a cornerstone for future advancements in software architecture. Understanding the future of Linux software architecture involves examining emerging trends, the community's collective vision, and the potential challenges that lie ahead.

As organizations and developers continue to adapt to cloud computing and containerization, Linux has proven its unparalleled ability to pivot in response to these technological shifts. The rise of microservices architecture, wherein applications are built as small, independent services that communicate with one another, aligns seamlessly with Linux's modularity. This approach allows developers to deploy updates swiftly without downtime, making Linux environments particularly attractive for businesses seeking agility in their software workflows. Looking ahead, we can anticipate that the architecture surrounding Linux will further embrace microservices as organizations continue to prioritize speed, scalability, and efficiency.

Moreover, the integration of artificial intelligence (AI) and machine learning (ML) into Linux software architecture is an inevitable progression. As these technologies grow in importance across various sectors—from healthcare to finance—Linux will likely serve as the preferred operational foundation for AI and ML applications. With robust support for programming languages such as Python and the widespread availability of scientific computing libraries, Linux environments will become indispensable for researchers and developers working on innovative AI solutions. This burgeoning intersection of Linux and AI will drive collaborative projects that push the boundaries of both fields, leading to the creation of smarter systems that adapt to user needs.

Continued community engagement and the ethos of open-source will be instrumental in shaping the software architecture of Linux. The strength of the Linux community lies in its diversity and willingness to embrace new ideas, creating an environment where innovation thrives. As developers contribute code, propose new features, and engage in discussions, the collective knowledge pool expands, refining the architecture of the operating system to better meet the needs of its users. The rise of collaborative tools and platforms that facilitate contribution and feedback will further embed open-source principles into the ongoing development of Linux, ensuring that the architecture remains adaptable and responsive to changes in technology and user demands.

Additionally, the future may see a more significant push towards interoperability and integration with other systems. As organizations increasingly adopt multi-cloud strategies and hybrid environments, the ability of Linux to seamlessly integrate with various technologies will become a critical requirement. The emergence of technologies like serverless computing will challenge Linux developers to conceptualize architectures that maintain efficiency while adapting to new deployment models. Embracing interoperability through APIs (Application Programming Interfaces) and service-oriented architecture (SOA) will be key to ensuring Linux's continued relevance in diverse computing landscapes.

However, as the landscape of Linux software architecture evolves, challenges will inevitably arise. The potential for fragmentation is one concern, as new distributions and forks emerge, each with different features and purposes. If not managed effectively, this fragmentation could lead to compatibility issues and dilute the collective strength of the Linux community. It is crucial for organizations and contributors alike to prioritize collaborative efforts, fostering a spirit of unity to ensure that advancements benefit the broader Linux ecosystem rather than splintering it.

Furthermore, security will remain a paramount concern as the sophistication of cyber threats continues to escalate. As Linux environments expand into cloud and IoT applications, maintaining robust security within software architecture will be essential. The community's focus on developing secure coding practices, auditing code, and collaborating on security standards will be pivotal in establishing Linux as a secure and trustworthy platform for businesses and end-users alike.

In summary, the future of Linux software architecture is characterized by adaptability, innovation, and a commitment to open-source collaboration. As trends in cloud computing, AI, and interoperability reshape the landscape, Linux stands poised to leverage its strengths to remain a leading operating system for diverse applications. By addressing challenges through community engagement and enhancing security measures, Linux will continue to pave the way for future advancements in technology, ensuring its relevance for generations to come. Together, the community and developers will shape the architecture of Linux, leaving an indelible impact on the ever-evolving world of technology.

10. Linux in Creative Industries: From Art to Animation

10.1. Animation and Film

In the vibrant world of animation and film, the Linux operating system has carved out an essential niche, significantly contributing to major productions and creative endeavors in the industry. Leveraging its robust capabilities and wide array of open-source software, Linux has become the go-to choice for many artists, animators, and filmmakers, allowing them to push the boundaries of creativity while accessing powerful tools without the prohibitive costs often associated with proprietary software.

The animation industry has witnessed a remarkable shift towards Linux, particularly in film production, where projects demand flexibility, scalability, and powerful rendering capabilities. Major film studios have adopted Linux-based systems for their production pipelines, resulting in enhanced collaboration among various teams and smoother integration of tools across different stages of animation production. The open-source nature of Linux allows studios to customize their environments to suit their unique workflows and needs, creating tailored solutions that optimize efficiency while accommodating the diverse requirements of animators, artists, and technical directors.

One notable example of Linux's impact can be seen in the Academy Award-winning film "Avatar." Renowned for its groundbreaking visual effects and stunning graphics, the production team at Weta Digital, which played a critical role in the film's animation, relied heavily on Linux-based systems for their rendering processes. The flexibility and performance of Linux-powered render farms enabled Weta Digital to handle the massive computational load required for such a highly detailed and visually intricate film. This collaborative environment also allowed for real-time feedback and iterative processes, crucial components of the animation workflow.

Furthermore, the influence of Linux extends beyond just large-scale productions; it also permeates independent films and smaller animation projects. Open-source software such as Blender, which operates seamlessly on Linux, has gained popularity among independent artists and creators, enabling them to produce high-quality animation and visual effects without being constrained by licensing fees. Blender's powerful suite of features, including modeling, animation, sculpting, rendering, and compositing, provides artists with a comprehensive toolkit for creating compelling narratives and visuals. The community-driven nature of Blender, coupled with its availability on Linux, empowers creators to collaborate, share resources, and continually enhance the software through user contributions.

Additionally, the adoption of Linux in animation brings a sense of community and collaboration that fosters innovation within the creative sector. Artists and developers often engage in discussions and share techniques through online forums and platforms dedicated to Linux animation software, enabling knowledge exchange and mentorship across varied backgrounds. This collaborative spirit inspires experimentation and cross-pollination of ideas, resulting in the gradual evolution of tools that empower creators to express their visions.

As the animation industry embraces technological advancements, tools for virtual reality (VR), augmented reality (AR), and 3D rendering increasingly require adaptable software solutions that can integrate seamlessly into existing workflows. The open-source nature of Linux positions it as a frontrunner in accommodating these innovations. For instance, software like Godot, an open-source game engine that supports both 2D and 3D graphics, can be employed on Linux platforms to create interactive experiences, paving the way for artists and developers to explore new forms of storytelling within the animation space that were previously inconceivable.

The rise of digital distribution platforms has also bolstered the role of Linux in film production and animation. Many independent filmmakers prefer utilizing Linux-based systems to create their films due to the significantly reduced costs and increased accessibility to professional-grade tools. The ability to produce and distribute content across multiple platforms without incurring high licensing fees resonates deeply with independent creators seeking to maintain control over their work.

However, while Linux's contributions to animation and film are significant, challenges remain in ensuring that Linux-based tools remain user-friendly and accessible to those new to the platform. As artists from varying backgrounds are introduced to Linux, it is important for the community to continue offering resources, tutorials, and support to facilitate their onboarding process.

In summary, Linux has emerged as a powerful ally in the world of animation and film, providing the backbone for major productions while empowering independent artists with free and open-source tools. Its adaptability, efficiency, and collaborative spirit create fertile ground for creativity, fostering innovation and pushing the boundaries of what is possible in animated storytelling. As the industry continues to evolve, Linux will undoubtedly play a crucial role in shaping the future of animation and film, inspiring a new generation of creators to explore their artistic journeys and realize their visions without constraints.

10.2. Linux in Music Production

In the world of music production, Linux has emerged as a powerful and versatile platform, transforming both the creative process and the technical landscape of audio engineering. With its open source ethos and robust community-driven software, Linux not only lowers the barriers to entry for aspiring musicians and producers but also fosters innovation in audio technologies. In this subchapter, we will explore the tools, applications, and advantages of using Linux for music production, illustrating how it has found its place within this dynamic industry.

One of the most significant factors contributing to the rise of Linux in music production is the wealth of professional-grade software applications available on the platform. Digital Audio Workstations (DAWs), often regarded as the cornerstone of modern music production, have made significant strides in adopting Linux as a viable operating system. Notable examples include Ardour, a powerful and flexible open-source DAW that rivals many proprietary options. With capabilities for multi-track audio recording, editing, and mixing, Ardour provides musicians with an extensive suite of tools to capture their creative ideas effectively. Users appreciate the intuitive interface and customizable features, allowing them to tailor their workflow according to personal preferences.

Additionally, other noteworthy DAWs such as Bitwig Studio and Reaper support Linux, illustrating the growing recognition of the operating system in the audio production arena. While some developers initially hesitated to embrace Linux due to concerns regarding compatibility and support, the increasing demand for alternative operating systems has prompted more creators to consider the benefits of developing their software for Linux users. As a result, musicians can now choose from a more extensive range of production environments tailored to their specific needs.

Beyond DAWs, Linux boasts a robust ecosystem of audio plugins and synthesis tools. Jack Audio Connection Kit, a professional sound server, epitomizes the versatility of audio routing in Linux. Jack provides musicians with the ability to connect multiple audio applications seamlessly, enabling complex signal routing and processing workflows. The modular nature of Jack allows producers to create custom audio setups, enhancing their productions by interconnecting the various applications they utilize.

Moreover, the rise of software synthesizers and samplers within the Linux community has expanded the sonic palette available to musicians. Renowned projects such as ZynAddSubFX, Helm, and Surge offer powerful synthesis capabilities that rival their proprietary counterparts. These tools empower artists to explore new textures, sounds, and creative possibilities without the financial constraints typically associated with commercial software. The open-source nature of these projects allows for ongoing community contributions aimed at refining and enhancing their features, driving continual innovation within the realm of audio synthesis.

Linux's dedication to fostering creativity also extends to its supportive ecosystems for music notation and editing. Software like MuseScore enables composers and musicians to create beautiful sheet music while benefiting from cross-platform functionalities and a vibrant community. These offerings empower artists to combine their technical skills with their musical ideas, transforming compositions into easily shareable and printable formats.

Another key aspect of Linux in music production lies in its compatibility with an array of hardware devices, from MIDI controllers to audio interfaces. The community of Linux audio users actively works to ensure that essential drivers for sound cards, USB interfaces, and other musical hardware are readily available. This compatibility allows musicians to utilize a range of devices without encountering the frustrating barriers often present in proprietary systems.

Additionally, the Linux platform is particularly well-equipped for collaborative projects. Many music producers are now turning to Linux to facilitate remote collaboration on music projects, harnessing the power of tools like Git as a version control system for their audio files. This approach enables multiple contributors to work on a shared project seamlessly, maintaining an organized workflow as files and changes are tracked effectively.

Despite the numerous advantages of using Linux for music production, there can be challenges that users encounter, particularly for newcomers. The learning curve associated with transitioning from proprietary operating systems can be daunting, especially if users are accustomed to the polished interfaces of widely-used commercial DAWs. However, many in the Linux community strive to create user-friendly resources, documentation, and tutorials, helping to bridge the gap for those starting their journey in Linux-based audio production.

Furthermore, while the growth of Linux in the music industry is undeniable, some proprietary software applications may still need to be available on the platform. As a result, some producers may opt to use cross-platform tools, including Wine, to run Windows-only software on Linux. While this can mitigate compatibility limitations, it may not provide the same level of stability that native Linux applications offer.

In conclusion, Linux has solidified its position as a formidable contender in the domain of music production, providing artists and producers with powerful tools and an open-source environment conducive to creativity and collaboration. With the ongoing growth of robust audio applications, a thriving community, and expanding hardware compatibility, Linux offers an accessible and innovative platform for musicians of all levels. As we look toward the future, the potential for further advancements in audio technology on Linux will continue to inspire creativity, ensuring that the platform remains at the forefront of music production for years to come. The infusion of collaborative energy, alongside the commitment to open-source principles, paves the way for a revolutionary era in music creation, where the possibilities are only limited by the imagination of its users.

10.3. Graphic Design on Linux

In the world of creative disciplines, graphic design on Linux has witnessed a remarkable evolution, driven by the abundance of powerful software and the community's openness to innovation. Graphic designers are increasingly turning to Linux for their design work due to the availability of robust applications, the customizability of the environment, and the significant cost savings associated with using open-source software. This subchapter will explore the diverse toolsets available for graphic designers working in Linux, highlight key applications that have gained traction in the design community, and discuss the overall impact of these tools on the creative process.

Linux has catalyzed a creative revolution with its assortment of design applications, rivaling those found on proprietary operating systems. One of the flagship programs for graphic design on Linux is GIMP (GNU Image Manipulation Program), a powerful image editing tool that offers a feature set comparable to Adobe Photoshop. GIMP supports a wide range of image formats, advanced manipulation techniques, and a plethora of plugins that enhance its functionality.

The program's versatility makes it suitable for a variety of tasks, from photo retouching to texture creation for 3D modeling. Moreover, the familiarity of GIMP's interface and tools allows users transitioning from other platforms to adapt more easily, encouraging its adoption among new users.

In addition to GIMP, Inkscape stands out as a premier vector graphics editor on Linux. With capabilities akin to Adobe Illustrator, Inkscape allows designers to create scalable vector graphics, making it an excellent choice for creating logos, illustrations, and professional layouts. Its extensive toolset includes path operations, advanced text manipulation, and support for various file formats, all of which position Inkscape as a go-to choice for creating high-quality vector graphics. The active community surrounding the software also contributes to its growth, enabling users to access a wealth of tutorials, resources, and plugins that enhance their design experience.

For those interested in 3D graphics, Blender has emerged as the leading open-source software for modeling, animation, and rendering. While initially celebrated as a powerful tool for animation, Blender has expanded its feature set to incorporate sculpting, video editing, and game creation, serving as a comprehensive solution for 3D design. Its high-quality rendering capabilities and support for complex environments have made it a popular choice among both independent creators and industry professionals. The Blender community has cultivated a culture of sharing knowledge and resources, enabling users to grow their skills and collaborate on projects seamlessly.

Furthermore, Linux's open-source ethos fosters a vibrant environment for collaboration and innovation in graphic design. As designers leverage these powerful tools, they can freely share their techniques, artwork, and resources with one another. Online platforms such as DeviantArt and ArtStation, combined with social media, enable artists to showcase their creations while inviting constructive feedback from peers. This interconnectedness not only enhances individual skills but also elevates the overall quality of design work produced within the Linux community.

Additionally, Linux users benefit from an array of cross-platform tools that facilitate design workflows. Creative software solutions like Scribus—an open-source desktop publishing application—enable users to create professional layouts for print and digital media. The ability to work on complex page layouts, along with support for various file formats, makes Scribus an attractive alternative to Adobe InDesign. Similarly, Krita has gained popularity among illustrators and concept artists for its powerful brush engines and intuitive interface designed primarily for digital painting.

Another notable advantage of using Linux for graphic design lies in the operating system's customizable nature. Designers can create workflows tailored specifically to their preferences, incorporating various tools, scripts, and configurations. The ability to fine-tune the Linux environment allows designers to optimize their productivity, significantly enhancing their creative processes.

Despite the numerous strengths associated with graphic design on Linux, there are still challenges that users may face. Some proprietary software options—while not available natively on Linux—can still be run via emulation or compatibility layers like Wine. However, these solutions may not provide the same stability and performance as native applications, which can be a deterrent for some users.

Moreover, entering the Linux arena may require a learning curve for designers accustomed to proprietary software. The transition can be daunting, as the design landscape on Linux may involve familiarizing oneself with alternative workflows, tools, and syntaxes. Nevertheless, the resources available through online documentation and community forums can mitigate this adjustment period, supporting new users as they navigate their journey into the Linux design ecosystem.

In conclusion, graphic design on Linux is an exciting and expanding field characterized by innovation, collaboration, and access to powerful tools. With applications like GIMP, Inkscape, and Blender paving the way, designers can realize their visions and express their creativity without the financial burdens associated with proprietary software. The customizable nature of Linux, paired with the wealth of resources and community support, makes it an appealing choice for both aspiring and seasoned designers. As the Linux design community continues to flourish, it will undoubtedly inspire further advancements that push the boundaries of digital artistry, fostering a culture of creativity and exploration in the realm of graphic design.

10.4. The Art of Open Source

In the world of open source, the art of collaboration and community-driven creativity takes center stage, enriching every experience, project, and individual involved in the landscape. At the heart of this artistic expression lies the collective belief that sharing knowledge and resources can amplify innovation across diverse domains, from software development to graphic design, and from education to research. The spirit of open source nurtures an environment where creativity flourishes, highlighting the importance of diverse contributions and the intersection of artistry and technology.

The Linux community serves as a prime example of how collaboration fosters creativity. With its open-source philosophy, Linux has cultivated a global community of developers, designers, and enthusiasts who actively contribute to the enhancement of the operating system and its applications. By harnessing the power of diverse perspectives —each influenced by unique backgrounds, experiences, and ideas— the community ensures that the landscape of Linux remains dynamic, inventive, and responsive to the needs of its users.

Projects that emerge from this community-driven model demonstrate the effectiveness of collaboration. Take, for instance, the development of editing software like GIMP or Inkscape. These powerful tools have been shaped by the contributions of numerous artists and developers who continually refine their features, create tutorials, and provide support. Through collaborative efforts, these applications have garnered acclaim for their capabilities and have become staples in the toolkit of digital artists across the globe.

Similarly, creative endeavors in other artistic fields benefit from Linux's collaborative spirit. Musicians utilizing Linux-based software such as Ardour or LMMS can share compositions, collaborate on projects, and access a wealth of free resources that enhance their musical journeys. This interconnected environment encourages artists to innovate and experiment, craft novel sounds, and push boundaries —all while fostering a strong sense of community that transcends geographical divides.

In the realm of education, Linux promotes collaborative creativity by providing tools that empower learners and educators alike. Platforms like Moodle, an open-source learning management system, enable institutions to create online courses, share resources, and facilitate communication between students and teachers. As educators collectively contribute to developing pedagogical strategies and resources, they instill a culture of sharing knowledge that enriches the educational experience. This same spirit extends to projects designed for young learners, where children's programming languages like Scratch allow students to collaboratively develop games and animations, igniting their interest in technology and fostering a passion for creativity.

Furthermore, the global impact of open source extends to humanitarian efforts, where Linux-based technologies are employed to create tools that address social issues and engage communities in creative solutions. Humanitarian open-source projects can be seen in emergency response systems, community-driven mapping tools, and educational initiatives that leverage technology to empower individuals in underserved areas. By embracing collaboration and inclusivity, these initiatives exemplify how creative problem-solving can make a positive difference in the world.

As we navigate through the complexities of an ever-evolving technological landscape, it is crucial to recognize the importance of community-driven creativity in our endeavors. The art of open source illustrates that when individuals come together to share ideas, skills, and resources, they can unleash unprecedented innovation and drive meaningful change that benefits all.

In summary, the art of open source is embodied by the creativity, collaboration, and community engagement that permeate the Linux ecosystem and its broader applications. This spirit cultivates a culture of sharing and inclusivity that empowers individuals to experiment, innovate, and grow, allowing art and technology to meld seamlessly. As the future unfolds, nurturing this creative collaboration will ensure that open source continues to inspire and propel advancements across diverse fields, paving the way for a world enriched by collective creativity and shared achievements.

10.5. Community Driven Creativity

In the vast landscape of technology and creativity, a phenomenon has emerged that celebrates the fusion of artistic expression with community collaboration: Community Driven Creativity within the realm of Linux. This subchapter examines how the principles of open-source software and a vibrant community spirit converge to empower artists, developers, and creators alike to harness their ideas, share their knowledge, and collaborate on tools and projects that advance the entire ecosystem.

At the heart of this narrative is an intrinsic belief in the potential of collective creativity. The Linux operating system itself, born from Linus Torvalds' vision of an open and collaborative platform, is a testament to the power of community-driven development. Torvalds' initial invitation to fellow programmers to contribute to what would become the Linux kernel kindled a global movement, inspiring countless individuals to embark on their journey of exploration, experimentation, and creation within this open environment.

The Linux community fosters creativity by providing a range of tools and resources that artists and developers can leverage. From graphic design applications like GIMP and Inkscape to audio production software like Ardour and LMMS, the available suite of open-source applications empowers individuals to approach their craft with the freedom to experiment, modify, and share their work. This accessibility enables artists—regardless of their technical expertise—to harness powerful capabilities without the burden of prohibitively expensive software licenses.

The community-driven aspect of creativity in Linux is not merely about access to tools; it encompasses the spirit of collaboration and knowledge-sharing that permeates this ecosystem. Users actively participate in forums, mailing lists, and online gatherings, where they can seek support, exchange ideas, and contribute to ongoing projects. Collaborations often blossom into unforgettable artistic endeavors—musicians teaming up to create new sounds, graphic designers joining forces to develop innovative applications, and developers pooling their expertise to build solutions that cater to a broader audience. This synergistic effect enhances not only individual skillsets but ultimately enriches the creative output of the entire community.

One striking example of community-driven creativity lies in the world of animation and game design, where artists and developers congregate to bring imaginative worlds to life. Open-source platforms like Blender have gained a dedicated following, enabling animators to produce intricate animations and 3D models while collaborating with fellow creators worldwide. The availability of extensive documentation, tutorials, and an engaged user base facilitates learning and experimentation, encouraging participants to share their projects, techniques, and findings. As projects evolve and improve through cooperative efforts, individuals become part of a greater narrative—collectively shaping the future of animation and game development.

In addition to visual arts, Linux has become a nurturing ground for musical exploration. Talents from diverse backgrounds contribute their knowledge, producing a myriad of open-source audio tools that enhance the music production landscape. Musicians work together to refine applications, develop plugins, and share samples—all while exchanging invaluable insights on their creative journeys. Platforms like Linux Audio Users (LAU) exemplify this collaborative endeavor, offering spaces for musicians to discuss their projects, showcase their work, and find inspiration from like-minded peers. This harmonious relationship between musical creativity and the Linux community is helping to dismantle barriers, allowing emerging artists to share their voices and innovations with the world.

Furthermore, in educational settings, community-driven creativity promotes engagement and collaboration among students and educators. Linux-based projects enable learners to explore coding and digital creation through hands-on experiences while actively contributing to open-source initiatives. The value of mentorship and collaboration among peers is reinforced, encouraging learners to take ownership of their educational journeys while building the skills and relationships necessary to thrive in the digital age. The principles of open-source provide students with the means to work collectively on projects, resulting in a dynamic learning environment that fosters creativity and innovation.

However, community-driven creativity is not without its challenges. As the Linux landscape evolves, ensuring inclusivity and diverse representation within the community remains a pressing concern. It is essential to create opportunities for individuals from all backgrounds to share their ideas and contribute to projects. Encouraging inclusivity fosters a flourishing environment where an appreciation for various perspectives fuels creativity, leading to innovative solutions and artworks with universal appeal.

In conclusion, Community Driven Creativity is the lifeblood of the Linux ecosystem, where collaboration, accessibility, and the shared pursuit of innovation intertwine. From artists and musicians to developers and educators, each participant has the opportunity to shape the narrative of creativity within Linux—transforming aspirations into reality, exploring the limits of possibility, and breaking down barriers through cooperative endeavors. As the community continues to grow and evolve, the potential for further artistic and technological advancements is boundless, reminding us that when creativity and collaboration come together, extraordinary achievements await. The Linux community stands as a beacon of inspiration—a place where open-source ideals fuel boundless imagination and collaboration for generations to come.

11. Harnessing Linux in Scientific Research

11.1. Linux in Astronomy

In the vast and intricate expanse of modern astronomy, Linux has firmly established itself as an invaluable ally, empowering researchers, universities, and organizations in their quest to unlock celestial mysteries. With a landscape increasingly defined by the sheer volume of data generated by telescopes and space missions, the adaptability, flexibility, and power of Linux provide the critical infrastructure needed to manage, analyze, and visualize astronomical data.

One of the most compelling reasons for Linux's prominence in the field of astronomy lies in its open-source nature. This characteristic not only encourages collaboration among researchers but also fosters an environment where scientists can freely share tools, software, and data. The ethos of open source is particularly beneficial in astronomy, where complex algorithms and sophisticated simulations often require collective input and diverse perspectives to refine and enhance methodologies.

The kernel of Linux serves as the backbone for an array of astronomical software tools that support tasks ranging from data acquisition and image processing to modeling and simulation. For instance, many astronomical observatories and institutions utilize customized Linux distributions tailored to manage their specific data needs. These distributions provide not only the operating environment but also come pre-loaded with vital libraries and frameworks necessary for analysis.

Moreover, well-known astronomical software packages such as AstroPy and the Virtual Observatory (VO) are built on Linux, enabling researchers to analyze celestial data effectively. AstroPy, a core package for Python, offers a unified and accessible framework for handling astronomical data, while the Virtual Observatory provides a collaborative network of datasets and tools that astronomers can access from anywhere in the world. These packages exemplify the strength of Linux as a platform designed for scientific inquiry.

Linux's ability to scale alongside advancements in technology is critical in astronomy. As new telescopes, such as the Square Kilometre Array (SKA) and the James Webb Space Telescope, prepare for their missions, vast amounts of data will flood in, requiring advanced computational solutions to process. The extensibility of Linux, coupled with high-performance computing (HPC) capabilities, allows researchers to harness powerful computing clusters to tackle the demands of data processing and analysis. This is particularly important when interpreting complex phenomena, such as gravitational waves or the cosmic microwave background radiation, which require advanced algorithms and significant computational resources.

Another significant aspect of Linux's contribution to astronomy is seen in its role within the realm of data visualization. Astronomers heavily rely on visual representations of data to draw insights and make discoveries. Applications like Blender, combined with libraries such as Matplotlib and Kitware's ParaView, enable the creation of three-dimensional models and visualizations of astronomical phenomena. The support that Linux provides for graphics drivers enables seamless interaction with these advanced tools, allowing researchers to portray their findings in compelling and insightful ways.

Furthermore, Linux facilitates collaboration on global initiatives that require the pooling of resources and shared expertise. Projects like Gaia, which aims to create the largest 3D map of our galaxy, exemplify how collaborative efforts in Linux environments allow astronomers worldwide to access cutting-edge data and analysis tools. As these expansive projects encompass institutions across continents, Linux's capability to provide a cohesive and interoperable platform is invaluable in aggregating efforts.

Additionally, Linux is not just limited to research institutions; it has practical applications in educational contexts, empowering the next generation of astronomers. Many universities integrate Linux-based software tools into their curricula, equipping students with the necessary skills and knowledge to navigate the complex landscape of modern astronomy. By offering access to powerful open-source software, students can undertake real astronomical research, analyze data, and even contribute back to the community, honoring the spirit of collaboration that Linux embodies.

Despite its prominent advantages, the journey of integrating Linux in astronomy is not without challenges. Users new to Linux may encounter a learning curve as they transition from proprietary systems. Continuing to provide thorough documentation, tutorials, and support resources is crucial in overcoming potential barriers for users venturing into the Linux domain.

In conclusion, Linux's role in astronomy is one of empowerment, collaboration, and innovation. Its flexibility, scalability, and open-source nature allow researchers and institutions to harness the power of modern technology, effectively tackling the challenges posed by vast astronomical datasets. As the field continues to evolve, Linux will remain at the forefront, facilitating groundbreaking research and unlocking the mysteries of the cosmos. Embracing such collaborative frameworks and powerful resources, the astronomical community can better understand the universe—one celestial discovery at a time.

11.2. Bioinformatics Breakthroughs

In the rapidly evolving field of bioinformatics, Linux has established itself as a pivotal platform, facilitating groundbreaking research and discoveries. The convergence of biology with information technology has necessitated the development of sophisticated software tools for analyzing vast amounts of biological data, and Linux has risen to meet these challenges with its robustness, flexibility, and open-source nature.

One of the primary advantages of utilizing Linux in bioinformatics lies in its ability to handle high-performance computing (HPC) environments. The sheer volume of data generated in genomic sequencing, proteomics, and transcriptomics has pushed computational requirements to new heights, and Linux-based systems are adept at managing these intensive workloads. Many research institutions and universities have adopted Linux-based clusters or supercomputers to process and analyze complex datasets efficiently. This infrastructure allows researchers to run parallel computations and perform analyses on a scale that would be unmanageable on less powerful systems.

Moreover, the open-source nature of Linux fosters a culture of collaboration and innovation, which is a cornerstone of the scientific community. Many bioinformatics tools and applications are developed as open-source software, enabling researchers from diverse backgrounds to contribute their expertise and enhance the functionality of existing tools. Projects such as Bioconductor and Galaxy exemplify this collaborative spirit. Bioconductor, built on the R programming language, provides tools for the analysis and comprehension of genomic data. Galaxy, on the other hand, offers a web-based interface that allows users to perform complex analyses without needing extensive programming knowledge. Both projects thrive on community contributions, promoting an ecosystem where knowledge is shared and innovations are built collaboratively.

The availability of a wide range of bioinformatics software packages specifically designed to run on Linux enhances its appeal among researchers. Popular tools such as BLAST (Basic Local Alignment Search Tool), Bowtie, and BWA (Burrows-Wheeler Aligner) are often optimized for Linux environments, ensuring compatibility and reliability during analyses. These cutting-edge programs facilitate tasks such as sequence alignment, variant calling, and functional annotation, allowing researchers to derive meaningful insights from their data quickly.

Furthermore, Linux's superior customization options enable researchers to tailor their environments to meet the specific needs of their projects. The ability to configure software, manage dependencies, and integrate various tools ensures that researchers can create workflows adaptable to their experimental designs. The modularity of Linux fosters innovation, prompting researchers to develop custom scripts and pipelines that streamline complex analyses and enhance reproducibility—key aspects of scientific research.

The role of Linux in bioinformatics extends to education and training, providing an accessible platform for students and upcoming professionals in the field. Many academic institutions incorporate Linux-based tools into their curricula, allowing students to gain hands-on experience with popular bioinformatics applications. With the rising interest in computational biology and bioinformatics, fostering familiarity with Linux empowers the next generation of researchers to navigate modern challenges in biological data analysis expertly.

While the benefits of Linux in bioinformatics are substantial, challenges remain. Some bioinformatics tools may initially lack user-friendly interfaces, posing hurdles for new users who may be transitioning from proprietary software. The community's commitment to improving documentation and providing support through forums and user groups plays a critical role in enhancing accessibility, ensuring users can gain proficiency over time.

In sum, the transformative impact of Linux on bioinformatics is evident. Its ability to support high-performance computing, foster collaboration within the scientific community, and provide a plethora of specialized tools makes it an invaluable asset for researchers. As the field continues to expand and evolve, Linux will undoubtedly play an even more prominent role in generating insights that drive our understanding of biology and the complex systems that govern life itself. With its commitment to open-source collaboration, Linux empowers researchers, educators, and students to push the boundaries of innovation in bioinformatics, enabling groundbreaking discoveries that have the potential to shape the future of healthcare, genomics, and beyond.

11.3. Data Science and Analytics

Data science and analytics are at the forefront of the tech revolution, reshaping industries and informing decision-making processes across various domains. Within this shifting landscape, Linux emerges as a powerful ally, providing a robust, flexible, and scalable platform for data scientists and analysts. This subchapter delves into how Linux supports complex data analysis and modeling, empowering users to leverage data-driven insights for transformative outcomes.

At its core, data science involves extracting knowledge and insights from structured and unstructured data through techniques such as statistical analysis, machine learning, and data visualization. The increasing amount of data generated by businesses, social media, and various sensors has led to an explosion of tools and technologies designed to process and analyze this data. The efficient orchestration of these tools often depends on the choice of operating system, and Linux has risen to prominence as the platform of choice for data scientists and analytics professionals.

One of the critical advantages of using Linux for data science is its performance and scalability. Linux is known for its ability to handle large datasets and complex computations efficiently. Many data science tools, such as Apache Hadoop and Apache Spark, were developed with Linux environments in mind. These distributed computing frameworks allow data scientists to manage and process large volumes of data across clusters of machines seamlessly, significantly accelerating the data processing pipeline.

Moreover, Linux's native support for high-performance computing (HPC) is particularly beneficial in data-driven fields. By leveraging Linux clusters, researchers and organizations can execute complex analyses rapidly, making it possible to model intricate systems and derive meaningful insights. The flexibility to configure various software tools and libraries tailored to specific analytical tasks enables data scientists to experiment and innovate unhindered by performance constraints.

The Linux ecosystem is rich with powerful programming languages and libraries commonly used for data analysis, including Python, R, and Julia. Python, in particular, has gained significant traction within the data science community due to its simplicity and versatility. With libraries such as NumPy for numerical computing, Pandas for data manipulation, and Matplotlib or Seaborn for data visualization,

Python integrates closely with Linux, allowing data scientists to perform comprehensive analyses within a unified environment.

R also boasts an impressive presence in statistical computing and graphics, serving as a preferred language for statisticians and data analysts. The availability of R tools and packages within Linux-based environments provides users with the full breadth of statistical tools necessary for deep exploratory data analysis. Its strong community support means that data scientists can easily access resources and packages that continue to enhance their analytical capabilities.

As data science progresses into the domains of machine learning and artificial intelligence, the support for frameworks like TensorFlow, PyTorch, and Keras on Linux further solidifies its relevance. These frameworks are essential for building and training machine learning models, providing extensive libraries and functions that facilitate experimentation and implementation. The open-source nature of these frameworks allows for continuous development and collaboration, propelling innovation within the field.

The commanding presence of Linux in the realm of data visualization tools also cannot be overlooked. Software such as Tableau and Power BI may dominate in some corporate environments; however, powerful open-source visualization libraries such as D3.js and Plotly are widely utilized within Linux, enabling data scientists to create impactful visual stories from their analyses. These visualizations can effectively communicate insights to stakeholders, thereby bridging the gap between technical findings and strategic decision-making.

Furthermore, Linux encourages collaborative engagement and community-driven projects, significantly enhancing data science practices. Open-source communities share techniques, algorithms, and datasets that empower researchers to learn from one another. Collaborative platforms such as GitHub and GitLab allow data scientists to share their projects, version control their code, and solicit feedback from peers, fostering an environment where collective intelligence drives further innovation.

With data increasingly recognized as a strategic asset across industries, the role of data science and analytics continues to grow. By choosing Linux as the operating system for data-driven work, organizations can harness the full potential of open-source tools, leverage community resources, and create scalable solutions that pave the way for impactful decision-making.

As we look toward the future, the synergy between Linux and data science will likely further deepen. Emerging technologies such as big data analytics, the Internet of Things (IoT), and cloud computing will rely on Linux as a cornerstone, enabling data scientists to explore uncharted territories and uncover insights that reshape industries. The foundations laid within the Linux ecosystem offer the promise of innovation and discovery, ensuring that data science remains an exciting and transformative field for years to come.

In conclusion, Linux plays an instrumental role in supporting complex data analysis and modeling, offering data scientists a powerful platform that enhances their ability to derive actionable insights from vast datasets. Through its performance capabilities, rich ecosystem of tools, and spirit of collaboration, Linux empowers data-driven decision-making across diverse sectors, positioning organizations to thrive in an era dictated by data. As the importance of data science continues to rise, the significance of Linux as the backbone of this evolving landscape is set to strengthen, ensuring that it remains a vital player in shaping the future of data analytics.

11.4. Supercomputing and Linux

As the intersection of technology advances, Linux has emerged as a vital player in the realm of supercomputing. The capabilities of Linux as a scalable and adaptable operating system uniquely position it to serve the world's most powerful computing systems, unlocking unprecedented processing power and ingenuity within various scientific and engineering fields. Organizations and institutions across the globe increasingly rely on Linux to maximize their computational resources, maintain efficiency, and drive innovation.

The foundation of supercomputing is predicated on the ability to tackle immensely complex problems that require vast amounts of calculation. Problems in fields such as climate modeling, genomics, astrophysics, and computational fluid dynamics produce data at scales that can only be managed by powerful clusters of servers operating in harmony. Linux provides the backbone for these super-computers, offering a lightweight, efficient, and open-source platform on which organizations can build their computing environments.

One of the primary reasons Linux is favored for supercomputing is its modularity and flexibility in configuration. This allows supercom-puting environments to tailor their systems to meet specific workload requirements. With Linux, administrators have the ability to optimize performance based on the tasks at hand—whether that entails tuning the kernel for specific hardware, optimizing memory usage, or con-figuring inter-process communication strategies. The open-source nature of Linux also means that organizations can modify and adapt it as necessary, allowing for bespoke solutions that are suitable for their unique computing needs.

Moreover, the networking capabilities of Linux lend themselves par-ticularly well to supercomputing environments. In modern cluster computing, Linux excels at managing the interactions between nodes within the cluster, allowing multiple CPUs to cooperate efficiently in executing complex tasks. The ability for Linux to seamlessly handle parallel processing is particularly advantageous for computational tasks that leverage multi-core architecture, enabling scientists to achieve results at unprecedented speeds.

The use of Linux is exemplified in some of the world's leading supercomputers, many of which run specialized distributions tailored specifically for high-performance computing (HPC). For example, CentOS and Ubuntu Server are popular choices in these environ-ments, providing high levels of performance and compatibility with the necessary software stacks for scientific computing. The ease of deploying different software packages on Linux, through its package management systems, further streamlines the configuration and maintenance of these powerful systems.

The scope of Linux's application within supercomputing also necessitates an emphasis on open-source scientific software. Tools such as OpenFOAM, TensorFlow, and NumPy are instrumental in carrying out simulations and performing analyses within supercomputing clusters. The cooperative nature of open-source development encourages researchers to enhance these tools collectively, refining them for optimal performance within the unique demands of HPC environments. This collaborative ethos encourages knowledge-sharing, allowing researchers to leverage each other's contributions and advancements in real-time.

Additionally, the prominence of containerization technologies, such as Docker and Singularity, further accentuates Linux's role in supercomputing. By allowing users to package applications along with their dependencies, these technologies enable more efficient allocation and management of resources across an HPC cluster. Researchers can run their applications consistently across diverse environments, minimizing compatibility issues that can arise from varying configurations. Containerization effectively encapsulates applications, ensuring reproducibility in research while optimizing resource utilization.

As supercomputing evolves, the intersection of Linux with cutting-edge technologies such as machine learning and artificial intelligence cannot be overlooked. Many supercomputers today are being purpose-built to accommodate complex machine learning frameworks, with Linux at the helm. This integration empowers scientists to leverage computational resources for training sophisticated models, processing astronomical datasets, and performing advanced simulations, revolutionizing numerous sectors ranging from healthcare and climate research to astrophysics.

However, despite its strengths, the Linux environment within supercomputing is not immune to challenges. Organizations must grapple with ensuring security and compliance within their clusters, given the sensitive nature of the data often processed. Linux offers robust security frameworks, but administrators must remain vigilant about configurations and access controls to mitigate potential vulnerabilities.

In conclusion, supercomputing demonstrates Linux's enduring position as the operating system of choice for high-performance computing environments. Its flexibility, adaptability, and performance make it indispensable to scientific research and engineering endeavors. As organizations increasingly demand more processing power and seek to solve complex problems at unprecedented scales, the capabilities inherent to Linux will propel innovation and foster discoveries that address some of the world's most pressing challenges. The future trajectory of supercomputing is undeniably linked to the Linux ecosystem, highlighting its foundational role in facilitating exploration, collaboration, and advancement in the age of high-performance computing.

11.5. Oceanic Exploration

In the field of oceanic exploration, the role of Linux has become increasingly essential as researchers seek innovative ways to monitor, understand, and protect marine ecosystems. The ability to process vast amounts of data collected from underwater sensors, drones, and remote-operated vehicles has positioned Linux as a vital operating system for various applications in oceanography, marine biology, and environmental science. From managing complex datasets to running sophisticated simulations, Linux is at the core of technological advancements that facilitate our understanding of the ocean's depths.

Marine research has traditionally been constrained by the high costs and limitations of proprietary software. However, with the adoption of Linux, scientists have gained access to powerful open-source tools that promote collaboration and innovation. Linux distributions, such as Ubuntu and Debian, provide researchers with the flexibility to customize their computing environments to suit the specific needs of their projects. This adaptability enables teams to efficiently deploy software for data collection, analysis, and visualization in oceano-graphic research.

One of the most prominent applications of Linux in oceanic explo-ration is in the realm of data acquisition. Various projects utilize Linux-based systems to manage the considerable data generated by underwater sensors and autonomous vehicles. For instance, the Ocean Observatories Initiative (OOI), a major initiative in ocean re-search, employs a network of sensors and monitoring systems, many of which run on Linux platforms. These systems collect data on water temperature, salinity, nutrient levels, and other parameters critical to understanding ocean conditions and their impacts on marine life.

Linux's resilience and high-performance capabilities also play a crucial role in data analysis related to marine environments. Tools such as R, Python, and MATLAB can run seamlessly on Linux plat-forms, enabling researchers to analyze complex datasets derived from oceanic studies. For example, Python libraries like SciPy and NumPy offer researchers mathematical functions and array operations to perform extensive statistical analyses and simulations, enhancing their ability to draw insights from collected data.

The open-source software movement within the Linux ecosystem has facilitated the development of specialized applications tailored to ma-rine research. Projects like Oceanographic Research Software (ORS) and ECOMAS (Ecological Modeling and Simulation) are specifically designed for studying marine ecosystems and simulating ecological dynamics. By fostering a collaborative environment, developers can access and improve upon these tools, making them more effective and accessible for researchers working in diverse areas of ocean exploration.

Furthermore, the adaptability of Linux makes it ideal for building and maintaining computational models that predict changes in oceanic systems. For instance, models that forecast ocean currents, monitor fish populations, and assess the impact of climate change on marine environments rely on the computational power that Linux offers. By utilizing powerful Linux clusters, researchers can run and refine these models, gaining insights that can aid in marine conservation efforts and ecosystem management.

Linux also shines in the area of remote sensing applications critical to ocean exploration. The use of satellite imagery, sonar data, and remote sensing from aerial drones has become integral to understanding marine environments. Open-source software projects, such as QGIS, enable researchers to visualize spatial data and produce maps that inform conservation planning. These tools can be easily integrated into Linux systems, allowing for efficient processing and analysis of geospatial information.

Moreover, the rise of the Internet of Things (IoT) in marine science has positioned Linux at the forefront of developing smart buoys and underwater vehicles equipped with advanced sensors. These devices collect real-time data on ocean conditions and wildlife, which can be sent to researchers for analysis. The flexibility of the Linux operating system supports the deployment of lightweight applications that can run efficiently on these low-power, remote devices, ensuring that valuable environmental data can be continuously gathered.

One important aspect of oceanic exploration lies in fostering collaboration among researchers, organizations, and institutions. The Linux community's commitment to open-source principles resonates well with the collaborative nature of scientific research, encouraging researchers in marine science to share their findings, datasets, and tools. Participating in forums, conferences, and collaborative projects allows for the cross-pollination of ideas and techniques, ultimately enhancing the quality of research conducted in oceanic science.

However, challenges remain, especially regarding the accessibility of Linux tools to researchers who may be unfamiliar with the operating system or open-source philosophy. Training programs and resources that focus on Linux-based applications in ocean research can help bridge this gap, empowering scientists with the skills needed to effectively utilize the technologies at their disposal.

In conclusion, the contributions of Linux to oceanic exploration are immense, facilitating marine research by providing access to powerful, customizable tools that promote collaboration and innovation. As the demands of understanding and conserving our oceans grow, the role of Linux in managing data, running simulations, and supporting research initiatives will only become more prominent. With its open-source foundation, Linux fosters a collaborative culture that encourages the sharing of knowledge and expertise, ensuring that the exploration of our seas continues to advance in the pursuit of sustainability and environmental stewardship. Together, the Linux community and scientific researchers hold the potential to unlock new understandings of the ocean's complexities, ultimately benefiting the ecosystems and the planet as a whole.

12. The Global Impact of Linux: From Developing Nations to Digital Giants

12.1. Empowering Developing Countries

In the current digital landscape, the influence of Linux extends significantly into the development trajectories of emerging nations, where technology access is critical in establishing sustainable economic growth and fostering innovation. As Linux serves as an accessible and versatile operating system, it empowers developing countries to leap over barriers typically associated with expensive proprietary software. By embracing Linux, these nations can cultivate local talent, increase computer literacy, and stimulate entrepreneurial endeavors that leverage technology for social and economic development.

One of the primary advantages of Linux is its cost-effectiveness. It eliminates the heavy licensing fees tied to proprietary operating systems, enabling schools, communities, and startups to access comprehensive computing solutions without incurring substantial financial burdens. This aspect is particularly crucial in developing countries where budgets for education and technology may be severely constrained. Educational institutions adopting Linux can provide students and communities with access to quality tools that facilitate learning and skill development, laying the groundwork for a tech-savvy workforce.

The abundant availability of open-source software in the Linux ecosystem allows users to find robust alternatives to conventional proprietary applications. Programs for word processing, spreadsheets, graphic design, and software development are available for free on Linux. OpenOffice, GIMP, and Blender represent some examples of powerful tools that serve high functionality while remaining accessible to individuals and organizations in developing nations. This accessibility reduces technological disparities and creates opportunities for local ingenuity and innovation.

Linux also reinforces the potential for collaboration and knowledge sharing within developing countries. The community-driven philosophy intrinsic to Linux encourages users to engage with one another through forums, online platforms, and local user groups. This communal learning experience empowers users as they share solutions, code, and best practices, fostering a collaborative spirit that can lead to technological advancements and innovations rooted in local contexts. Grassroots movements often emerge within these communities, driving awareness, motivation, and technological literacy among users.

Moreover, as countries strive to integrate technology into various sectors—education, agriculture, healthcare, and governance—Linux-based systems serve as flexible and customizable solutions. Consider agricultural cooperatives that can leverage Linux to analyze crop data, market prices, and environmental conditions, thus enhancing productivity and decision-making. In healthcare, Linux-based software can support patient records management systems critical in improving healthcare delivery and access to information. These implementations highlight how Linux serves as a pragmatic means to drive progress and efficiency across diverse fields.

The role of Linux goes beyond mere accessibility; it can facilitate the establishment of local tech startups. Aspiring entrepreneurs seeking to develop software solutions can leverage Linux technologies to create innovative applications tailored to their communities' needs. By fostering a culture of innovation and entrepreneurship, developing countries can harness the potential of technology to address pressing local issues while creating economic opportunities, employment, and sustainability.

Furthermore, the adaptability of Linux positions it well within the context of technological advancements. Cloud computing and IoT technologies are increasingly accessible through Linux infrastructure, empowering developing countries to harness these tools meaningfully. By developing and deploying IoT solutions on Linux, for example, local enterprises can monitor resources, enhance supply chains, and boost productivity. The potential use cases for cloud-based solutions also illustrate how Linux can support remote learning, telemedicine, and other applications that play crucial roles in modern infrastructure.

However, the journey of empowering developing countries through Linux is not without challenges. Systematic barriers, such as internet connectivity issues and limited technical training, can hinder the adoption of Linux technologies. As a result, initiatives that promote training, mentorship, and community engagement are vital for bridging these gaps. Encouraging partnerships between local organizations, educational institutions, and government bodies can facilitate comprehensive training programs and awareness campaigns that empower individuals with the skills they need to thrive in a digital world.

In conclusion, Linux emerges as a powerful catalyst for change in developing nations, championing access, collaboration, and innovation. By eliminating costs associated with proprietary software, providing a rich environment for open-source alternatives, and fostering community-driven initiatives, Linux empowers individuals and organizations alike to harness technology's potential to drive economic growth and societal advancement. As the impact of Linux continues to resonate across borders, its role in shaping the future of technology in developing countries is significant, building a resilient and empowered workforce ready to tackle the challenges of the modern digital landscape. With continued support and access to the resources surrounding Linux, developing nations can create a more equitable technological ecosystem that benefits all individuals and communities.

12.2. Government Adoptions

Government adoptions of Linux represent a significant chapter in the narrative of open-source software, illustrating how public institutions have embraced this flexible operating system to enhance their operations, reduce costs, and empower citizens. As governments worldwide grapple with the growing need for technological solutions at a time when budgets are often constrained, the proactive switch to Linux has positioned many administrations on the path toward better resource management, increased security, and greater independence from proprietary software vendors.

The adoption of Linux by governments can be traced back to its roots in the ethos of collaboration and transparency that underpin open-source development. The concept of using and contributing to software that is freely available aligns closely with public sector values, appealing to policymakers who prioritize transparency, security, and budgetary responsibility. By choosing Linux, governments signal their commitment to fostering an environment where technology serves the public good without the reliance on expensive licenses associated with proprietary software.

One major advantage of moving to Linux is the significant cost savings associated with operating and maintaining IT infrastructures. Public institutions can avoid licensing fees tied to proprietary operating systems, which often escalate alongside changes in technology. Instead, they can significantly reduce expenditures by deploying various Linux distributions tailored to specific needs—be it enterprise resource planning, data management, or web services. Governments across different regions have demonstrated this shift: from France's a2e project, which sought to deploy open-source software in various public agencies, to India's ambitious plans to promote the use of Linux in educational institutions, the trend is evident.

In education, for instance, many school districts have implemented Linux-based systems to provide students and educators with access to robust computing resources without incurring extensive licensing costs. Initiatives such as "Linux in Schools" have emerged, seeking to introduce Linux to students and teachers and create a more sustainable educational model. The availability of free, high-quality educational tools on Linux ensures that students receive a comprehensive tech education without being limited by budget constraints. This aspect empowers educational institutions to nurture digital literacy while allocating resources toward other critical areas, such as teacher training and program development.

Moreover, the robust security features inherent in Linux have attracted government entities concerned about cyber threats and data breaches. The open-source nature of Linux allows public institutions to audit the code, identify vulnerabilities, and make necessary adjustments—an increasingly vital capability in an era of heightened scrutiny regarding data privacy. Governments in countries like Germany, which embraced Linux for their public institutions, have experienced improved security postures as a direct result of adopting an open-source operating system.

Another critical area where governments utilize Linux is in systems integration and interoperability. Many governmental prompt systems require various software solutions to communicate seamlessly with one another. Linux's flexibility allows public institutions to create customized solutions that integrate with existing infrastructure, reducing downtime and improving operational efficiency. Linux also enhances data portability across platforms, an essential quality for agencies that manage complex projects requiring collaborative inputs from multiple stakeholders.

The international community's collaboration on Linux-related projects also signifies its impact in the realm of governance. Open-source initiatives in software development promote global discourse among governments, NGOs, and citizen scientists, encouraging shared knowledge on best practices, security measures, and resource sharing. The administration of data-driven projects that address societal challenges—such as monitoring public health or environmental conditions—often involves using Linux as the enabling technology. The collaborative atmosphere nurtured in open-source environments amplifies efforts among disparate entities, resulting in synergistic approaches to solving challenges faced by many countries.

From a geopolitical perspective, the adoption of Linux reinforces digital sovereignty, enabling nations to maintain control over their local IT systems while lessening reliance on foreign technology providers. This becomes critical in regions where geopolitical tensions or trade imbalances may justify the need for self-sufficiency in software resources. By embracing Linux, governments effectively safeguard their digital assets while fostering local skill development, thereby bolstering national security.

While there are many benefits to government adoptions of Linux, challenges persist. Resistance to change, potential interoperability issues with proprietary systems, and the requirement for skilled technical staff to manage Linux-based infrastructure can complicate the transition. However, as success stories of governments leveraging Linux continue to emerge, these hurdles are increasingly being addressed through strategic partnerships, training programs, and dedicated community support.

In conclusion, the trend of government adoptions of Linux reflects the operating system's profound impact on public sector technology management. By embracing open-source solutions, governmental entities worldwide can realize significant cost savings, improve security, promote transparency, and nurture local innovation. As Linux continues to evolve and adapt to the changing technological landscape, its role in shaping government policies and practices will undoubtedly remain central to efforts geared toward fostering an inclusive, democratized digital future. As we move forward, the governance of technology will increasingly echo the principles of open collaboration and shared prosperity that lie at the heart of the Linux movement.

12.3. Digital Giants Embrace Linux

In the contemporary technological landscape, digital giants are increasingly recognizing the power and flexibility of the Linux operating system, leading to its widespread adoption across various sectors, including tech, finance, healthcare, and beyond. This embrace of Linux signifies not merely a change in operational tools but a strategic shift in how these companies view collaboration, innovation, and cost efficiency. From major corporations like Google, Facebook, and Amazon to startups aiming to maximize their potential within a competitive industry, the transition to Linux has become a hallmark of modern business practices that prioritize agility and sustainability.

At the heart of this trend is the recognition that Linux, as an open-source operating system, offers a significant advantage in terms of customization. Major tech firms have embraced the ability to tailor Linux to their specific needs, allowing them to create tailored solutions that align with their proprietary technologies or internal processes. This adaptability has led to enhanced performance and operational efficiencies, as companies can optimize Linux systems to better suit their infrastructure demands. For example, companies developing large-scale applications often rely on modified versions of Linux to handle increased traffic loads, ensuring that their services remain responsive and reliable.

Furthermore, the cost-effectiveness of Linux cannot be overstated. In an era where tech giants are constantly seeking to streamline expenses, the absence of licensing fees associated with proprietary systems presents a compelling financial argument for moving to Linux. Companies can deploy and scale their operations without incurring hefty upfront costs, allowing for greater flexibility in resource allocation. This financial strategy aligns perfectly with the increasing emphasis on sustainability in corporate practices, enabling organizations to invest more strategically in innovation and talent rather than software licenses.

Another factor driving the embrace of Linux among big tech companies is its remarkable security architecture. As concerns surrounding data breaches and cyber threats escalate, businesses are turning to Linux for its proven security features. The open-source nature of Linux means that potential vulnerabilities are often identified and patched promptly by a global community of developers, enhancing the robustness of its security posture. Companies like Amazon Web Services (AWS) have relied on Linux to underpin their cloud infrastructure, with security and privacy as a top priority. As such, Linux has become a trusted foundation for countless organizations operating in sensitive industries where data integrity is paramount.

Moreover, the flexibility of Linux extends to its compatibility with cutting-edge technologies such as cloud computing, machine learning, and artificial intelligence. Digital giants are increasingly adopting Linux-based solutions to power their cloud infrastructures, allowing them to scale operations seamlessly and embrace the myriad of applications that are transforming industries. Containerization technologies, such as Docker and Kubernetes, which thrive in Linux environments, further facilitate the deployment of applications within diverse infrastructures, permitting businesses to innovate without barriers.

In addition to operational efficiencies, the adoption of Linux fosters collaboration and community-driven innovation—a principle that perfectly aligns with the ethos of many tech giants. Companies like Google have not only utilized Linux to power their services but have also invested in its development, contributing code and resources to projects like Android and Chrome OS. By actively participating in the open-source community, these companies amplify the collaborative potential inherent in Linux, encouraging innovation that benefits all users and paving the way for advancements that push the technology envelope.

As more corporations recognize the merits of Linux and contribute to its ecosystem, we will likely see an accelerated rate of innovation across sectors. The collective effort of these digital giants to enhance and refine Linux fosters a culture of collaboration that will lead to better, more secure, and highly adaptable solutions for businesses large and small.

However, it is essential to recognize that while the embrace of Linux by these companies is a positive development, it also raises questions about the sustainability of the open-source model. As commercial interests increasingly overlap with community-driven projects, navigating the delicate balance between profit motives and the open-source ethos of collaboration will be crucial for the future of Linux. Engaging in conversations about corporate responsibility, community contributions, and the long-term sustainability of the ecosystem will be vital for fortifying Linux's foundation as a resource for all users.

In conclusion, the embrace of Linux by digital giants signifies a transformative shift in how organizations operate, innovate, and engage with technology. Through customization, cost-effectiveness, robust security, and a commitment to collaboration, Linux stands as a powerful alternative to proprietary systems, empowering businesses to thrive in an ever-changing technological landscape. As the community continues to grow and evolve, the journey ahead for Linux users and advocates will be rich with opportunities, challenges, and the promise of collective innovation.

12.4. Linux in International Organizations

In the realm of international organizations, Linux plays a pivotal role in enhancing operational efficiency and fostering collaboration in a world that increasingly relies on technology for communication and project execution. The adaptability, security, and cost-effectiveness of Linux have made it the operating system of choice for various global entities, including non-governmental organizations (NGOs), intergovernmental organizations (IGOs), and multinational corporations. As these organizations navigate complex global challenges, the capabilities afforded by Linux empower them to streamline processes, maximize resources, and reinforce their commitments to transparency and community engagement.

One of the defining attributes of Linux is its open-source nature, which allows international organizations to access powerful software solutions without incurring the high costs typically associated with proprietary systems. This affordability is particularly crucial for NGOs and charitable organizations operating on limited budgets. By leveraging Linux-based distributions, these organizations can deploy computing solutions that enhance their operations while conserving funds for their core missions. For instance, popular distributions such as Ubuntu, Fedora, and Debian offer robust software packages tailored to various needs, providing organizations with the tools necessary to manage data, conduct research, and collaborate effectively.

Security is paramount in the operations of international organizations that handle sensitive data and communications. Linux has garnered a reputation for its robust security features, including strong user permission settings, regular updates, and the ability to audit code for vulnerabilities. Given the potential risks of cyber attacks in today's digital landscape, these security capabilities are ideal for organizations that prioritize data integrity and confidentiality. By choosing Linux, organizations minimize risk while ensuring compliance with regulations relevant to data protection and privacy.

Moreover, Linux's flexibility allows international organizations to customize their systems to meet specific needs. The ability to modify open-source code fosters a culture of innovation, enabling teams to create tailored applications or workflows that align with their unique operational requirements. For example, an international non-profit may develop specialized software solutions to track field data, manage aid distributions, and facilitate communication among staff. The adaptability of Linux provides these organizations the freedom to innovate without being bound by the restrictions that often come with proprietary software licenses.

As international organizations increasingly rely on cloud computing solutions, Linux seamlessly integrates into these environments as well. Many cloud service providers offer Linux-based solutions suitable for hosting applications, managing data, and ensuring scalability. By adopting Linux in cloud deployments, organizations can effectively respond to fluctuating demands and access computing power on a pay-as-you-go basis, optimizing their resource management. This scalability is especially valuable for organizations that may handle large datasets or run complex simulations in their projects.

The collaborative nature of Linux fosters a sense of community among international organizations, enabling them to share tools, knowledge, and experiences. Open-source communities thrive on the principle of collaboration, allowing organizations to pool resources and enhance the functionality of software solutions collectively. For example, different NGOs may contribute to and refine advocacy tools or data management systems, amplifying their impact on the communities they serve while minimizing redundancy in development efforts. By working together, organizations can produce solutions that benefit a broader range of users.

In the education and training arenas, international organizations utilizing Linux can harness a wealth of resources to cultivate digital literacy and technological skills among their staff and constituents. Training programs that leverage open-source platforms empower individuals to engage with technology while boosting their employability and skill sets. Programs emphasizing Linux facilitate learning in developing regions, enabling participants to gain valuable expertise that carries into future career opportunities in technology and beyond.

Nonetheless, challenges remain in the landscape of Linux adoption among international organizations. The transition from proprietary systems to Linux may require significant investment in training and support as individuals adapt to new workflows or technologies. Ensuring comprehensive training resources and community support is vital for overcoming these hurdles and maximizing the benefits of Linux.

In conclusion, the role of Linux in international organizations represents a transformative force, amplifying their ability to communicate, collaborate, and innovate in a technology-driven world. By embracing Linux, these organizations can access cost-effective, robust solutions that enhance their operational capabilities while remaining committed to principles of security, transparency, and community engagement. As digital technologies continue to evolve, the capacity for Linux to facilitate collaboration and adaptation within international organizations positions it as an essential tool for addressing global challenges and fostering positive change across borders. The future of Linux in this context is bright, paving the way for enhanced cooperation and sustainability in the efforts of international organizations striving to make a lasting impact.

12.5. Linux as an Agent of Change

Linux is more than just an operating system; it is an agent of change, reshaping the technological landscape and paving the way for future innovations. From its inception in the early 90s to its current status as a dominant force in various sectors, Linux embodies a philosophy of collaboration and freedom that has fundamentally altered how society interacts with technology.

The narrative of change begins with the core tenet of open-source software, where the ability to view, modify, and redistribute code has democratized software development. This shift enables individuals and organizations to actively participate in the software creation process, leading to an environment where innovation is nurtured, and barriers are dismantled. The impact of this democratization is particularly vivid in developing countries, where communities can leverage Linux and its extensive ecosystem to access powerful tools without the financial burdens of proprietary software. Schools, startups, and tech hubs have sprung up, showcasing how Linux empowers local talent and fosters a culture of creativity and collaboration.

The success of Linux is also reflected in its adoption by major corporations and organizations. Many tech giants, including Google, Facebook, and Amazon, have harnessed the power of Linux to drive their infrastructure and services, signifying not only trust in the platform but also its effectiveness in managing vast amounts of data and delivering robust performance. This embrace has heralded an era of technological progress marked by efficiency, scalability, and rapid deployment, enabling businesses to remain agile and responsive to market needs.

Furthermore, Linux's adaptability to modern technological trends —cloud computing, containerization, and artificial intelligence—is a testament to its resilience. As industries evolve, Linux continues to be at the forefront, offering solutions that meet the rapidly changing demands of technology. For instance, with the proliferation of Internet of Things (IoT) devices, Linux has provided a strong foundation for developing scalable and secure applications that can operate across diverse hardware platforms. This versatility ensures that Linux remains a crucial player in the next wave of technological advancements, driving innovation in various domains.

The ongoing collaboration within the Linux community demonstrates the power of collective effort. Developers from around the world unite to contribute to projects, share knowledge, and enhance the functionality and security of the operating system. This sense of community is underscored by initiatives such as Google Summer of Code, which invites students to engage with open-source projects, ensuring that the spirit of collaboration continues to flow through generations of developers.

Moreover, the cultural impact of Linux extends beyond technology into societal narratives. It has inspired fresh perspectives on transparency, openness, and collaboration. As organizations adopt and promote open-source principles, they contribute to a changing landscape that prioritizes collective problem-solving over proprietary control. This cultural shift reflects a growing awareness of the need for ethical technology practices—ensuring that users are not merely consumers but active participants in shaping the tools they rely upon.

Nevertheless, challenges remain on the horizon. The rapid advancements in technology introduce complexities that Linux must navigate to maintain its relevance. Fragmentation within the ecosystem, the need for continued funding, and addressing security concerns in a multi-device, interconnected world require sustained attention and collaboration within the community. Addressing these challenges will be paramount in ensuring that Linux continues to thrive as an agent of change.

To encapsulate, Linux stands as a transformative force, reshaping not only the world of technology but also the broader societal and cultural landscape. By embodying open-source principles, it has empowered numerous individuals and organizations across the globe to embrace innovation and creativity, promoting a culture of collaboration that transcends borders. As we move forward into an increasingly digital future, the legacy of Linux will undoubtedly inspire generations to come, reinforcing the notion that shared knowledge, community engagement, and technological empowerment can ignite profound change across society. The future of Linux lies in its adaptability, collective mindset, and unwavering commitment to democratizing access to technology—an essence that will continue to drive it as an agent of change in the years to come.

13. Command Line and Usability: Mastering the Terminal

13.1. History of the Command Line Interface

The Command Line Interface (CLI) holds a central place in the history and functionality of Linux, embodying the spirit of efficiency and power that the operating system has come to represent. To understand its significance, we must trace its evolution from the rudimentary input/output systems of early computing to the sophisticated command environments we interact with today. The CLI embodies a philosophy of direct interaction with the operating system, offering users unparalleled control over their computational tasks.

The roots of the command line can be found in the early days of computing during the 1960s and 1970s, and it was initially designed for highly technical users: computer scientists, engineers, and programmers who had the expertise to navigate cryptic commands and syntax. Early systems, such as those developed by IBM and the use of the TECO (Text Editor and COrrector) by MIT, introduced users to the concept of issuing text commands to perform operations. As computers transitioned from mainframes to more accessible personal machines, the necessity of an interaction model that did not rely on graphical representations became evident.

Throughout the late 1970s and the early 1980s, various forms of command line interfaces took shape, culminating in the development of the UNIX operating system. UNIX and its derivative systems laid the groundwork for modern command-line interfaces. The ability to execute commands through typed input became a fundamental aspect of how users interacted with UNIX systems. Its design philosophy emphasized simplicity and modularity, allowing users to chain commands together to perform complex tasks—an essential quality of the command line that has persisted into the present day.

The birth of Linux in the early 1990s heralded a new chapter for the command line. Linus Torvalds, motivated by the principles of collaboration and accessibility, saw the command line as an essential tool for empowering users to interact with their systems without heavy reliance on graphical interfaces. As Linux gained traction, its command line interface became a powerful vehicle for users and developers to harness the full potential of the operating system. The flexibility offered by the CLI allowed users to manage not only file systems and applications but also network configurations, user permissions, and system operations—all with a few keystrokes.

As the Linux community flourished, so did the complexity and sophistication of the command line tools available. Utilities like Bash (Bourne Again SHell) emerged, cementing the CLI's role as an integral part of the Linux experience. Bash provided scriptable environments, allowing users to automate tedious tasks, create complex workflows, and extend their command-line capabilities through user-defined functions and aliases. The ability to write shell scripts transformed the command line into a productive environment that elevated user efficiency, enabling users to leverage their creativity in new and innovative ways.

The command line also became the bedrock for many of the development tools that define modern software production. Version control systems, such as Git, heavily rely on command-line interactions. Developers can manage code, track changes, and collaborate seamlessly through straightforward command structures. The prominence of devops practices, which emphasize continuous integration and deployment, further bolster the importance of command-line proficiency for modern developers.

However, while the command line is celebrated for its power and flexibility, usability and accessibility have also been topics of discussion within the community. As Linux continues to welcome a diverse user base, efforts to enhance the command line experience have gained momentum. The introduction of user-friendly shells, command completion, and interactive command history features has made the CLI more approachable for newcomers, ensuring that the complexity is tempered by intuition and ease of use. The growth of visual command-line interfaces through tools such as Terminator or fish shell further bridges the gap between power users and newcomers, allowing users to enjoy the strengths of command-line interfaces without sacrificing user-friendliness.

Looking to the future, the command line will continue to hold relevance in the ever-evolving technological landscape. As cloud computing, artificial intelligence, and containerization technologies gain traction, command lines will remain essential for interfacing with sophisticated systems, driving automation, and enhancing productivity across various sectors. As the Linux community continues to thrive, the CLI will serve as a powerful gateway, inviting users to explore the depths of their operating systems while providing them with the tools necessary to innovate, create, and collaborate.

In conclusion, the history of the Command Line Interface illustrates its foundational role in the evolution of Linux, shaping how users interact with systems and express their creativity. As we reflect on its journey from early computing to its present-day applications, it becomes evident that the command line embodies the very essence of Linux— open, collaborative, and infinitely adaptable. As we look ahead, the command line will remain a cornerstone, empowering users to harness the full potential of their technological endeavors while ensuring that the spirit of exploration and innovation continues to thrive.

13.2. Essential Command Line Tools

In the ever-evolving landscape of software development and system administration, mastering essential command line tools in Linux is crucial for enhancing productivity and efficiency. The command line interface (CLI) empowers users with the ability to interact directly with their operating system, providing granular control over system operations that graphical user interfaces (GUIs) may not offer. This subchapter will delve deeply into several essential command line tools that form the backbone of a powerful Linux user experience along with techniques for improving usability.

To begin, the `bash` shell, which is the default command-line interpreter for many Linux distributions, is the foundation for executing commands. Familiarity with bash commands such as `ls` (list files), `cd` (change directory), `cp` (copy files), and `mv` (move or rename files) establishes a solid base for navigating the filesystem. Understanding file permissions and ownership commands like `chmod` and `chown` is also essential for managing access control, ensuring that users can efficiently manage and secure their files and directories.

One of the most powerful tools available in command line environments is `grep`, which stands for "Global Regular Expression Print." `grep` works by searching through text input for lines that match a given pattern, making it an invaluable tool for filtering and analyzing data. For instance, combining `grep` with other commands using pipes allows users to sort through command outputs effectively. For example, running `ps aux | grep firefox` quickly identifies running instances of the Firefox browser, showcasing how `grep` simplifies monitoring processes.

The use of `find` is also imperative for locating files and directories within the Linux filesystem. Given the potential complexity of large directory trees, `find` allows users to search for files based on a multitude of criteria: name, size, modification time, and more. For instance, `find /home/user/docs -name "*.pdf"` effectively locates all PDF documents within a specified directory, enabling users to perform file management tasks with ease.

Another essential command line tool is `tar`, which provides functionality for archiving and compressing files. This is particularly useful for system backups and file transfer over networks. Using `tar` in conjunction with `gzip`, users can create compressed archives that save disk space while preserving file integrity. A command such as `tar -czvf archive.tar.gz /path/to/directory` efficiently compresses a directory, demonstrating how this tool streamlines data management and distribution.

For users who require additional functionalities, awk emerges as a flexible programming language that excels in text processing and data extraction. Often referred to as a "data-driven scripting language," awk enables users to execute operations on structured data files, such as CSV files, making it invaluable for data analysis tasks. For example, using awk to calculate the sum of a specific column in a CSV file allows for quick data manipulation that would otherwise require dedicated software.

The installation and management of software packages are vital components of using Linux, and tools like apt, yum, and dnf enhance this experience. For instance, the command apt install package_name allows Debian-based users to easily fetch and install software from repositories, ensuring that they can access the latest applications while seamlessly managing dependencies.

Beyond these core tools, aliases and custom scripts can greatly enhance user productivity in the command line environment. With the use of alias, users can create shortcuts for commonly used commands, reducing time and effort expended on repetitive tasks. For example, configuring an alias alias ll='ls -la' allows users to simply type ll to view a detailed directory listing. Similarly, writing shell scripts enables users to automate sequences of commands, significantly reducing manual effort and facilitating complex workflows.

Improving usability within the command line environment involves employing techniques such as command completion and history navigation. Utilizing the Tab key for command and file name completion streamlines workflow, while the command history combined with ! n (where n is the history number) enables quick execution of previously run commands. These features underscore the command line's potential for enhancing user experience.

In conclusion, mastering essential command line tools in Linux is foundational for enhancing productivity, efficiency, and system management capabilities. Understanding the plethora of available commands, their functionalities, and how to streamline workflows can empower users to harness the full power of the command line interface. The ongoing engagement with command line tools fosters a deeper understanding of the Linux operating system, ensuring users can adapt to various environments while maximizing their productivity. The CLI is not just a tool—it's an art, where the mastery of commands leads to enhanced creativity, efficiency, and innovation in the world of technology.

13.3. Improving Usability and Accessibility

In the realm of usability and accessibility, Linux has made significant strides in recent years, aiming to provide a more inclusive experience for users of all abilities. While historically viewed as a platform primarily for experienced users, Linux distributions have evolved to embrace catalogs of features that enhance usability and address barriers faced by individuals with disabilities. This transformation reflects a commitment to fostering an ecosystem where everyone, regardless of their technical expertise or physical capabilities, can effectively engage with technology.

The journey towards improved usability in Linux begins with the user interface. Many distributions, such as Ubuntu and Linux Mint, have adopted graphical user interfaces (GUIs) that prioritize simplicity and intuitiveness. These GUIs feature user-friendly elements such as straightforward menus, logically organized settings, and visually appealing layouts that make navigating the system easier for newcomers. Desktop environments like GNOME and KDE have incorporated accessibility tools into their designs, such as screen magnifiers and customizable keyboard shortcuts, ensuring users can tailor their environments to meet their specific needs.

Accessibility features play a vital role in leveling the playing field for users with disabilities. Speech recognition tools, screen readers, and braille displays have become increasingly integrated with Linux distributions, allowing users with visual impairments to interact with their systems effectively. Screen readers such as Orca enable text-to-speech functionality, converting on-screen content into audio cues that assist users in navigating applications, web pages, and documents. By bundling these essential tools within the operating system, Linux embraces the principle of inclusivity, enabling all users to harness the power and versatility of the platform.

Installation processes have also been streamlined to ease the transition for users. Most distributions now offer live environments, allowing users to boot from USB drives or CDs to test the system before installation. These environments highlight key features and demonstrate usability, making it easier for users to evaluate whether a specific distribution meets their needs. Additionally, many distributions incorporate guided installation wizards that provide clear, step-by-step instructions, minimizing potential points of confusion during setup.

The Linux community's commitment to inclusivity is reflected in ongoing efforts to develop documentation and resources that cater to users with varying levels of expertise. Beginner-friendly guides, video tutorials, and community forums provide invaluable support for users embarking on their Linux journey. Notably, organizations like the Ubuntu Accessibility Team actively work to improve accessibility features and promote awareness around assistive technologies, ensuring that potential barriers are continuously addressed.

In fostering an inclusive software environment, usability and accessibility considerations extend beyond initial interactions with the operating system—they permeate the applications available within the Linux ecosystem. Many open-source programs, including LibreOffice, GIMP, and VLC Media Player, have integrated accessibility features that facilitate easier usage for people with disabilities. These applications cater to a broad audience, ensuring that individuals can create, edit, and share documents, images, and media without encountering hurdles.

Moreover, developers are encouraged to adopt best practices related to accessibility during the application development process. Open-source licensing allows contributors to build upon existing projects to address usability concerns, identify gaps, and enhance overall functionality. By mobilizing the community around usability, Linux perpetuates a cycle of improvement that ultimately leads to a more inclusive user-base.

As technology advances, usability and accessibility on Linux will continue to evolve. The integration of artificial intelligence, machine learning, and natural language processing will facilitate the development of more intuitive interfaces that cater to users' individual needs. Additionally, continuous advocacy for inclusivity within the tech community will push the envelope for assistive technologies, allowing a more accessible digital world.

In summary, improving usability and accessibility in Linux is an ongoing commitment that embodies the core philosophy of the open-source community. By prioritizing user-friendliness, actively promoting assistive technologies, and fostering ongoing collaboration, the Linux ecosystem ensures that individuals from all walks of life can engage with and benefit from this powerful operating system. As we look towards the future, the strides made in usability and accessibility reflect the dedication to inclusivity—a reminder that technology serves to empower, uplift, and unite us all.

13.4. Advanced Terminal Tips and Tricks

In the realm of technology, the command line has long been a powerful tool for users, particularly for those tapping into the flexibility and depth of the Linux operating system. While many may initially view the command line as a daunting experience, developing a mastery of terminal operations is a gateway to unlock the true potential of a Linux system. This section aims to provide you with advanced terminal tips and tricks that enhance productivity and streamline your interactions with Linux.

One fundamental aspect of effective command-line usage is understanding the importance of command history. When working in the terminal, every command you type is saved in a history file, which allows you to recall previous commands without having to retype them. The `history` command displays the list of recent commands, while using the arrow keys can help you easily navigate through them. To execute a command from your history, you simply can type ! n, where n is the number assigned to the command in the list. For instance, typing !25 would execute the command listed as number 25 in your command history. This feature greatly enhances efficiency, particularly during longer sessions in the terminal.

Shell expansion is another powerful feature that allows for greater efficiency with your commands. For example, if you are routinely navigating to a specific directory or running a series of commands involving files within a directory, using braces is an efficient method. For instance, you can use the syntax {file1,file2,file3} in commands to operate on the specified files all at once. A command like cp {file1,file2,file3} /destination/path/ would copy all three files to the specified destination in one simple operation.

Furthermore, command chaining can significantly enhance your command line productivity. By using operators like && and ||, you can chain multiple commands together based on the success or failure of preceding commands. For example, if you want to compile a program and then execute it only if the compilation succeeds, you can write: make program && ./program. Alternatively, you can run a backup command if an operation fails by using: cp original.txt backup.txt || echo "Backup failed.". This feature allows you to create more efficient and streamlined workflows without needing to repetitively type in commands.

Another effective approach to boost productivity involves using wildcards and regular expressions. For instance, wildcards like * can be utilized to represent any sequence of characters, allowing users to perform operations involving multiple files easily. Instead of running a command on each file individually, you can execute rm *.tmp to remove all temporary files in a directory, significantly speeding up file management tasks. Mastering regular expressions can take this capability to a new level as they allow for more complex pattern matching in commands, letting you address specific needs within your workflow.

Command-line utilities are a treasure trove of features that can help automate and simplify tasks. Utilizing utilities such as `awk`, `sed`, and `xargs` expands your toolkit significantly. For example, `awk` can be used for sophisticated data manipulation within text files; with a command like `awk '{print $1}' file.txt`, you can extract the first column from a file. Adjusting how you handle data within your scripts can amplify your productivity and streamline repetitive tasks within the command line environment.

Another powerful feature to incorporate into your workflow is the use of aliases. Creating aliases helps shorten complex commands into simpler, more memorable terms. For instance, adding an alias like `alias ll='ls -la'` to your `.bashrc` file allows you to type `ll` to access detailed directory listings, simplifying your command input. This customization not only saves time, but it also allows you to tailor your command line to suit your working style.

Finally, enhancing usability in the terminal can also involve integrating terminal multiplexer tools like `tmux` or `screen`. These tools enable you to create multiple terminal sessions within a single window, allowing for better organization and multitasking. Users can detach from sessions, switch between them, or even share sessions with collaborators—all features that significantly boost productivity and collaboration when working on complex projects.

In conclusion, mastering advanced terminal tips and tricks is essential for enhancing productivity and efficiency in the Linux environment. By harnessing command history, shell expansions, command chaining, and powerful utilities, users can streamline their workflows and maximize interaction with their systems. As you continue to explore the potential of the Linux command line, these tools will undoubtedly empower you to navigate, manipulate, and innovate with confidence and creativity. The command line is a gateway into the deeper realms of what Linux offers, and with practice, you will ascend to a level of expertise that allows you to engage with your system like never before.

13.5. Scripting and Automation

In the rapidly evolving technological landscape, scripting and automation are pivotal processes that empower users to optimize workflows and streamline operations within the Linux operating system. The power of automation lies in its ability to reduce human intervention, enhance reliability, and improve efficiency across various tasks, transforming not only the way users interact with their systems but also how organizations manage their resources.

At the core of scripting and automation in Linux is the shell, which serves as the command-line interface where users can input commands to execute operations directly. Scripting allows users to write sequences of commands within a file, known as a script, which can be executed to perform a variety of tasks without manual input. Shell scripting, primarily performed in environments like Bash (Bourne Again SHell), provides users with a powerful means of communicating with the operating system, enabling them to automate repetitive tasks, manage system configurations, and enhance productivity.

The beauty of shell scripts lies in their simplicity and versatility. Developers and system administrators can harness scripts to manage everything from file manipulations and system monitoring to application installations and user account management. For example, a script can be written to automate the process of backing up critical files, creating a single-line command to execute an entire series of operations for efficient backup management.

A common starting point for beginners interested in scripting is learning the syntax and fundamental constructs of shell scripting, including variables, conditionals, loops, and functions. By understanding these constructs, users gain the foundation needed to create more complex scripts tailored to their specific needs. For example, a bash script might use a `for` loop to iterate over a list of files and perform an operation on each, improving workflow and reducing time spent on manual intervention.

Another key component of scripting in Linux involves utilizing command-line tools and utilities that are deeply integrated within the environment. Tools such as sed, awk, and grep are invaluable companions for users engaged in data manipulation, text processing, and structured reporting. By incorporating these tools into their scripts, users can execute powerful operations, such as extracting specific patterns from a file or transforming data formats effortlessly.

Further enhancing the potential of automation within Linux are task schedulers like cron. Using cron, users can schedule scripts and commands to run at specified intervals, automating tasks such as system maintenance, backups, and data collection. For instance, a system administrator can create a cron job to automate daily backups by running a shell script during off-peak hours, thereby minimizing the impact of resource usage on system performance.

Python, often hailed for its simplicity and readability, has also become a popular choice for scripting within Linux environments. Adopted widely by developers and data scientists alike, Python scripts can be utilized to execute more sophisticated automation tasks that involve libraries for data analysis, networking, and web scraping. As a versatile scripting language, Python seamlessly integrates with various Linux applications, presenting a formidable environment for both beginners and seasoned professionals in automating their workflows.

Another facet of automation in Linux is the inclusion of configuration management tools like Ansible, Puppet, and Chef. These tools allow users to define their infrastructure as code, enabling automated deployment, configuration, and management of servers and applications. By leveraging these tools, organizations can ensure consistency across environments, minimize configuration drift, and enhance productivity in resource management.

While the benefits of scripting and automation within Linux are immense, challenges exist that users may need to navigate. Learning to script effectively requires a foundational understanding of programming concepts, which might appear daunting to newcomers.

However, the vast array of resources available—from community forums and tutorials to online courses—ensures that users can access support as they build their skills.

Moreover, debugging scripts can sometimes prove to be a challenge, particularly when errors arise. Employing techniques such as code comments, echo statements, and the use of debugging tools can significantly alleviate these challenges, empowering users to create functional and reliable scripts.

In summary, scripting and automation are vital components of the Linux ecosystem, providing users with powerful means to optimize their workflows and enhance productivity. By leveraging shell scripts, command-line utilities, task schedulers, and advanced scripting languages, users can automate mundane tasks, streamline operations, and focus on higher-level processes that drive innovation. As the demand for efficiency and agility continues to grow in today's fast-paced technological landscape, mastering scripting and automation in Linux will be foundational for both individual users and organizations striving to thrive in a competitive digital world. The journey into scripting represents not just a technical endeavor but a pathway toward greater creativity and productivity in the dynamic environment of Linux.

14. Security and Linux: Beyond the Surface

14.1. Foundations of Linux Security

In the vast and intricate realm of Linux security, building a solid foundation is paramount. Understanding the principles that govern security measures, as well as the systems in place to uphold them, prepares users and administrators alike to effectively protect their Linux environments from various threats. The foundations of Linux security not only encompass technical measures but also constitute a broader understanding of the principles of security, risk management, and community collaboration that underpin the open-source ecosystem.

At the most basic level, Linux security hinges on the principle of least privilege, which dictates that users should have the minimum level of access necessary to perform their tasks. This principle reduces the risk of misuse or accidental damage by limiting what users and processes are able to do within the operating system. In Linux, user accounts are organized into groups, allowing system administrators to manage permissions effectively. This granularity enables detailed control over who can access specific files, directories, and system functions.

Central to the security architecture of Linux is the concept of user and group permissions. Each file and directory in a Linux system has associated read, write, and execute permissions, determining who can access it and what actions they can perform. This setup allows for effective resource management, as administrators can tailor permissions to suit the needs of different users. Mastery over the chmod, chown, and chgrp commands is essential for implementing and managing permissions, ensuring that only authorized users can modify critical system resources.

Moreover, Linux employs role-based access control (RBAC) mechanisms, particularly in enterprise environments. RBAC allows administrators to assign permissions based on roles within an organization, further promoting security by associating specific privileges with user roles rather than individual accounts. For example, a role defined for a developer might allow access to certain directories and files necessary for their work while restricting access to sensitive information.

Another cornerstone of Linux security is the kernel's inherent architecture, which is designed to mitigate risks associated with system vulnerabilities. The separation of user and kernel space is a key feature that protects the operating system from unauthorized access and malicious activities. User programs operate in user space, while the kernel has full control over system resources. This architecture prevents malicious code from executing at the kernel level, thus safeguarding the integrity of the operating system.

Moreover, tools like SELinux (Security-Enhanced Linux) or AppArmor further enhance security by implementing mandatory access controls (MAC). These systems enforce policies that dictate how processes interact with each other and with files, providing an added layer of security. SELinux, for instance, includes pre-defined policies that define roles and permissions for processes and users, preventing unauthorized access and limiting the impact of any potential exploits.

The importance of regular updates and patches cannot be overstated when it comes to maintaining Linux security. Vulnerabilities in software can expose systems to threats, and the proactive management of software updates is essential for mitigating these risks. The Linux community is known for its responsiveness when it comes to addressing security vulnerabilities, with many distributions providing timely releases of security patches. Utilizing tools like apt or yum to keep packages up to date, and employing utilities like unattended-upgrades to automate the process, can significantly enhance a system's security posture.

The concept of community collaboration also plays a vital role in the foundations of Linux security. The open-source model allows security researchers, developers, and users from around the world to contribute to identifying vulnerabilities and developing patches collaboratively. Projects like the Linux Security Module (LSM) framework demonstrate how collective efforts can create effective security solutions that benefit innumerable users. Participating in open-source communities can empower users to report issues, propose fixes, and engage in discussions that advance the overall security landscape of Linux.

To culminate this exploration, building a security foundation in Linux requires a multi-faceted approach rooted in an understanding of permissions, user roles, system architecture, access control, regular updates, and community collaboration. By fostering a culture of security consciousness and implementing best practices, users and organizations can create resilient environments that effectively manage and mitigate security risks. As the landscape of threats continues to evolve, remaining vigilant and proactive in securing Linux systems is essential for safeguarding vital resources against potential vulnerabilities and breaches. Through the lens of foundational security principles, Linux emerges as a robust operating system, prepared to embrace the challenges and complexities of the digital age.

14.2. Security Models and Systems

In the vast and interconnected landscape of technology, security models and systems form the bedrock of safeguarding sensitive data and ensuring the integrity of computational environments. As Linux continues to thrive as a dominant operating system for servers, personal computers, and embedded devices, its security frameworks must adapt to the evolving threats posed by the digital age. This examination explores the principles, architectures, and practices that underlie Linux security, illuminating how the operating system fosters secure environments while remaining accessible to users of all skill levels.

At the heart of Linux security is its foundational architecture, which emphasizes user permission management and access controls. Linux employs a multi-user model where each user account operates within a defined scope of permissions. Access control is enforced using read, write, and execute (rwx) permissions, which can be assigned to individual users or groups. Understanding how to manipulate these permissions through commands like chmod and chown is essential for system administrators seeking to uphold security measures. By adhering to the principle of least privilege, administrators can limit user access to only the resources necessary for fulfilling their roles, reducing the risk of unauthorized access or accidental damage to critical files.

Enhancing its architecture further, Linux integrates mandatory access control (MAC) systems like SELinux (Security-Enhanced Linux) and AppArmor. These powerful frameworks enable fine-grained access control policies that can limit the permissions granted to applications and processes well beyond the traditional UNIX permission model. SELinux employs security contexts and policies to restrict how applications interact with files and other resources, effectively creating an additional layer of defense against potential vulnerabilities or exploits. By enabling administrators to define detailed security policies, SELinux strengthens the security posture of Linux systems through proactive enforcement of resource access.

Another salient aspect of Linux security involves timely updates and vulnerability management. As new security threats emerge, maintaining an up-to-date system is crucial for mitigating risks. The Linux community is known for its agile response to vulnerabilities, with distributions frequently releasing patches and updates that address emerging security issues. Utilizing package managers, users can swiftly install updates without manual oversight—ensuring their systems remain secure. Commands like apt update && apt upgrade or dnf upgrade exemplify the ease with which users can bolster their defenses against newly identified threats.

In addition to core security measures, Linux provides a rich set of tools for monitoring and auditing system activity. Utilities like auditd (the Linux Auditing System) and system logging tools enable administrators to track access attempts, system calls, and user actions within the system. By maintaining thorough logs and employing intrusion detection systems (IDS), users can identify abnormal patterns or unauthorized access attempts, allowing for timely interventions to safeguard critical data.

Moreover, the modular approach of Linux security enables organizations to customize their security frameworks based on varying operational needs. Depending on the specific use case—be it web servers, cloud environments, or desktop systems—Linux can adapt its security measures accordingly. For instance, deploying firewalls (like `iptables` or `firewalld`) can protect against unauthorized external access, while VPN support can secure remote connections for users accessing the network from outside.

The community aspect of open-source is vital to the ongoing evolution and improvement of Linux security. Researchers, developers, and users contribute to security discussions and share their findings across forums and mailing lists, creating a robust network of knowledge. Collaborative efforts result in the development of security-enhancing tools, such as ClamAV (an open-source antivirus solution) or Fail2Ban (a utility that monitors logs and automatically bans IP addresses engaging in malicious behavior). This spirit of cooperation ensures that Linux security continues to adapt to meet new challenges as they arise.

Linux security models and systems do not merely emphasize the reactive aspect of cybersecurity; they also prioritize education and awareness. A solid understanding of security principles, threats, and risk management strategies is essential for both users and administrators. Educational initiatives, resources, and community-driven awareness campaigns foster a security culture around Linux environments, encouraging ongoing vigilance and proactive measures.

In conclusion, the security models and systems integrated within Linux represent a dynamic and comprehensive framework that transcends the mere protection of data. By embodying principles of collaboration, customization, and proactive defense, Linux not only stands as a powerful operating system but as a resilient fortress in the face of emerging threats. As users continue to innovate and evolve the Linux landscape, the commitment to security remains steadfast, ensuring that Linux can fulfill its promise as a versatile and secure platform in the ever-changing digital ecosystem. The role of security in Linux is paramount, reinforcing the understanding that safeguarding resources is not just an individual effort but a community-driven endeavor, where knowledge, strategy, and technology converge to foster a reliable and secure computing environment for all.

14.3. Mitigating Threats and Vulnerabilities

Mitigating threats and vulnerabilities in the Linux environment is a critical undertaking that requires diligent attention, proactive measures, and a comprehensive understanding of the unique challenges faced by both users and system administrators. As Linux continues to gain traction across a myriad of applications—ranging from personal desktops to enterprise servers and cloud infrastructures—the imperative to ensure enhanced security has never been greater. This section explores various strategies, best practices, and tools for effectively mitigating threats and vulnerabilities in Linux systems.

One of the foundational steps in establishing a secure Linux environment is the principle of maintaining least privilege. By ensuring that users and applications only have the minimum permissions necessary to perform their designated tasks, organizations can significantly reduce the attack surface. This practice extends to the management of user accounts, where administrators should regularly review permissions and access levels, revoke unnecessary privileges, and utilize role-based access controls (RBAC) whenever feasible.

Regular software updates play a crucial role in mitigating vulnerabilities. The Linux community is known for its proactive approach to identifying and patching security vulnerabilities, and it is essential that administrators stay vigilant in keeping their systems updated. Using package managers, such as APT or YUM, administrators can automate updates or establish regular schedules to ensure that both the operating system and all installed applications are continuously maintained at the latest secure versions. Commands such as `apt update && apt upgrade` and `yum update` facilitate this process and are fundamental practices that every Linux administrator should incorporate into their routine.

Firewalls serve as a vital line of defense in securing Linux systems. Utilizing tools like iptables or firewalld allows administrators to control incoming and outgoing traffic based on defined rules. Establishing a robust firewall configuration ensures that only necessary services are exposed to the internet and that unauthorized access attempts are blocked. For example, configuring a firewall to allow traffic only on specific ports used for required services (e.g., SSH on port 22 or web services on port 80/443) greatly enhances the security posture of any Linux system.

Moreover, implementing security extensions like SELinux or AppArmor can enhance system security by enforcing stringent access controls. SELinux, in particular, allows administrators to define policies that dictate how processes interact with files and resources in a Linux environment. This capability adds an additional layer of protection, making it much harder for attackers to exploit vulnerabilities and execute malicious code. Understanding and configuring these security measures can take time, but investing in personnel training and knowledge-sharing within the community pays dividends in creating more secure systems.

Vulnerability scanning tools are essential for identifying potential weaknesses within a Linux environment. Tools such as OpenVAS, Nessus, or Lynis provide administrators with insights into misconfigurations, outdated software, and potential exploits. Regularly running these scans enables organizations to stay ahead of threats by addressing vulnerabilities before they can be exploited. Implementing a policy of routine scanning—whether weekly or monthly—ensures that vulnerabilities are tracked and remediated promptly.

The importance of logging and monitoring cannot be overstated. Utilizing tools such as the Linux Auditing System (`auditd`) or Logwatch helps to maintain visibility into system activities and user actions. Staying informed of unusual activity can alert administrators to potentially malicious attempts at unauthorized access. Additionally, integrating third-party monitoring solutions, such as Splunk or ELK (Elasticsearch, Logstash, Kibana), offers enhanced capabilities for analyzing logs, detecting anomalies, and responding to incidents in real-time.

Educating all users about security best practices is another essential layer in threat mitigation. Users are often the weakest link in the security chain; therefore, promoting awareness around common threats, such as phishing, social engineering, and insecure password practices, can bolster overall security. Organizations should conduct regular training sessions that instill a security-first mindset, empowering all users to recognize potential threats and adhere to established protocols.

Despite the numerous defenses that can be put in place, security cannot be entirely absolute. Organizations need to develop incident response plans that define processes for containing, investigating, and recovering from breaches. Establishing clear communication channels and responsibilities within an incident response team enables a coordinated approach to threat management. Regularly testing these plans through drills will ensure that users and administrators are prepared to act quickly and effectively when security incidents occur.

In conclusion, mitigating threats and vulnerabilities in Linux environments is a multifaceted process that requires a blend of strategic planning, diligent practices, and community collaboration. By focusing on principles such as least privilege, maintaining updated software, establishing strong firewalls, utilizing security extensions, and fostering user awareness, organizations can create a resilient security posture around their Linux systems. Additionally, incorporating vulnerability scanning, logging, monitoring, and well-defined incident response plans enables proactive management of evolving threats. As the technology landscape continues to change, remaining vigilant and adaptable in security practices will be essential to safeguarding Linux environments and preserving the integrity of crucial digital assets.

14.4. Technology Evolutions in Security

In the ever-evolving landscape of digital technology, few domains experience transformation as dynamically as security. Over the past few decades, the rapid advancement of technology has not only reshaped our methods of communication and interaction but has also influenced how we approach the security of our systems and data. Among those at the forefront of this change is the Linux operating system, which continues to evolve in response to emerging threats and new paradigms in security.

At its core, Linux has long been recognized for its strong security features, which are integral to its design philosophy. The principles of open-source development underpin a robust security model, where users benefit from transparency, community involvement, and collaborative problem-solving. This model encourages immediate identification and resolution of vulnerabilities, empowering developers worldwide to engage in proactive security practices. Yet, as technology evolves, so do the threats that Linux faces, necessitating continuous adaptation and innovation within its security framework.

As we examine the journey of Linux security, several fundamental changes have been occurring. For one, the internet's proliferation and the ubiquity of connected devices have expanded the attack surface significantly. The Internet of Things (IoT) presents unique security challenges, as a multitude of devices interact on the same network, many of which lack stringent security measures. This phenomenon has prompted Linux developers to innovate new standards and frameworks tailored for IoT, striving to maintain security in increasingly complex environments, while also addressing concerns about third-party integration and data privacy.

Moreover, the rise of cloud computing has introduced new avenues for exploitation, compelling security professionals to rethink traditional defense mechanisms. The architecture of cloud services requires robust identity management, data encryption, and network security protocols to safeguard data in transit and at rest. Linux remains a primary operating system for cloud infrastructures, yet its security posture must adapt to ensure that organizations can confidently leverage cloud resources without compromising sensitive information.

Recent advancements in artificial intelligence and machine learning are reshaping how security measures are implemented within Linux environments. These technologies introduce new solutions for identifying anomalies, detecting intrusions, and automating responses to threats. By employing machine learning algorithms, Linux systems can analyze vast amounts of data to uncover patterns and identify potential vulnerabilities in real-time, enhancing their resilience against sophisticated attacks.

Additionally, the approach to patch management and vulnerability assessment has evolved significantly, with the integration of automated tools and processes to ensure timely updates and fixes. The Linux community has long had a reputation for rapid response to discovered vulnerabilities, but the advent of automated patching utilities and continuous integration/continuous deployment (CI/CD) frameworks further exemplifies the commitment to safeguarding systems and data integrity.

As security concerns escalate among users and organizations, the emphasis on training and awareness for Linux administrators and users has become crucial. Investing in education around best practices and emerging threats fosters a culture of vigilance and encourages proactive security measures within the community. The Linux ecosystem thrives on collaboration and knowledge-sharing, making it essential for users to stay informed about the latest security challenges and defenses.

The legacy of security in the Linux environment is marked by an ongoing commitment to improvement. The adaptability ingrained in its open-source nature has created an environment where security innovations emerge not only from core developers but also from a diverse array of contributors. The collaborative spirit encourages individuals to share their findings, tools, and methodologies with the community, continuously enhancing the collective understanding of security threats and solutions.

In summary, technology evolutions in security represent both opportunities and challenges within the Linux ecosystem. As Linux continues to adapt and respond to the rapidly changing landscape, the operating system remains dedicated to fostering secure environments characterized by transparency, collaboration, and innovation. By addressing emerging threats, embracing advancements in technology, and nurturing awareness among users, Linux will undoubtedly continue its legacy as a powerful and secure platform within the digital realm. As we venture into this new territory, the spirit of cooperation will serve as a catalyst, enabling the Linux community to rise to the occasion and meet the demands of a complex, interconnected world.

14.5. Security in Open Source Projects

In the realm of open-source projects, security is a vital consideration that calls for deliberate attention and proactive measures. Unlike proprietary software, where source code is tightly controlled, open-source projects enable anyone to access and modify code, resulting in a collaborative spirit that fosters innovation. However, this openness is also a double-edged sword, as it requires a well thought out approach to ensure the integrity and security of the project. Understanding security in open-source projects entails a multifaceted perspective that encompasses best practices, community engagement, and the balance of openness with effective risk management.

At the forefront of security concerns in open-source projects is the issue of code vulnerability. With the ability for anyone to contribute, there exists a risk that poorly written or malicious code could be introduced into the project. To mitigate these risks, it is crucial for open-source projects to establish a code review process that emphasizes scrutiny and testing of contributions. By maintaining a clear structure for code submission, including automated testing and peer review mechanisms, projects can reduce the likelihood of vulnerabilities making their way into the production environment. Implementing robust testing frameworks allows for the rapid identification and resolution of issues, enhancing the overall security of the project.

Furthermore, the ability of the community to actively monitor and audit the code is a defining characteristic of open-source security. The transparency of open-source projects allows contributors and users alike to scrutinize code and report vulnerabilities or exploits. This collaborative effort through mailing lists, forums, and issue trackers fosters an environment of shared responsibility and vigilance. By harnessing the diverse skillset within the community, projects can address security concerns in a timely manner and cultivate a culture that prioritizes security as a fundamental principle.

Community engagement extends beyond code review; it also involves establishing clear communication channels for vulnerability reporting and incident response. Open-source projects must provide guidelines for users to report security vulnerabilities responsibly. By creating a transparent communication strategy that acknowledges the contributions of individuals who identify vulnerabilities, projects foster trust within the community while encouraging a proactive stance toward security measures.

Beyond the code itself, it's important for open-source projects to consider the security of their deployment environments. Often, the components of an open-source project involve multiple software dependencies, each of which may introduce potential vulnerabilities. It is essential for maintainers to conduct regular audits of the libraries and tools used within the project, ensuring that they are up to date and free from known security flaws. Utilizing tooling and frameworks designed for dependency management can help streamline this process, providing insights into the health of the project's dependencies and their associated security issues.

As the digital landscape evolves, so too do the threats that open-source projects face. Keeping abreast of new attack vectors—such as supply chain attacks, ransomware, and sophisticated exploitation techniques—demands ongoing vigilance and education within the community. Organizations and contributors involved in open-source security must prioritize knowledge sharing, attending conferences, participating in workshops, and collaborating with cybersecurity experts to better understand the dynamics of emerging threats. Engaging in discussions around secure coding practices, threat modeling, and incident response within the community not only raises awareness but also reinforces a culture of accountability.

The role of governance structures in open-source projects also merits attention. Establishing clear guidelines around contributions, coding standards, and security policies helps create a cohesive security model that encompasses the entire lifecycle of the project. By drafting formal governance documents, projects articulate their commitment to security and can outline processes for handling vulnerabilities, code contributions, and incident management.

Furthermore, security training and education for contributors, maintainers, and users can significantly bolster project security. By providing awareness about common security pitfalls, best practices, and available resources, open-source projects empower individuals to adopt proactive measures in their engagement with the code. Workshops focused on secure coding practices, threat modeling, and incident response can foster a knowledgeable community, enabling its members to navigate the complexities of security within the open-source ecosystem.

In conclusion, security in open-source projects is a multifaceted endeavor requiring collaborative efforts from both contributors and users. By implementing robust code review processes, maintaining open communication channels, and engaging in proactive community-driven security practices, open-source projects can improve their resilience against threats. While the principles of openness foster collaboration and innovation, it is imperative for the community to prioritize security and lay a solid foundation for building trust, integrity, and sustainability. Emphasizing the balance between openness and effective risk management will ensure that open-source projects can thrive within a secure environment, empowering their communities to continue fostering innovation and creativity while safeguarding their collective contributions.

15. Linux and the Internet of Things (IoT): Sewing Connectivity

15.1. Connecting Devices with Linux

Connecting devices with Linux is a pivotal aspect of the ever-evolving landscape of technology, particularly with the rise of the Internet of Things (IoT). The transient nature of how devices communicate, share information, and operate autonomously in coordinated networks can significantly improve operational efficiency and enhance user experiences. Linux, with its open-source flexibility, customization capabilities, and resilience, is at the forefront of this connectivity revolution, allowing developers and engineers to create a vast array of smart devices that are both functional and user-friendly.

The foundation of connecting devices with Linux starts with its broad support for various hardware architectures. Linux can seamlessly run on a plethora of embedded devices, sensors, microcontrollers, and single-board computers like the Raspberry Pi and Arduino platforms, which are often used in IoT applications. This compatibility across diverse hardware promotes innovation, enabling manufacturers to integrate Linux into devices intended for environments ranging from industrial automation to smart home solutions.

Moreover, the Linux kernel is specifically designed to be highly modular, allowing developers to incorporate only the necessary components for their applications. This modularity is invaluable in the IoT realm, where efficiency is crucial, and resource constraints may limit the capabilities of devices. Developers can build lightweight Linux distributions, optimizing them for specific tasks such as monitoring environmental conditions, controlling machinery, or managing home security systems. The ability to customize the operating system to suit the minimal needs of IoT devices ensures efficient use of processing power and memory, enhancing overall performance.

Networking protocols also play a critical role in connecting devices with Linux. Linux supports a wide array of networking technologies, including TCP/IP, Bluetooth, MQTT (Message Queuing Telemetry

Transport), and Zigbee, among others. The flexibility of Linux allows developers to choose the appropriate protocol for specific applications, facilitating effective communication between devices in a network. For example, the lightweight MQTT protocol is ideal for IoT environments, as it is efficient in terms of bandwidth and power consumption, making it suitable for devices that are subject to limited connectivity or battery constraints.

In addition to these advantages, Linux's extensive development community continues to foster innovation in the IoT space. Numerous open-source projects focus specifically on IoT frameworks and solutions, providing developers with resources and tools to create connectivity applications. Platforms such as Home Assistant and OpenHAB emphasize interoperability among smart devices, enabling users to control and automate their environments effortlessly. These frameworks support a variety of protocols and devices while leveraging Linux to provide a cohesive user experience.

The versatility of the Linux operating system extends beyond traditional IoT devices, as it is also capable of integrating advanced technologies such as artificial intelligence and machine learning into connected systems. By utilizing tools such as TensorFlow and PyTorch, developers can enhance their IoT solutions through intelligent decision-making and data analysis capabilities. This could manifest in scenarios such as smart agriculture—where connected sensors analyze soil conditions and adjust irrigation systems or predictive maintenance—where machinery anticipates service requirements based on usage patterns.

Enhancing connectivity with Linux may also involve addressing security challenges inherent in IoT networks. As multiple devices communicate and exchange sensitive data, ensuring that these interactions are secure becomes paramount. Linux security features, such as SELinux and AppArmor, provide mechanisms for enforcing security policies, ensuring that only authorized devices can connect and communicate within the network. Regular updates and community discourse around vulnerabilities allow IoT developers to harness the collective wisdom of the Linux community, resulting in more secure devices and applications.

In conclusion, connecting devices with Linux empowers the creation of innovative IoT solutions that enhance the way we interact with technology in our daily lives. Linux's adaptability, extensive support for networking protocols, and robust security features make it an ideal choice for developing the next generation of connected devices. As the demand for IoT solutions continues to expand across industries —from smart homes and healthcare to industrial applications—Linux stands at the forefront, offering the versatility and performance needed to build resilient and effective systems. The future of IoT connectivity is undeniably intertwined with the continued evolution and unwavering contribution of the Linux community.

15.2. IoT Frameworks and Distributions

In the context of the entire book 'Bashing the Myths: An Explosive Journey through Linux Trivia', the subchapter focusing on IoT Frameworks and Distributions presents an exciting intersection of technology and innovation facilitated by Linux. As the Internet of Things continues to expand its reach and influence over our daily lives and industry processes, Linux remains at the heart of many successful implementations thanks to its unique adaptability, security, and open-source principle.

Linux distributions specifically optimized for IoT applications have fundamentally changed how we approach connectivity and smart environments. Distributions like Raspbian (now Raspberry Pi OS), Ubuntu Core, and Yocto Project are prime examples of tailored operating systems designed to run efficiently on low-powered devices and embedded systems. These distributions provide a complete package that addresses the unique constraints often found in IoT contexts— from low energy consumption and limited computing resources to hardware compatibility issues.

Raspberry Pi OS is particularly popular in educational settings, empowering students and hobbyists to create and experiment with their IoT projects. The lightweight nature of this distribution makes it ideal for running on single-board computers like the Raspberry Pi, allowing users to engage with hardware programming and application development concurrently. Users can turn these small devices into sophisticated IoT applications such as weather stations, media centers, and home automation systems, promoting a culture of innovation and creativity.

Ubuntu Core, on the other hand, focuses on containerized applications designed for IoT environments. This snap-based distribution decentralizes applications and their dependencies, allowing for seamless updates and enhancing security by minimizing the attack surface of each application. Ubuntu Core is gaining traction in industrial IoT projects where device management, security, and maintainability are crucial for operational success. The use of snap packages further simplifies deploying applications across various devices, making it an attractive option for organizations scaling their IoT deployments.

The Yocto Project offers another level of flexibility for developers creating customized Linux distributions tailored to their IoT hardware and software requirements. By providing a comprehensive set of tools and workflows, Yocto allows developers to build and customize Linux images that can run on various architectures. This modularity and adaptability make Yocto particularly appealing for organizations with specialized needs, such as automotive or aerospace applications, where precise customization of the software stack is often necessary.

In conjunction with the development of distributions, frameworks such as Node-RED and OpenHAB demonstrate how Linux can be utilized to facilitate connectivity, automation, and monitoring of IoT devices. Node-RED specializes in visual programming and allows developers to create flows and connections between different devices and services through an intuitive web-based interface. This approach lowers the barrier to entry for users who may not have extensive programming expertise but still want to engage with IoT technologies meaningfully.

On the other hand, OpenHAB serves as a home automation platform that gives users the ability to integrate various devices from different manufacturers into a cohesive smart home system. By leveraging Linux, OpenHAB provides the necessary infrastructure for device communication and interoperability, allowing users to control everything from smart lights to security systems from a centralized application.

Despite the numerous advantages of utilizing Linux frameworks and distributions in IoT, challenges remain, particularly regarding security and standardization. With the proliferation of devices connected to the internet, securing these systems against potential cyber threats becomes paramount. The responsibility for implementing security measures often falls on developers and organizations that must remain informed about common vulnerabilities and evolving threat landscapes.

Standardization remains another pressing concern, given the diversity of IoT devices and protocols. Fragmentation can lead to compatibility issues as different manufacturers adopt their solutions. Initiatives promoting interoperability, such as the AllSeen Alliance and the Open Connectivity Foundation, aim to address these challenges by establishing common standards that improve communication between devices regardless of the operating systems they run.

In conclusion, the frameworks and distributions built on Linux for IoT applications reveal a landscape rich with possibilities for innovation and creativity. With specialized solutions like Raspberry Pi OS, Ubuntu Core, and Yocto Project, users can navigate the intricacies of connectivity while addressing the unique constraints of the IoT ecosystem. As the demand for smart devices and connected solutions continues to grow, Linux's importance as a backbone for IoT infrastructure will only strengthen, establishing it as a driving force in shaping the future of technology-enabled environments. Through continued collaboration, innovation, and mindful attention to security, the Linux community will contribute significantly to the success of IoT, transforming how we live and work in an increasingly connected world.

15.3. Security Concerns in IoT Ecosystems

In the rapidly evolving landscape of the Internet of Things (IoT), security is a pressing concern that has significant implications for every connected device. The potential for vulnerabilities to be exploited in the growing number of IoT devices underscores the need for robust security measures, particularly in those running on Linux—the operating system that has become the backbone of many IoT solutions. This subchapter delves into the key security concerns in IoT ecosystems, examining the unique challenges these devices face, the security frameworks available in Linux, and strategies for mitigating threats.

IoT devices, from smart thermostats and wearable fitness trackers to industrial sensors, often operate in environments where they interact with a vast array of networks and other devices. This complexity and interconnectivity create an expansive attack surface, leaving IoT systems vulnerable to various cyber threats including unauthorized access, data breaches, and even physical tampering. How these devices communicate, store data, and share information becomes critical in identifying potential vulnerabilities and implementing effective security measures.

One of the fundamental security challenges in IoT ecosystems is the sheer diversity of devices and platforms involved. Each device may have its own set of hardware, software, and networking protocols, complicating the establishment of uniform security standards. Linux, embraced for its flexibility and customization, often serves as the operating system of choice for many IoT devices. However, this variability means that security practices must be tailored to the unique characteristics and functions of each device. The lack of a comprehensive security framework across different devices can lead to inconsistencies in how security measures are implemented, increasing vulnerability.

Additionally, many IoT devices come with limited computing resources, which can hinder the implementation of sophisticated security measures. Developers often face trade-offs between functionality and security; for instance, resource-constrained devices may struggle to support complex encryption algorithms or security features. This situation necessitates the development of lightweight security protocols and solutions that adequately protect devices without severely impacting their performance.

Deployment practices further complicate security in IoT ecosystems. Often, many devices are deployed without regular monitoring or updates, leaving them susceptible to emerging vulnerabilities. Without diligent management of firmware updates, devices may remain on outdated software, exposing themselves to known security flaws. The responsibility increasingly falls upon manufacturers, developers, and users to prioritize regular updates and maintenance to ensure that devices remain secure against newly discovered threats.

Linux provides several frameworks and features aimed at bolstering the security of IoT devices. One such feature is AppArmor, which serves as a Mandatory Access Control (MAC) system, allowing administrators to define and enforce specific security policies for individual applications. By confining applications to designated permissions, AppArmor minimizes the potential damage that could result from an exploited vulnerability, protecting critical system resources.

Additionally, Security-Enhanced Linux (SELinux) enforces access controls that extend beyond traditional UNIX permissions. SELinux allows system administrators to define policies governing how processes can interact with files and system resources. By leveraging SELinux, IoT developers can impose strict access controls that harden devices against common exploit vectors, ensuring that potentially compromised applications cannot extend their reach throughout the system.

The use of secure communication protocols is also paramount in mitigating risks in IoT ecosystems. Encrypting data in transit using protocols such as HTTPS (Hypertext Transfer Protocol Secure) or MQTT (Message Queuing Telemetry Transport) with TLS (Transport Layer Security) enhances the confidentiality and integrity of communications between devices and servers. Implementing secure authentication methods, such as OAuth and JSON Web Tokens (JWT), further safeguards against unauthorized access to IoT platforms.

Another pivotal aspect of securing IoT devices involves diligent monitoring and logging practices. By utilizing tools that monitor device behavior in real time, administrators can quickly detect anomalies that may signify a security breach. These insights enable swift responses to potential threats, limiting the damage and restoring secure operations promptly.

Security training and awareness programs are integral to promoting safe practices among those involved in IoT development and deployment. Raising awareness of common threats—such as phishing, insider threats, and insecure configurations—can empower engineers, users, and organizations to take proactive measures in safeguarding their IoT environments.

In conclusion, securing IoT ecosystems running on Linux involves addressing a complex web of challenges tied to device diversity, resource limitations, deployment practices, and evolving threats. By leveraging the security features inherent in Linux, enhancing communication protocols, and fostering a culture of awareness and vigilance, developers and organizations can create resilient IoT solutions that not only perform effectively but also protect the integrity and privacy of users. As we continue to witness the proliferation of IoT devices, the commitment to security will be paramount in ensuring a safe and connected future.

15.4. Smart Homes and Linux

In today's ever-evolving technological landscape, smart homes are increasingly becoming a focal point for innovation and convenience. At the forefront of this revolution, Linux has emerged as a critical player, powering a diverse array of smart devices and home automation systems. With its open-source flexibility, reliability, and extensive community support, Linux is well-positioned to address the challenges and opportunities presented by this growing sector.

The integration of Linux into smart home solutions starts with its ability to run on a wide range of hardware platforms, from single-board computers like the Raspberry Pi to IoT devices and smart hubs. This versatile compatibility allows manufacturers, hobbyists, and developers to tailor Linux-based solutions to meet a variety of needs, such as managing lighting systems, climate control, home security, and energy consumption—all while remaining cost-effective. The accessibility of hardware components, paired with the availability of Linux distributions optimized for embedded systems, empowers users to create customized smart home ecosystems that enhance the overall living experience.

Moreover, the open-source nature of Linux encourages collaboration and innovation, resulting in a rich ecosystem of software applications designed specifically for smart home management. Home automation platforms such as Home Assistant and OpenHAB exemplify this trend by allowing users to connect and control various smart devices from different manufacturers through a single interface. Users can create custom automations—such as programming their lights to turn on when they come home or setting the thermostat based on their daily routines. The flexibility of these platforms allows for easy integration of devices that use different communication protocols, fostering interoperability and delivering a seamless user experience.

An additional benefit of using Linux in smart homes is the continuous evolution of software capabilities through community contributions. Open-source software projects thrive on the collective efforts of developers, who actively contribute features, bug fixes, and new integrations based on user feedback. This collaborative spirit ensures that smart home solutions are not only continually improved but also responsive to the changing needs of users. For instance, through regular updates and enhancements, users can integrate newly released smart devices or advanced technologies into their existing setups without requiring comprehensive overhauls.

Further enhancing the security of smart home systems is Linux's inherent architecture, which can be configured to enforce strict security measures and permissions. By employing tools such as Firewall, fail2ban, or app-specific security policies like AppArmor or SELinux, users can protect their networks and devices from potential threats. As smart homes increase in popularity, the importance of applying robust security practices when using Linux-based systems becomes paramount to safeguard private data and ensure user trust.

While the integration of Linux into smart home solutions brings many advantages, challenges do persist. Interfacing with proprietary devices or systems may create compatibility issues, as many manufacturers tend to produce products that may not seamlessly integrate with open-source platforms. Addressing these challenges requires active community engagement, where users can share experiences, solutions, and workarounds for effectively connecting various devices.

Moreover, educating users about the capabilities and limitations of Linux in the context of smart homes is essential for empowering them to harness the full potential of their systems. Providing clear documentation, tutorials, and support resources will ensure that users, whether seasoned developers or new adopters, feel confident in deploying Linux-based solutions for their smart home applications.

In conclusion, Linux serves as a vital operating system in the development of smart home solutions. Its flexibility, security features, and collaborative spirit foster an environment where users can create customized experiences that enrich their lives while offering robust control over their home technology. As the smart home landscape continues to grow, Linux's role will undoubtedly expand, paving the way for innovative solutions that enhance convenience, security, and energy efficiency. Through continuous community engagement and an emphasis on user education, Linux can sew connectivity into the fabric of smart homes, guaranteeing that these technologies remain accessible and beneficial for all.

15.5. Industrial IoT and Linux Deployments

In the modern landscape of industrial IoT, Linux has emerged as a foundational pillar, providing the necessary infrastructure and tools to support an interconnected network of smart devices, sensors, and machinery. The combination of Linux's open-source flexibility, strong community backing, and robust performance positions it as the preferred operating system for industrial applications and deployments. This environment not only enhances operational efficiencies but also fosters innovation, creating intelligent systems that can intelligently respond to real-time data.

Central to Linux's role in industrial IoT is its adaptability to various hardware and networking protocols. From single-board computers, such as Raspberry Pi and Arduino, to edge gateways and sensor nodes, Linux can be deployed on a multitude of devices, making it a versatile option for diverse industrial settings. The ability to customize distributions—like Yocto and OpenWrt—tailored for specific hardware requirements allows engineers to optimize the performance of IoT devices, ensuring efficient energy use and processing capabilities.

Furthermore, Linux's compatibility with many connectivity protocols, including MQTT, CoAP, and Modbus, enables fluid communication between different IoT devices and the centralized systems that monitor and control them. The lightweight nature of these protocols allows devices to transmit data with efficiency, supporting real-time decision-making processes that are critical in industrial environments. For example, predictive maintenance systems can be deployed on Linux-based devices, capturing sensor data and using it to foresee equipment failures before they occur, thus averting costly downtime.

One of the advantages of Linux in industrial IoT deployments is the open-source ecosystem that fosters collaboration and community-driven development. Many companies and research institutions contribute to platforms and applications within the Linux community, continuously enhancing their capabilities. Projects like Eclipse IoT and Home Assistant allow companies to build and manage applications that facilitate device management and data visualization, promoting interconnectivity and smarter operations across industrial systems.

Security is another key aspect of industrial IoT deployments where Linux shines. With its extensive suite of security features, Linux empowers organizations to implement strict access controls, encrypted communications, and regularly updated security patches. For instance, incorporating technologies such as SELinux and AppArmor restricts access permissions and ensures that only authorized processes can interact with sensitive data or critical system functions. These measures are paramount in industrial settings, where data integrity and privacy are crucial.

Additionally, the documentation and community support surrounding Linux provide invaluable resources for developers and engineers working on IoT projects. The ability to tap into collective knowledge, access tutorials, and engage with forums significantly eases the learning curve, enabling teams to troubleshoot issues effectively and rapidly develop innovative solutions.

The integration of Linux in industrial IoT extends to large-scale applications such as smart factories, energy management systems, and supply chain optimization. By gathering actionable insights from connected devices, analytics, and machine learning algorithms, organizations can achieve greater operational efficiency and reduce costs. For example, energy management systems employing Linux can analyze power consumption patterns to optimize energy use across facilities, resulting in significant cost savings and reduced carbon footprints.

However, challenges remain in harnessing the full potential of Linux in industrial IoT. Interoperability issues may arise when integrating devices from various manufacturers that use different protocols or standards. Ensuring seamless communication between diverse components necessitates ongoing collaboration within the IoT community to establish and adhere to common open standards.

In conclusion, Linux's contributions to industrial IoT deployments redefine how industries operate, innovate, and respond to the dynamic demands of modern technology. Its adaptability to various hardware configurations, robust security features, and a vibrant community foster an environment where intelligent connectivity thrives. As organizations invest in harnessing the power of Linux for their industrial IoT initiatives, they position themselves at the forefront of technological advancement, enabling smarter operations and sustainable practices that benefit not only their enterprises but also society at large. As we look to the future, the role of Linux in industrial IoT is poised for continued growth, innovation, and transformative impact across a multitude of industries.

16. The Future of Linux: Challenges and Opportunities

16.1. Predicting Technological Trends

In the dynamic landscape of technology, predicting future trends is an essential endeavor that impacts both individual users and organizations alike. Linux stands at a crucial intersection, where its adaptability and versatility position it to play pivotal roles across diverse fields, ushering innovations and solutions to emerging challenges. As we explore the trajectory of Linux within the context of technological evolution, we will delve into possible trends that may shape its future and the implications of these shifts for users worldwide.

The growing reliance on cloud computing stands out among the most significant trends impacting Linux. As enterprises increasingly migrate their operations to the cloud, they leverage the scalability and flexibility offered by Linux-based environments. Linux distributions like Ubuntu, CentOS, and Red Hat Enterprise Linux are already deeply embedded in cloud infrastructures due to their performance, security features, and active community support. Moving forward, we can anticipate a further integration of Linux in cloud-native technologies, particularly with the rise of container orchestration platforms like Kubernetes. As organizations strive for efficiency and cost-effectiveness, expecting Linux to be at the heart of cloud deployments seems inevitable.

Additionally, the surge of artificial intelligence and machine learning is likely to foster Linux's expansion in these domains. The increasing demand for robust data processing capabilities and analysis tools will lead to more advanced open-source frameworks built on Linux. Tools such as TensorFlow, PyTorch, and Scikit-learn are becoming more prevalent, and developers will rely on Linux systems to build and train machine learning models effectively. This trend may also encourage greater collaboration in creating libraries and resources that will support the next generation of AI applications, reinforcing the spirit of community-driven innovation.

Moreover, as the Internet of Things (IoT) continues to proliferate, Linux will undoubtedly remain at the forefront of this technological revolution. The versatility of Linux in connecting numerous devices —from industrial sensors to smart home appliances—positions it as an ideal operating system for IoT applications. The future will likely witness the development of specialized Linux distributions tailored for IoT environments, focusing on minimizing resource use while ensuring security and connectivity. As industries recognize the immense potential of IoT, aligning their strategies with Linux's capabilities will pave the way for smarter, more interconnected systems.

In tandem with these trends, privacy and security concerns will occupy a central role in Linux's future developments. As cyber threats become increasingly sophisticated, the Linux community will emphasize security enhancements and initiatives to protect users' data and privacy. Implementations of advanced security frameworks, such as Security-Enhanced Linux (SELinux), will continue to evolve, and the community will remain vigilant in patching vulnerabilities while educating users on secure practices. The commitment to transparency inherent in Linux offers users more control over their data and security, further enhancing its appeal and relevance.

Given the increasing emphasis on sustainability in technology, the future of Linux could also intersect with eco-friendly solutions. As organizations become more attuned to the impacts of technology on the environment, leveraging Linux to create energy-efficient systems will be essential. Additionally, supporting environmentally sustainable practices through resource-efficient programming and server management can ultimately contribute to a greener future.

The collaborative nature of the open-source community will continue to drive Linux's evolution. Projects dependent on community engagement will likely gain traction as enthusiasts and professionals leverage their collective expertise to enhance the capabilities and functionalities of Linux. This will foster an environment where innovation flourishes, leading to exciting developments driven by the contributions of users who actively shape the future of the operating system.

In summary, the future of Linux is marked by trends that encompass cloud computing, AI, IoT, security, sustainability, and community collaboration. As technological advancements continue to reshape industries, Linux is poised to remain a dynamic and indispensable force —catalyzing innovation while empowering individuals and organizations with accessible, secure, and adaptable solutions. By staying attuned to these evolving trends, both the Linux community and its users can embrace the transition and participate in shaping a vibrant technological future. The potential for Linux to adapt and thrive ultimately hinges on the synergy between its foundational principles of open-source collaboration and the drive for continuous improvement in an ever-changing world.

16.2. Linux in Emerging Industries

In the landscape of technology, Linux has undeniably carved its place as a transformative force across various emerging industries. As businesses and organizations adapt to rapid market changes and technological advancements, the appeal of Linux as an adaptable, cost-effective, and secure operating system has become increasingly prominent. From its early days as a niche alternative to proprietary software, Linux has grown into an extensive ecosystem that fuels innovation and fosters collaboration. This subchapter delves into how Linux is shaping and catalyzing change within emerging industries.

A prime example of Linux's impact can be seen in the healthcare sector. As healthcare systems worldwide endeavor to streamline operations, improve patient outcomes, and enhance data management, Linux has emerged as a dependable backbone for various applications. Health IT solutions, like electronic health record (EHR) systems, are being developed on Linux due to its robustness and security features. The use of Linux in this capacity not only minimizes operational costs by reducing licensing fees but also enhances patient data privacy— an increasingly critical aspect in the face of growing cyber threats. Additionally, Linux's open-source model allows healthcare organizations to customize software solutions to align with specific needs, ultimately enabling them to improve service delivery and health management.

The financial services sector is also experiencing a seismic shift thanks to Linux. As the demand for agility, security, and low latency continues to burgeon, financial institutions are turning to Linux-based systems to manage complex trading and analytics processes. High-frequency trading platforms and financial analytics tools, often running on Linux clusters, leverage its efficiency to process large datasets in real-time. The ability to incorporate advanced machine learning and AI algorithms on Linux allows these institutions to gain insights faster and make data-driven decisions, ultimately improving operational efficiencies and competitive advantages in the constantly evolving financial landscape.

In the world of scientific research, particularly in bioinformatics, Linux has established itself as a critical OS for managing and analyzing vast laboratory datasets. Researchers rely on Linux-based tools to conduct genomics studies, collaborate on large-scale experiments, and share findings with the global scientific community. Open-source biocomputing tools and frameworks, such as Bioconductor and Galaxy, have gained traction within this domain, allowing researchers to harness the power of collaborative open-source innovation across a myriad of bioinformatics projects. By leveraging these tools on Linux, scientists can conduct sophisticated analyses that drive breakthroughs in genetics, ecology, and personalized medicine.

The manufacturing industry has also begun to embrace Linux for its operational advantages, particularly in the context of the Industry 4.0 movement. The advent of smart factories, reliant on connected devices and IoT technology, has created a demand for scalable, reliable, and flexible operating systems to manage production and logistics. Linux has become the default choice for many industrial IoT applications due to its robustness in handling real-time data streams and ability to integrate seamlessly with various protocols and devices. As manufacturers deploy Linux-based systems, they gain the ability to enhance productivity, monitor equipment health, and optimize supply chain processes—all of which are critical for maintaining competitive edge in a rapidly changing market.

Moreover, the world of entertainment and gaming has witnessed a significant uptick in Linux adoption, particularly among independent developers and studios. The open-source ethos encourages innovation and experimentation, enabling smaller creators to build high-quality games and applications without the financial constraints associated with proprietary solutions. Linux-based game engines, such as Godot, are gaining traction in the gaming community, allowing developers to create engaging experiences while promoting cross-platform compatibility. Furthermore, major streaming services are beginning to support Linux users, further solidifying its presence in the entertainment realm and expanding access for gamers on this platform.

The education sector is another area where Linux is making substantial strides. Schools and universities are increasingly implementing Linux in classrooms to enhance digital literacy and equip students with essential technology skills. By providing access to open-source tools and applications, educators are fostering creativity and collaboration among their students. Initiatives promoting "Linux in schools" encourage the utilization of Linux labs, where students can engage with programming, data analysis, and graphic design projects, nurturing an interest in technology from an early age.

However, the journey of Linux in emerging industries is not without challenges. Organizations must confront interoperability issues arising from the fragmented software ecosystem, including the need to integrate multiple platforms and devices. To successfully navigate this complexity, industry stakeholders must advocate for open standards and collaboration across organizations, ensuring that advancements benefit the broader community.

In conclusion, Linux is shaping emerging industries by providing an agile, cost-effective, and secure platform for innovation and collaboration. As sectors such as healthcare, finance, manufacturing, entertainment, and education increasingly adopt Linux, they unlock new possibilities for efficiency, productivity, and creativity. The continued growth of Linux relies on a dedicated community and an ongoing commitment to collaboration, transparency, and shared knowledge. As organizations harness the potential of Linux to create adaptable solutions for emerging patterns and challenges, its legacy as a transformative agent is poised to endure, bringing about positive change across diverse industries and communities worldwide.

16.3. Sustainability and Community Growth

In the modern landscape of technology, sustainability and community growth within the Linux ecosystem play pivotal roles in shaping its future. As users and developers increasingly advocate for open-source principles, the connection between sustainability and community engagement becomes ever more pronounced. This synergy not only ensures the continuity of the Linux user base but also fosters an environment where innovation thrives, ultimately benefitting both individuals and organizations connected to this vibrant ecosystem.

At the heart of this discussion lies the principle of sustainable software development. As Linux continues to expand its reach across various fields—such as cloud computing, Internet of Things (IoT), artificial intelligence, and more—establishing sustainable practices is essential. Developers are called upon to create software that not only meets the immediate demands of users but also considers its long-term impact on resources, performance, and security. The ethos of sustainability emphasizes responsibility towards users, communities, and the environment, ensuring that advancements contribute positively to all stakeholders involved.

The Linux community is inherently characterized by collaboration and inclusivity, driving growth by channeling diverse perspectives into the development process. Engaging users from different backgrounds, industries, and geographical locations allows for the generation of innovative ideas that address a multitude of challenges. This inclusive approach facilitates the development of tools tailored to the unique needs of various sectors, creating a versatile ecosystem in which organizations can thrive. As communities grow and contribute their insights, Linux's adaptability remains its strongest asset, enabling it to evolve alongside advancements in technology.

Furthermore, the focus on community growth is intrinsically linked to the principles of open-source software. By providing users with free access to software and resources, Linux empowers individuals and organizations to harness technology without the constraints typically associated with commercial products. This democratization of technology encourages entrepreneurship and fosters local development initiatives, particularly in emerging markets. The collaborative nature of open-source also nurtures a sense of belonging among users who participate in ongoing projects and discussions, as they collectively shape the directions of the software they use.

Sustainability within the Linux user community is further exemplified by initiatives aimed at increasing awareness and education around open-source software. Educational programs, workshops, and mentoring opportunities play an essential role in encouraging prospective users to delve into the world of Linux. By removing barriers to entry—such as technical jargon and intimidating interfaces—community-led initiatives can create more inclusive spaces for individuals to learn and engage with open-source technologies. This proactive approach ensures that new and diverse contributors can emerge, injecting fresh ideas and perspectives that drive sustainable growth.

As we venture into a future increasingly characterized by digital transformation, the need for ongoing collaboration, education, and knowledge-sharing will become paramount. With the shift towards remote working, the adoption of cloud-based systems, and the demand for adaptable technologies, Linux's community-driven approach will serve as a vital resource for users striving to navigate this evolving landscape. The reciprocal relationship between sustainability and community growth serves to empower the Linux ecosystem, allowing it to respond dynamically to the emerging challenges and opportunities present in the tech world.

In conclusion, sustainability and community growth are inextricably linked to the future vitality of the Linux ecosystem. By nurturing an environment built on collaboration, inclusivity, and shared purpose, the Linux community not only ensures its continued relevance but also leads the charge towards a more sustainable and equitable technological landscape. By focusing on these principles, the Linux movement can inspire the next generation of innovators to embrace open-source software, fostering an enduring legacy that champions accessibility, creativity, and progress in the digital age. The potential for Linux to thrive amidst evolving challenges is not solely a reflection of its technical capabilities but a testament to the power of community as the heartbeat of this remarkable operating system.

16.4. Contributions and Innovations Ahead

In the rapidly changing landscape of technology, Linux has consistently served as a catalyst for contributions and innovations that shape the future of computing. As we look ahead, it is evident that the strengths of Linux as an open-source platform, combined with vibrant community participation and adaptability, will continue to drive significant advancements across various fields.

One of the promising avenues for future innovation lies in the continued evolution of cloud computing. With organizations increasingly shifting their operations to cloud-based infrastructures, Linux-based solutions become indispensable in managing scalability and performance. As technologies such as Kubernetes and containerization gain traction, we can expect Linux to lead the charge through its robust support for these modern deployment methodologies. Innovations in serverless architectures and multi-cloud strategies may further enhance Linux's capabilities in this regard, positioning it as the foundation for next-generation cloud services.

Equally, the intersection of Linux with artificial intelligence and machine learning represents another frontier ripe for exploration. As the demand for AI-driven applications continues to surge, Linux will remain central to the development of sophisticated machine learning frameworks. Projects like TensorFlow, PyTorch, and Scikit-learn are just the beginning, as community members collaborate on enhancing existing libraries and developing new algorithms tailored for Linux environments. This collaborative innovation will enable researchers and developers to harness the power of Linux to augment their AI capabilities, driving advancements in computer vision, natural language processing, and more.

The domain of the Internet of Things (IoT) is another area where the contributions of Linux are expected to flourish. As smart devices proliferate and become integrated into everyday life, the need for an adaptable operating system that can power a multitude of connected devices will only continue to grow. Linux-based frameworks and distributions designed for IoT will likely evolve, focusing on optimizing resource usage while ensuring security and interoperability. The community's commitment to open standards will be paramount in tackling the challenges of fragmentation, enabling devices from various manufacturers to coexist and communicate effectively.

Moreover, as society becomes more attuned to the discussion surrounding digital privacy and ethical data usage, the open-source nature of Linux positions it favorably. Users will gravitate toward Linux solutions that prioritize transparency and security, allowing individuals and organizations to maintain control over their data. Innovations in privacy-focused distributions and applications emphasize the need for secure computing environments, which can empower users against increasingly sophisticated cyber threats.

Additionally, the continued growth of Linux in education signifies a vital source of contributions and innovations ahead. As educational institutions expand access to technology, initiatives that integrate Linux into curricula can inspire future generations of technologists and developers. By encouraging students to engage with open-source software and contribute to community-driven projects, we foster a culture of collaboration that nurtures creativity and innovation within the field.

The global movement toward sustainability enhances the relevance of Linux contributions as well. As organizations seek eco-friendly solutions, Linux's open-source nature allows for the development of efficient software or hardware solutions that minimize energy use and waste. The community's emphasis on collaboration can lead to creative approaches for addressing pressing environmental challenges while promoting sustainable practices in technology use.

Ultimately, the future of contributions and innovations within the Linux ecosystem is bright, fueled by the collaborative spirit that defines its community. As we move forward, we will witness the ongoing evolution of Linux as a platform capable of accommodating new technologies and responding to the complex demands of users and society alike. By nurturing an inclusive and engaged community, Linux continues to serve as a powerful catalyst for innovation, inviting users to become active contributors to a dynamic and ever-changing technological landscape that champions collaboration, transparency, and adaptability.

These advancements will not only carry Linux forward but also ensure that the open-source movement remains a driving force within the realms of computing, paving the way for interactive and transformative experiences that benefit individuals and organizations around the globe. The ongoing commitment to contributing to innovation will undoubtedly place Linux at the forefront of the next generation of technological breakthroughs.

16.5. Maintaining the Ideals of Open Source

In the realm of technology, the concept of open source has evolved into a profound phenomenon characterized by community collaboration and shared innovation. At its heart, the ideals of open source embrace the principles of transparency, accessibility, and collective contribution, offering an invitation for individuals around the world to engage in the development of software. Maintaining these ideals is essential to ensuring that the open source movement continues to flourish and expand into new domains, influencing the next generation of developers and users.

The battle for ideals in open source is not merely about maintaining a free software license or a set of ethical guidelines. It encompasses a broader responsibility to cultivate a vibrant community where diverse participants feel empowered to contribute their unique perspectives and talents. For many individuals, the essence of open source serves as a catalyst for personal growth, creativity, and empowerment. By upholding the ideals of open source, communities can foster an environment that nurtures innovation and encourages collaboration.

As we reflect on the core values that define open source, it is important to consider the role of documentation and support. A transparent framework that provides clear resources ensures that newcomers feel welcomed and supported in their journey. Comprehensive manuals, tutorials, and community forums create a nurturing environment where users can ask questions, share experiences, and learn from one another. Maintaining an inclusive and knowledgeable community helps cultivate a sense of belonging and encourages ongoing engagement, reinforcing the foundational principles of open source.

In parallel, the promotion of diverse representation within the open-source community is paramount to maintaining ideals. Inclusive practices allow individuals from various backgrounds—whether based on gender, race, socioeconomic status, or geographical location —to contribute to the collective knowledge base and engage actively in development efforts. Initiatives aimed at promoting diversity and inclusion within open-source spaces—through education, mentorship, and sponsorship opportunities—foster a community that is both resilient and innovative.

Sustainability is also a crucial aspect of maintaining the ideals of open source. Encouraging contributors and projects to adopt practices that ensure long-term viability can help keep the movement relevant in an ever-evolving technological landscape. This entails not only addressing potential funding and resource challenges but also fostering a culture that recognizes and rewards contributions, whether financial or technical. By nurturing the foundations of sustainability—financial, technological, and community-focused—open-source projects can continue to thrive and drive innovation for generations to come.

Additionally, engaging in proactive advocacy for open-source principles helps solidify the legacy of the movement. This means actively participating in conversations surrounding technology policy and intellectual property rights while promoting transparency and ethical practices both within the community and in broader technology discourse. By articulating the benefits of open source, advocates can build bridges to other sectors, illustrating how collaboration, flexibility, and community engagement drive progress and innovation.

As technology continues to evolve, the ideals of open source must also adapt to address new challenges and opportunities. The growing complexities of topics such as data privacy, cybersecurity, and environmental sustainability require open-source communities to rethink their approaches to innovation and advocacy. By integrating these values into the fabric of the movement, the open-source community can reinforce its commitment to fostering a more inclusive, just, and sustainable technological future.

In conclusion, maintaining the ideals of open source is a multi-faceted endeavor that requires careful consideration, collaboration, and advocacy. By nurturing a vibrant community centered around transparency, inclusivity, and sustainability, we can ensure that the movement thrives while continuing to empower individuals and organizations alike. The open-source journey is one marked by shared growth, mutual support, and boundless creativity—an ethos that will undoubtedly inspire future generations to contribute to a collective narrative of innovation and progress for all. As we continue crafting the landscape of technology, the ideals of open source will remain a guiding light, beckoning individuals from all walks of life to explore, create, and innovate together.

17. User Stories: Testimonials from the Open Source Trenches

17.1. A Beginner's Journey

As we embark on the journey of exploring a beginner's encounter with Linux, we find ourselves delving into a world where curiosity meets profound technical potential. For many newcomers, the initial experience with Linux can resemble stepping into a dense forest filled with unexplored trails and hidden treasures. The vast landscape of options, commands, and communities can be as intimidating as it is intriguing. Yet, this very uncertainty often transforms into a rich tapestry of learning, discovery, and empowerment that embodies the Linux experience.

The journey often begins with a simple motivation—an eagerness to overcome the limitations associated with familiar operating systems like Windows or macOS. Many individuals are drawn to the idea of an operating system that embodies freedom, flexibility, and the potential for customization. Early introductions through online tutorials, community forums, or even friend recommendations fuel the desire to install Linux on a personal computer or a virtual machine. The world of Linux beckons each newcomer, promising an exhilarating voyage filled with opportunities for personal and professional growth.

One of the remarkable aspects of this beginner's journey is the accessibility of Linux distributions, carefully designed to accommodate varying skill levels. Distros like Ubuntu and Mint stand at the forefront, often heralded as gateways for novices. The process of installation typically unfolds as a straightforward experience, guided meticulously by installation wizards that demystify partitioning and software selection. For our protagonist, choosing Ubuntu becomes an intuitive decision, driven by its reputation for user-friendliness and extensive community support.

Upon completing the installation, the excitement of booting into a fresh Linux environment is palpable. The desktop interface introduces a breath of familiarity while hinting at the unique features

Linux has to offer. The initial moments are spent exploring the Activities overview in GNOME or the menu in Cinnamon, uncovering preinstalled applications ranging from web browsers to media players. Yet, it is the terminal—the command line interface—that elicits both fascination and trepidation among newcomers. The command line appears as an enigmatic door through which vast knowledge and capabilities await, inviting experimentation and discovery.

A common first interaction with the terminal involves simple commands, such as `ls` to list directory contents or `mkdir` to create a new folder. As the beginner grows comfortable with these commands, they stumble upon the concept of package management, which unlocks a wealth of possibilities for software installation. The allure of accessing repositories brimming with applications beckons them to explore further; commands like `sudo apt install [package-name]` become second nature, placing a powerful suite of tools at their fingertips.

Throughout this journey, community engagement plays a pivotal role in transforming uncertainty into empowerment. Engaging with various forums, such as Ask Ubuntu or Reddit's Linux community, opens gateways to advice, shared experiences, and troubleshooting support. Encountering common challenges, like driver issues or software compatibility, leads to a sense of camaraderie as fellow users offer guidance and encouragement. The ethos of open-source collaboration seeps into each interaction, reminding beginners that they are part of a vast and welcoming network that spans the globe.

As confidence builds, individuals delve into projects that take their enthusiasm a step further. Many begin customizing their Linux environment, exploring themes, icon sets, and alternative desktop environments. The ability to mold the computing experience to their preferences serves as a testament to Linux's flexibility, fostering creativity and personal expression. Compiling their first software from source or writing a simple shell script becomes a rite of passage, marking the transition from novice to confident user.

With time, many beginners find their initial fears dissipating as they recognize the power at their command. The security features, comprehensive documentation, and responsive community all contribute to transforming Linux from an intimidating realm into an essential tool for productivity and creativity.

The journey does not culminate at the beginner stage but serves as the foundation for ongoing exploration. Whether diving into system administration, contributing to open-source projects, or experimenting with programming languages, Linux continues to offer new paths for adventurous users willing to embrace its potential.

In conclusion, the beginner's journey through Linux encapsulates the essence of exploration, innovation, and community-driven collaboration that lies at the heart of this operating system. Linux empowers individuals to break free from traditional constraints and forge their paths within the tech landscape. As we share these stories of discovery, learning, and growth, we celebrate each new user's commitment to embracing the transformative power of Linux, ensuring that this journey remains dynamic, inclusive, and rich with opportunity. The spirit of curiosity ignited from that first interaction with Linux reverberates, inspiring the next generation of users to explore, engage, and contribute to the ever-evolving landscape of open-source technology.

17.2. Experts' Perspectives

In the vast realm of technology, the perspectives of experts in the field of Linux provide invaluable insights into its evolution, adoption, and future trajectory. Individuals who have navigated the challenging landscapes of open-source software have experienced firsthand the transformative effects of Linux, watching as it has developed into the powerhouse that it is today. The experts' perspectives bring to light the nuances of community dynamics, technological innovations, and the core philosophies that define Linux.

Among these thought leaders are system administrators, software developers, and educators, each contributing their unique vantage points to the broader narrative of Linux. Their stories not only reflect personal journeys of growth and discovery but also illustrate how the communal spirit inherent in Linux inspires collaboration and inclusivity.

One recurring theme shared among experts is the power of collaboration within the Linux ecosystem. Many highlight their experiences participating in forums, mailing lists, and collaborative projects, attributing much of their success to the knowledge shared among members of the community. One senior software engineer recounts how his initial ventures into Linux were marked by apprehension, yet the encouragement and support from the community empowered him to contribute to significant projects. The spirit of collective development instilled in him a sense of belonging and purpose, transforming a once solitary experience into one rich with shared accomplishments.

The realm of education also underscores the importance of community and collaboration, as educators witness the impact of Linux on their students' learning experiences. Experienced teachers embrace Linux for its affordability and accessibility, allowing them to offer expansive computing resources in classrooms that would otherwise be financially prohibitive. They share stories of students, often from diverse backgrounds, who find confidence in their abilities to use and contribute to open-source software. This generational shift toward open-source ideals fosters a culture of curiosity and exploration that shapes the next wave of technology leaders.

Additionally, industry veterans often reflect on how Linux has revolutionized their organizations by facilitating innovation and operational efficiency. CEOs and CTOs of tech companies discuss how adopting Linux led to significant reductions in software licensing costs, allowing them to redirect resources toward research and development initiatives. The sheer flexibility provided by Linux empowers businesses to rapidly adapt to changing market demands, ultimately positioning organizations to remain competitive in an ever-evolving landscape.

Through discussions about the future of Linux, experts express optimism regarding the evolution of open-source technologies. They highlight emerging trends in cloud computing, AI, and IoT, all of which present exciting opportunities for Linux adoption across varying sectors. This sentiment is echoed loudly within the community, which thrives on collective innovation and collaboration. Experts emphasize the importance of maintaining the core principles of open-source development—transparency, inclusivity, and volunteer contributions—as these values will enable Linux to continue to evolve and meet the demands of tomorrow.

Yet the insights of experts also caution against complacency. As Linux solidifies its place across industries, maintaining engagement and encouraging new contributors are seen as vital to the long-term sustainability of the platform. Advocating for diversity in the Linux community is critical, as it fosters creativity and innovation, reflecting the demographics of the global user base. Experts underscore the need for mentorship programs that help newcomers navigate their journeys, ensuring that opportunities for contribution are both accessible and equitable.

In conclusion, the perspectives of experts illustrate the profound impact of Linux on the world of technology, collaboration, and community growth. As they share their stories, it becomes evident that Linux is not merely an operating system, but a movement fueled by the collective drive for openness, accessibility, and innovation. Their insights inspire both current and future users to engage with Linux actively and contribute to its legacy as they explore the depths of technology and ignite the flames of creativity and progress. Through these expert insights, we understand that Linux's evolution is an ongoing journey—one where every contribution, story, and collaboration enriches the vibrant tapestry of the open-source community.

17.3. Linux for Humanitarian Efforts

Linux has become a catalyst for humanitarian efforts across the globe, demonstrating its versatility and adaptability in addressing some of the most pressing issues affecting communities. As an open-source operating system, Linux empowers individuals and organizations to leverage technology without the prohibitive costs often associated with proprietary software. This democratization of technology enables humanitarian initiatives to operate more efficiently, effectively connecting people, resources, and solutions in transformative ways.

One prominent example of Linux's impact on humanitarian efforts is its role in emergency response systems. During natural disasters, organizations need to establish communication networks quickly and efficiently. Linux-powered systems can provide the backbone for establishing local networks that facilitate communication among emergency responders and affected communities. The Debian-based open-source project "OpenStreetMap" showcases how volunteers can utilize Linux to create maps and coordinate logistics when traditional services may be unavailable. By providing mapping data and visualization tools, Linux helps communities mobilize resources and assess needs in real time.

Furthermore, the health sector has experienced significant benefits from Linux deployments in humanitarian contexts. Organizations like Médecins Sans Frontières (Doctors Without Borders) rely on Linux systems to manage patient records, collect data in the field, and coordinate medical assistance. The affordability of Linux allows these organizations to channel more financial resources into their core missions—delivering care and support to vulnerable populations —rather than being tied down by expensive software licenses.

In the realm of education, Linux has been instrumental in empowering marginalized communities with digital literacy. Programs designed to introduce Linux in schools not only alleviate the burden of licensing costs but also offer students valuable skills in technology and software development. Projects like "OLPC (One Laptop Per Child)" leverage Linux-based systems to provide educational resources to children in underprivileged areas, ensuring that young learners can access quality educational materials and computing tools.

Moreover, Linux fosters innovation and collaboration among activists and grassroots organizations. Open-source platforms enable these groups to form networks, share resources, and develop tailored applications that cater to unique social challenges. For instance, utilizing Linux for building custom applications related to food distribution systems helps streamline operations, ensuring that aid reaches those most in need with efficiency and transparency. The spirit of collaboration embedded in the Linux community encourages individuals to contribute their expertise and knowledge, thus amplifying the impact of humanitarian efforts.

The ability of Linux to adapt to different hardware configurations is also a crucial factor in its success for humanitarian projects. Many regions face hardware constraints, and Linux's lightweight distributions can run effectively on older machines or low-powered devices often found in rural or resource-limited settings. This compatibility allows humanitarian organizations to make the best use of available resources, maximizing the value of their investments.

Nevertheless, despite its advantages, challenges remain when deploying Linux for humanitarian purposes. Limited access to technology, lack of training on open-source systems, and potential connectivity issues in remote regions might hinder these initiatives. Therefore, organizations must invest in training and educational outreach to equip local communities with the skills needed to effectively utilize Linux-based technologies.

In conclusion, Linux serves as a powerful tool in humanitarian efforts, enabling organizations to address social issues, improve operational efficiencies, and enhance access to crucial resources. Its open-source nature fosters collaboration, drives innovation, and democratizes technology, allowing individuals and organizations to take charge of their solutions. As we navigate a world filled with challenges rooted in inequality, access, and sustainability, Linux remains a steadfast companion for those working toward a brighter future, reinforcing the notion that technology can be harnessed for the collective good and empowering communities globally.

17.4. Educators and Students on Linux

In today's technological landscape, the use of Linux within educational institutions has become increasingly significant, particularly in instilling foundational computer skills among both educators and students. Linux offers a unique and accessible platform that equips individuals with a wealth of knowledge and practical experience in handling operating systems, programming, and collaborative development. This subchapter explores the influence of Linux from the perspectives of educators and students alike, shedding light on how this powerful operating system is shaping learning experiences and creating opportunities for success.

For educators, the integration of Linux in the classroom presents numerous advantages. First and foremost, Linux operates on the principle of open-source software, enabling educators to access powerful tools without the financial constraints typically associated with proprietary software. By leveraging Linux, educational institutions can provide comprehensive computing resources that support a variety of subjects while ensuring equitable access for all students. This affordability alleviates budget pressures, allowing schools to allocate funds toward enhancing educational materials, improving infrastructure, or offering additional training opportunities.

Additionally, Linux supports a wide range of educational software that fosters creativity and engagement. From programming environments to data analysis tools, many applications are designed to run seamlessly on Linux. For instance, educators can introduce students to programming languages such as Python or C++ using available integrated development environments (IDEs) and provide practical experience that is highly relevant in today's job market. Moreover, Linux-based tools, such as GIMP for graphic design and Blender for 3D modeling, empower students to explore various creative fields without incurring costs for expensive licenses.

Linux also nurtures a culture of collaboration and community engagement among students. Open-source projects provide students with opportunities to contribute to real-world initiatives, engaging them in collaborative coding and project development. By participating in projects hosted on platforms like GitHub, students not only gain technical skills but also learn the values of teamwork, accountability, and inclusivity. These experiences prepare them for the workforce, fostering the skills and mindsets necessary for navigating an increasingly interconnected world.

The flexibility of Linux allows educators to customize their teaching approaches to suit the needs and learning styles of their students. With an array of distributions available, educators can choose a version of Linux that aligns with the curriculum objectives and the comfort level of their students. For example, user-friendly distributions like Ubuntu or Linux Mint facilitate a smooth learning curve for beginners, while advanced users can explore more customizable and feature-rich distributions, such as Arch or Fedora. This adaptability fosters a sense of ownership and autonomy among students, encouraging them to engage deeply in their learning experiences.

Engagement with Linux also empowers students to pursue their interests in technology and innovation. As they gain familiarity with the command line interface, scripting, and system management, students become equipped to tackle challenges, troubleshoot issues, and experiment creatively within their projects. The opportunity to learn skills that go beyond the surface level of technology not only enhances students' readiness for careers in STEM fields but also instills confidence in their ability to contribute meaningfully to their communities through technology.

Moreover, educators benefit from the continuous learning opportunities that Linux offers, enabling them to stay updated with technological advancements. Many administration and management tasks can be streamlined on Linux through powerful command line tools and scripting capabilities. Educators who engage with the technology themselves can empower their students more effectively and foster a culture of innovation within their classrooms. Additionally, networking and partnerships with local tech communities often lead to collaborative initiatives, enriching the learning environment even further.

Despite the numerous benefits of adopting Linux in education, some challenges remain. A learning curve may exist for both educators and students as they transition from familiar proprietary systems to Linux environments. However, with the abundance of resources available—ranging from online tutorials to community forums—solving issues and overcoming obstacles becomes a shared endeavor, reinforcing the collaborative ethos of the Linux community.

In conclusion, the influence of Linux in education extends far beyond mere access to technology. Through its affordability, flexibility, and open-source framework, Linux creates opportunities for students and educators to learn, innovate, and collaborate. The skills gained by engaging with Linux not only prepare students for success in their future careers but also foster a culture of inclusivity and community engagement. As Linux continues to evolve and adapt, its impact on education will undoubtedly pave the way for future generations of innovative thinkers and creators who will harness technology to champion positive change in their communities and beyond.

17.5. Future Leaders and Ambassadors of Linux

In the world of technology, the future of leadership and advocacy will be heavily shaped by individuals who are not just users of Linux but are also passionate ambassadors of its innovative potential. These future leaders will play pivotal roles in championing Linux as they build on the foundation laid by the pioneers of the open-source movement. Through their efforts, they will continue to drive the ideology of collaboration and community engagement, ensuring that Linux remains not only relevant but also at the forefront of technology in an increasingly connected world.

Becoming a leader in the Linux community often starts with a journey marked by personal exploration, curiosity, and a desire for knowledge. Many future leaders emerge from grassroots involvement —whether contributing to projects, developing new applications, or participating in local user groups. Their stories exemplify a shift from being mere users to becoming active contributors who want to make a difference. This transformative path is one that inspires others to recognize their potential within the community and take steps to engage, learn, and grow.

An ambassador of Linux is someone who advocates for open-source principles in wider contexts, from educational institutions to corporate environments. The impact of these ambassadors can be far-reaching, as they often pave new pathways for the adoption of Linux in various sectors—demonstrating how it can enhance productivity, foster innovation, and reduce costs. By sharing their experiences, knowledge, and successes, they can dispel misconceptions about Linux, illustrating its capabilities and real-world applications. For instance, educators who integrate Linux into their curricula inspire students to explore technology deeply and confidently, ensuring that future generations carry the torch of innovation forward.

Collaboration stands as a key pillar upon which the future of Linux leadership will be built. Today's leaders must harness the power of community engagement, fostering networks that encourage knowledge sharing and cross-functional collaboration. Events such as conferences, hackathons, and workshops will remain crucial in nurturing this collaborative spirit. Future leaders can take inspiration from the community-oriented approaches that have defined Linux's journey thus far, actively seeking opportunities to mentor newcomers, engage with diverse voices, and advocate for inclusivity within the Linux ecosystem.

Innovation is another essential aspect of leadership in the Linux community. As technology continues to evolve, future ambassadors will need to remain attuned to emerging trends and advancements, embracing adaptability and openness to change. By fostering innovation and creativity, they can guide the community in exploring new horizons—whether through addressing contemporary challenges, investigating the potential of AI and machine learning within Linux, or adapting to the growing landscape of IoT. The spirit of exploration will be critical in ensuring that Linux evolves continually to meet the needs of users and industries alike.

Furthermore, future leaders will have the opportunity to advocate for Linux in jurisdictions and sectors that may have traditionally overlooked or undervalued open-source solutions. By consistently showcasing the advantages of Linux in areas such as security, cost-effectiveness, customization, and community collaboration, they can influence discussions on technology policies and funding allocations. Engaging policymakers, industry stakeholders, and educational institutions will be paramount in solidifying Linux's position as a viable and preferred solution.

As these future ambassadors continue to share their stories of success, challenge misconceptions about Linux, and promote its use, they will collectively shape a brighter, more inclusive future for this technology. By actively fostering collaboration, mentoring newcomers, and advocating for innovative approaches, they can help ensure that Linux thrives for years to come.

In summary, the future leaders and ambassadors of Linux will play a crucial role in shaping the trajectory of open-source software, fostering a collaborative environment that encourages participation and innovation. Through their passion and commitment, they will inspire a new generation of users and contributors, ensuring that Linux remains a vibrant, dynamic force within technology. As this journey unfolds, it will undoubtedly be marked by creativity, community spirit, and the shared conviction that collaboration can drive meaningful change in an ever-evolving digital landscape.

18. Cross-Platform Ventures: Linux and Other Operating Systems

18.1. Linux and Windows: Coexistence

In the ever-evolving digital landscape, the coexistence of Linux and Windows represents a fascinating chapter in the annals of operating systems, showcasing how diverse platforms can thrive alongside each other. This harmonious interaction reflects both historical context and the current demand for flexible, adaptable technologies in various environments, from personal computing to enterprise applications. As we delve into this coexistence, it becomes evident that the intricate interplay between Linux and Windows is driven by collaborative spirit, interoperability strategies, and shared user needs.

Historically, the rivalry between Linux and Windows has epitomized the dichotomy between open-source and proprietary software philosophies. Linux emerged as a response to the constraints of proprietary systems like Windows, aiming to provide a more customizable, transparent, and community-driven alternative. For many users and organizations, the limitations of Windows ignited interest in exploring Linux distributions such as Ubuntu, Fedora, and CentOS, each intended to empower users with greater control over their computing environments.

Despite the perceived friction between these two operating systems, their coexistence has become increasingly beneficial for users. The emergence of cross-platform applications, tools, and development frameworks has blurred the lines between Linux and Windows, allowing users to leverage the strengths of both systems. Software development environments often utilize a mixed approach, wherein code may be written and tested on Linux systems before being deployed on Windows servers. The flexibility afforded by virtual machines enables users to run Windows applications within a Linux host or vice versa, bridging the gap that may have historically divided both ecosystems.

One of the key strategies that promote the coexistence of Linux and Windows is the implementation of robust interoperability solutions. Technologies such as Samba facilitate file and printer sharing between Linux and Windows systems, allowing seamless collaboration in mixed-OS networks. Additionally, tools like Wine, which allows Windows applications to run on Linux, grant users the ability to leverage familiar software without being tethered to Windows-based systems. This adaptability elevates the Linux experience for those who rely on specific applications that may not have native Linux alternatives.

Moreover, the dominance of cloud computing has further united Linux and Windows in a shared ecosystem. Many organizations opt for hybrid cloud environments that take advantage of both operating systems depending on business needs. Cloud service providers often support Linux for server-side solutions while also providing Windows-based offerings, allowing organizations to tailor their infrastructure to align with specific applications and workloads. This dual strategy not only maximizes performance and efficiency but also reduces vendor-lock and dependence on single platforms.

The use of containerization technologies—such as Docker and Kubernetes—exemplifies how developers can build, deploy, and manage applications across both operating systems. By employing containers, developers can ensure that their applications function correctly regardless of whether they are deployed in Linux or Windows environments. This flexibility streamlines workflows and encourages innovation, as organizations can choose the components optimize their technology stacks while drawing from both ecosystems.

In the realm of end-user computing, the coexistence of Linux and Windows supports diverse user needs. For instance, educational institutions and tech boot camps commonly adopt a dual OS approach, providing students with the opportunity to learn both environments. This exposure fosters adaptability, allowing learners to cultivate skills that are increasingly valuable in a technology-driven job market.

As we look to the future, the coexistence of Linux and Windows is likely to become even more pronounced as industries continue to evolve and embrace digital transformation. The integration of artificial intelligence, machine learning, and Internet of Things (IoT) technologies will necessitate cross-platform cooperation, presenting individuals and organizations with the opportunity to harness the strengths of both operating systems to drive innovation and address complex challenges.

In conclusion, Linux and Windows exemplify the potential for cooperation within the technology landscape, transforming what may have been a competitive relationship into a collaborative partnership. By fostering interoperability, supporting cross-platform tools, and adapting to user needs, the ecosystems surrounding these operating systems can thrive together. As we navigate this hybrid landscape, it becomes clear that the future promises exciting opportunities for innovation and creativity through the coexistence of Linux and Windows.

18.2. Linux on Mac Hardware

Linux on Mac Hardware offers a distinctive perspective on using an operating system typically associated with computers designed by Apple. The fusion of Linux and Mac hardware represents a compelling intersection of two influential tech worlds—one cultivated on principles of open-source development and community participation, the other characterized by proprietary design and exclusivity. This subchapter delves into the unique experience of running Linux on Mac devices, identifying challenges, benefits, migrations strategies, and the resultant contributions to the evolving Linux landscape.

Historically, the landscape of computing has seen users of Mac hardware express a desire for the flexibility and robustness offered by Linux. While Apple's macOS provides a polished and intuitive user experience, some users find themselves seeking the freedom of customization, the power of open-source software, and the vast repositories of applications available in the Linux world. These desires contribute to an emerging trend of multi-boot setups, virtual machines, and even complete swaps of macOS for a Linux distribution.

One of the most significant steps in running Linux on Mac hardware is the installation process. Users often opt for popular distributions known for ease of use and extensive community support, such as Ubuntu, Fedora, or Debian. These distributions typically feature installation wizards that streamline the process, yet unique considerations must be taken into account for Mac users due to hardware compatibility concerns. For instance, during installation, users may need to alter disk partitioning schemes or consider specific drivers and kernel parameters to tailor the Linux installation to their Apple hardware.

Once Linux is installed on a Mac, users can enjoy several advantages. One notable benefit lies in the performance of Linux on Mac hardware. Many Linux distributions handle processes efficiently, capitalizing on the robust hardware capabilities of Macs. Users may notice improved performance for resource-intensive applications, particularly in contexts such as data science, software development, or multimedia production. Furthermore, the user-friendly interface of desktop environments like GNOME or KDE can provide a novel aesthetic while still maintaining responsiveness despite the potential complexity behind the scenes.

Compatibility with Mac hardware, however, is not without challenges. Certain drivers—especially for graphics or wireless components—may require manual installation or configuration to ensure they work correctly with Linux. This experience can be complicated for less technically inclined users, but the Linux community actively supports users navigating these issues through forums, wikis, and documentation. Maintaining a strong presence in these support networks significantly aids Mac users running Linux, while discussions can often lead to innovative solutions that enhance compatibility.

Moreover, the open-source nature of Linux encourages collaborative contributions from users around the globe, leading to ongoing developments that facilitate better interactions with Apple hardware. Open-source drivers are continually being updated and improved, allowing users to experience greater stability and functionality with their devices over time. This process exemplifies the importance of fostering community-driven innovation in bridging gaps between hardware and software ecosystems.

Additionally, utilizing Linux on Mac gives users a unique opportunity to engage with the conceptual foundations of open source. Familiarizing oneself with the terminal and command-line operations becomes essential for optimizing the Linux experience, and this practice can deepen users' understanding of their systems. As they learn to adapt, troubleshoot, and customize their environments, Mac users can draw parallels to Apple's model while finding empowerment in the context of Linux.

Running Linux on Mac hardware also encourages a discussion surrounding the democratization of technology. As more users embrace this hybrid approach, they challenge the notion that high-performance computing must be confined to proprietary systems. By showcasing the versatility of Linux in diverse hardware environments, users contribute to shifting cultural narratives around technology access and ownership. This movement reinforces the intrinsic values of both platforms, illuminating the potential for collaboration beyond established lines.

As we look to the future of this intersection, we can anticipate a continued rise in the popularity and effectiveness of running Linux on Mac hardware. The ever-improving compatibility between Linux distributions and Mac hardware will likely lead to a growth in dedicated resources for users navigating this path. Furthermore, with the rise of virtual machines and containerization technologies, users will find it increasingly feasible to run both operating systems concurrently, illuminating new opportunities for creativity and collaboration.

In conclusion, Linux on Mac hardware represents a merging of two powerful worlds—an exploration of flexibility, performance, and open-source principles. While challenges exist, the advantages of utilizing Linux on Mac systems cannot be overstated, enabling users to leverage both environments to their advantage. As the community continues to support and contribute to this collaboration, the potential for innovation and creative exploration is boundless, underscoring the dynamic relationship between Linux and Mac. Ultimately, this intersection offers exciting opportunities for users to embrace technology's transformative power while celebrating the best of both ecosystems.

18.3. Virtualization: Bridging OS Worlds

In the contemporary innovation landscape, virtualization has emerged as a critical technology resource, facilitating seamless cross-platform interactions and integrations. This capability is of immense value in the Linux ecosystem, as diverse operating systems coexist and need to communicate effectively for a variety of tasks. Virtualization supports the bridging of operational silos, allowing organizations to leverage the strengths of different operating systems within integrated environments while optimizing resource utilization.

Virtualization allows users to create and run virtual instances of different operating systems using a single physical hardware platform. For Linux users, this means that they can deploy Windows, macOS, or even other distributions within the Linux ecosystem, all accessible through virtualization software like VirtualBox, VMware, or KVM (Kernel-based Virtual Machine). This enables users to develop, test, and run applications across different platforms without the need for multiple physical machines, adding invaluable flexibility and efficiency to the development workflow.

One of the most significant benefits derived from virtualization is the ease of environment creation for developers and testers. The ability to spin up virtual machines on their Linux home system allows developers to recreate production-like environments easily, test applications in isolation, and debug cross-platform issues. Virtualization provides an efficient sandboxing mechanism, allowing user isolation from primary systems where critical configurations or sensitive data exist. Moreover, shared folders and clipboard functionalities in virtual environments enhance ease of use, fostering smooth interactions between host and guest systems.

Moreover, virtualization fosters collaboration and resource sharing across teams within an organization. Teams can develop applications on their preferred operating system while still accessing shared resources, configurations, and databases without the need for uniformity in their physical machines. This capability is especially prominent in diverse work environments where team members have different operating systems based on personal and professional preferences.

In IT operations, virtualization enhances disaster recovery and system redundancy strategies. Organizations can create snapshots of their virtual machines, preserving the state of an operating system at a specific point in time. These snapshots serve as backup points from which administrators can restore systems quickly in the event of a failure. The capacity to replicate entire virtual machines for redundancy supports system resilience, enabling organizations to safeguard their operations against potential disasters effectively.

The rise of cloud computing is inextricably tied to the advancements in virtualization technologies, as cloud service providers often utilize virtualized environments to deliver services. Large-scale cloud infrastructures, such as those provided by AWS, Azure, and Google Cloud, rely heavily on virtualization to aggregate resources, minimize overhead, and maximize efficiency. For Linux systems, cloud providers frequently deploy Linux-based virtual machines to serve applications while ensuring robust performance and security.

However, challenges do persist in virtualization implementations. Users must carefully navigate issues that can arise from resource allocation, such as CPU and memory overutilization. Moreover, network configurations can become complex as multiple virtual machines communicate across various networks. Proper management and understanding of network virtualization principles become essential to ensure optimal performance within these environments.

As we look forward, the future of virtualization technology holds exciting possibilities. Advancements in containerization—epitomized by technologies like Docker and Kubernetes—are likely to further enhance cross-platform interactions. Containers encapsulate applications and their dependencies, allowing them to run consistently across different environments. This portability highlights the potential for users to create highly efficient, cross-platform solutions while optimizing resources beyond traditional virtualization methods.

In conclusion, virtualization serves as a powerful enabler of cross-platform integration within the Linux ecosystem and beyond. By facilitating the coexistence of various operating systems, virtualization enhances flexibility, collaboration, and resource optimization across diverse computing environments. As organizations increasingly embrace virtualization to navigate the complexities of today's technological landscape, Linux stands poised to lead the charge in driving innovation, adaptability, and resilience while bridging operational silos through seamless integrations. The ongoing evolution of virtualization technologies will continue to empower users and organizations alike, expanding opportunities for creativity and innovation in a rapidly changing world.

18.4. Challenges in Multi-OS Environments

In the realm of technology, the abundant potential of Linux faces numerous challenges, particularly when it comes to the integration of various operating systems in multi-OS environments. The widespread usage of diverse platforms—ranging from Windows and macOS to different Linux distributions—calls for solutions that facilitate effective collaboration and smooth interoperability. While Linux embodies ideals of flexibility and openness, the practical realities of maintaining harmonious interactions in multi-OS settings can be fraught with complexities.

One significant challenge in multi-OS environments arises from the differences in file systems and data access. Linux primarily utilizes file systems like ext4, XFS, and Btrfs, while Windows relies on NTFS and FAT32. These variations in file systems can impede seamless file sharing and access, leading to potential data corruption or loss during transfers. As users attempt to engage in shared workflows across platforms, they often find that permissions and ownership structures differ significantly, complicating effective collaboration. For instance, executing commands on files created in a Windows environment may yield different results when accessed via Linux, leading to confusion and frustration among users.

Networking also poses unique considerations when integrating Linux with other operating systems. Each OS typically employs its networking stack and protocols, which can result in disparate handling of network configurations. Different firewall configurations, network settings, and security protocols can complicate the straightforward exchange of data. Users might encounter difficulties in connecting Linux machines to Windows-based networks, especially when traversing different domains or employing distinct authentication methods. These inconsistencies necessitate thoughtful planning around network strategies and protocols to ensure smooth connections.

In addition to compatibility challenges, users may encounter variance in software applications between operating systems. Proprietary or specialized applications developed for one OS may lack equivalent counterparts on others, limiting user options. While many cross-platform applications exist, the unique feature sets of various operating systems can create hesitancy among users to adopt Linux fully if they are reliant on specific tools only available on a different platform.

The learning curve associated with utilizing multiple operating systems can also present a challenge. Users accustomed to a particular platform may struggle when transitioning to Linux, leading to a lack of confidence and productivity. The command-line interface (CLI) in Linux, while extraordinarily powerful, may intimidate users from different backgrounds, reinforcing the need for education and support resources to facilitate this transition. As multi-OS environments grow in prevalence, the demand for training initiatives that bridge knowledge gaps will become increasingly critical.

Despite the challenges faced in multi-OS environments, opportunities abound for community-driven solutions aimed at fostering compatibility and collaboration. One approach involves focusing on universal standards in file formats and protocols across different platforms. Initiatives that encourage adopting open standards can mitigate fragmentation and enhance interoperability, allowing users to navigate multi-OS landscapes more seamlessly.

Additionally, utilizing virtualization and containerization technologies presents a pragmatic way to navigate compatibility issues. By running applications in isolated environments on Linux, organizations can continue leveraging proprietary applications while utilizing the power of Linux for other tasks. Employing tools like VirtualBox or Docker allows users to create layered environments, expanding their capabilities while optimizing resources.

In closing, while multi-OS environments present unique challenges for Linux and its users, these hurdles can be effectively mitigated through a combination of innovation, collaboration, and open-source practices. By emphasizing compatibility, fluidity, and shared knowledge, the Linux community has the opportunity to shape the dynamics of multi-operating system interactions, paving the way for enhanced collaboration, creativity, and flexibility among diverse users. The future will undoubtedly require an adaptive approach to thriving in these environments—one where Linux serves not as a standalone entity but as an essential player within a collaborative technological ecosystem.

18.5. Future Perspectives on OS Interactions

In the ever-evolving realm of operating systems, the interaction between different platforms presents a fascinating landscape filled with opportunities and challenges. As we gaze into the future of OS interactions, particularly in a world increasingly dominated by the digital realm, the implications for Linux and its coexistence with other operating systems like Windows, macOS, and emerging environments will play a pivotal role in shaping technological adoption and user experiences.

First and foremost, interoperability will become a cornerstone of future OS interactions. As businesses adopt multi-cloud strategies and complex infrastructures that utilize various systems, the ability for these systems to communicate and operate seamlessly will be paramount. Linux, known for its strong networking features and compatibility with open standards, is well-positioned to bridge gaps between disparate environments. Advancements in API development, microservices architectures, and containerization technologies will further enable Linux to integrate with other systems effectively, fostering collaboration and enhancing overall functionality.

Moreover, the rise of remote work and distributed teams will necessitate a rethinking of how multiple operating systems coexist to support work environments. The growth of tools that promote universal access to applications—and the efficiency of cross-platform capabilities—signals an opportunity for Linux to carve out a significant role. Building solutions that facilitate streamlined workflows across diverse platforms will enhance user satisfaction while promoting productivity, allowing organizations to harness the benefits of each OS. As users find Linux as a viable option for their systems, the interactions will continue to proliferate, resulting in environments where different operating systems enrich collaborative efforts.

As the Internet of Things (IoT) continues to expand, the security aspect of operating system interactions will gain increasing importance. With countless devices reliant on diverse platforms interconnected in a larger ecosystem, safeguarding data and security will be paramount. Linux's commitment to security, through comprehensive frameworks and continuous community vigilance, will position it as a trustworthy OS within this interconnected realm. Future advancements in blockchain technology may offer exciting possibilities for enhancing security in inter-OS communications, paving new pathways for secure interactions.

In parallel, educators and trainers will have an essential role in shaping how users engage with multiple operating systems. Training programs focusing on cross-platform skills—ranging from basic troubleshooting to advanced administration—will create a generation of technologists equipped to flourish in an increasingly varied digital landscape. By highlighting Linux and its interoperability in educational curricula, the foundation is laid for users to embrace diverse environments, navigating each OS with confidence and proficiency.

However, alongside these opportunities come challenges related to compatibility and user experience. The continued fragmentation of software ecosystems, where different organizations develop and maintain proprietary solutions, may pose hurdles to interoperability. Encouraging collaboration among developers and organizations to establish open standards will be critical in overcoming these barriers, promoting seamless communication across systems while respecting user needs.

The rise of AI and machine learning will undoubtedly influence future OS interactions as well. As algorithms become increasingly integrated into everyday applications, OS interactions may become more sophisticated, with systems capable of adapting to user behaviors and preferences in real-time. Linux is already at the forefront of these developments, with popular machine learning frameworks such as TensorFlow and PyTorch running effectively on Linux environments. As we look ahead, the collaboration between operating systems will likely transition toward more intelligent, adaptive platforms that leverage these technologies for enhanced user engagement.

In conclusion, the future perspectives on OS interactions present a landscape rich with possibilities for Linux in an interconnected world. By embracing interoperability, fostering community collaboration, prioritizing security, and investing in education and training, Linux can thrive alongside other operating systems. The opportunities that lie ahead will require continuous adaptation, creativity, and a shared commitment to progress within the vibrant open-source community. As new technologies and standards emerge, Linux will continue to play a critical role in shaping the dynamics of OS interactions, ultimately creating environments that empower users and drive innovation across various sectors.

19. Bashing the Biggest Myth: The Unseen Heartbeat of Linux

19.1. Demystifying the Linux Kernel

In the realm of computing, the Linux kernel stands as a cornerstone, an unseen heartbeat that powers an expansive network of devices and systems. Yet, despite its critical importance and influence, the essence and inner workings of the Linux kernel remain misunderstood or obscured within the community. For many users and even seasoned developers, the kernel is often perceived as a complex, esoteric component—a black box that operates in the background while they interact with more visible aspects of the operating system. Demystifying the Linux kernel, therefore, is essential to forming a comprehensive understanding of how Linux operates and grows.

At its core, the Linux kernel is the core component of the Linux operating system, responsible for managing hardware resources and allowing software applications to communicate with the physical hardware of the computer. Unlike user-space applications, which provide interfaces for users, the kernel operates in a privileged mode, handling essential tasks such as memory management, process scheduling, and device management. This foundational role places the kernel as the bridge between user applications and the hardware, translating requests from high-level software down into the low-level operations required to access memory, storage, and processing resources.

The technical architecture of the Linux kernel is designed around the principle of modularity. This means that components of the kernel can be loaded or unloaded dynamically, allowing for flexibility in accommodating various hardware, functionalities, and features. This modular architecture supports a diverse array of devices—from desktops and servers to embedded systems (like routers, smart appliances, and IoT devices)—enabling a consistent experience across different hardware platforms. This adaptability is one reason Linux has gained traction across the globe—its ability to transcend boundaries and support various contexts has made it the operating system of choice for many tech enthusiasts and companies alike.

However, navigating through the intricacies of kernel configurations, compilation, and extensions can be daunting for newcomers. Tailoring the kernel to meet specific user needs often involves understanding how to compile the kernel from source, select necessary modules, and configure settings that facilitate optimized performance for the intended applications. For developers or system administrators, this process can yield significant benefits—an optimized kernel can lead to improved performance, enhanced security through lean configurations, and the incorporation of custom features that cater specifically to particular environments or use cases.

Updating and upgrading the Linux kernel similarly plays a vital role in maintaining system performance and security. Staying current with kernel versions ensures that devices benefit from the latest security patches, features, and bug fixes, thus enhancing stability and performance. The process of upgrading is typically straightforward on most Linux distributions, coordinating across package managers to facilitate seamless updates. This practice, however, also requires a proactive approach to manage potential compatibility issues with existing hardware and applications. Users must remain aware of changes that accompany new kernel releases, understanding how updates may impact their systems and workflows.

The vitality of the Linux kernel is further bolstered by the contributions of the community—an expansive, collaborative entity that shapes its evolution. The open-source nature of the kernel encourages users and developers to engage actively with its development, report bugs, submit patches, and propose new features. A transparent process of community-driven input allows the kernel to grow more resilient and innovative, adapting to the ongoing shifts in technology and user needs. Developers who contribute to the kernel often feel a sense of ownership and pride in their work, fostering an environment where collaboration and shared vision lead the way toward meaningful advancements.

Yet, the journey of understanding and navigating the complexities of the Linux kernel is ongoing. To fully appreciate its role, individuals must not merely view it as a technical construct but as a dynamic ecosystem shaped by contributions and innovation—a living manifestation of the open-source spirit that permeates the Linux community.

In summary, demystifying the Linux kernel is pivotal to grasping the essence of the Linux operating system as a whole. Its architecture, responsibilities, and the collaborative community driving its advancement reveal that the kernel is far more than an obscure component— it's the lifeblood of Linux, continuously evolving to meet the demands of its users and the ever-changing technological landscape. By understanding the kernel's role, features, and community contributions, users can forge a deeper connection with Linux, setting the stage for meaningful engagement with this powerful operating system. As we navigate the complexities and wonders of the Linux ecosystem, it's essential to recognize that the kernel isn't merely an unseen force— it's a vibrant, collective achievement that embodies the power of open collaboration and innovation.

19.2. Handling Kernel Panics and Debugging

In dealing with kernel panics and debugging in Linux, there is a distinct necessity to strike a balance between equipping users with the fundamental knowledge necessary for effective system management while also ensuring they have advanced techniques at their disposal for deeper troubleshooting. Understanding kernel panics— unexpected failures in the operating system's kernel that lead to system crashes—can be daunting. Yet, with the right approach and tools, users can manage and troubleshoot these challenging scenarios effectively.

A kernel panic is a critical failure that occurs when the kernel encounters an unrecoverable error, preventing the operating system from continuing to function. This situation often results in a system halt, usually accompanied by a cryptic error message displayed on the screen. These messages are often technical and can appear overwhelming; however, understanding their components is essential for effective troubleshooting.

The first step in resolving a kernel panic is to analyze the messages displayed during the event. The information presented typically includes a stack trace—a list of function calls leading to the panic —which can provide invaluable insight into the source of the issue. Key identifiers, such as the kernel version and any error codes, can also guide users towards more targeted searches, whether through documentation or community support. In many instances, the exact cause of the panic can be traced back to driver issues, faulty hardware, or misconfigurations within the system.

Upon encountering a kernel panic, one of the most effective approaches is to create a remote logging or debugging environment to capture diagnostic information. By configuring the kernel parameters to log events leading up to the panic, users can accumulate data that is invaluable in diagnosing the issue. Linux supports several options for logging, such as the Kernel Crash Dump (Kdump) facility. Kdump allows users to save the memory image of the crashed system, enabling detailed analysis post-event. Users can enable Kdump through configuration in the Grub bootloader and ensure that the right tools —such as crash utility for postmortem debugging—are installed in advance.

Additionally, utilizing a serial console can be beneficial for capturing kernel messages when a panic occurs. Through a serial connection, users can redirect kernel output, making it easier to record and analyze information directly from the boot process. This technique can be particularly useful in production environments where GUI access is limited or where remote management is preferred.

Bug tracking tools, such as GDB (GNU Debugger), can also assist in debugging kernel panics. Developers can leverage GDB to analyze the core dump generated by a panic. This process can involve cross-referencing the loaded modules and tracking down erroneous code. The integration of debugging symbols can provide additional context, enabling developers to step through code execution leading to the panic.

While all these methods contribute to efficient debugging, it's essential to emphasize preventative measures in kernel management. Regularly updating the kernel, troubleshooting drivers, and maintaining the hardware health of systems can mitigate the occurrence of kernel panics. System monitoring tools, such as Nagios or Prometheus, can help track system performance and detect irregular behavior that may precede critical failures.

The community aspect of Linux also plays a significant role in addressing kernel panics. Resources such as mailing lists, forums, and online documentation allow users to share experiences and solutions related to similar issues. Engaging actively with these communities can foster a collaborative spirit where users learn from one another's struggles and successes.

In conclusion, handling kernel panics and debugging in Linux necessitates a comprehensive understanding of the underlying issues contributing to these events. By analyzing kernel messages, utilizing crash dump facilities, and employing effective debugging tools, users can navigate the complexities of system failures. While these techniques address immediate concerns, fostering a proactive approach through system maintenance, kernel updates, and community engagement will enhance users' ability to manage and mitigate future kernel issues, ensuring a more resilient Linux environment. Embracing the collaborative nature of the Linux community further empowers users to share knowledge and solutions, reinforcing that overcoming challenges is not a solitary endeavor but a shared journey within the open-source landscape.

19.3. Customizing the Kernel

Customizing the kernel in Linux opens up a world of possibilities for users who wish to tailor their operating system to meet specific needs, optimize performance, and enhance system functionality. The kernel acts as the core of the operating system, responsible for managing hardware resources and facilitating communication between software and hardware. By customizing it, users can gain greater control over how their system operates, be it for enhanced security, improved resource management, or to support specialized applications. This subchapter explores the various aspects of customizing the kernel, from understanding the need for customization to practical steps and considerations involved in the process.

To begin with, the necessity for kernel customization arises from the diverse use cases Linux supports. Different users may require unique configurations—be it a lightweight kernel for embedded devices, a kernel optimized for high-performance computing, or a version with specific modules enabled for proprietary hardware. Customizing the kernel can help eliminate unnecessary components, reduce overhead, and improve system responsiveness. This capability is especially crucial for users in the fields of gaming, data science, and software development, where optimizing the operating system can significantly impact performance.

When customizing the kernel, the first step is to obtain the kernel source code. Linux distributions typically provide the necessary packages for downloading the kernel source through their package management system. For instance, on a Debian-based system, you can use commands like `apt-get install linux-source` to download the kernel source code to your machine. After obtaining the source, users can navigate to the directory containing the kernel's source files, which serves as the starting point for customization.

Configuring the kernel is arguably the most critical step in the customization process. Using configuration tools like `make menuconfig`, users can access a user-friendly interface to define which features, modules, and drivers should be included in their kernel build. Users can enable or disable specific functionalities based on their requirements—whether adding support for specific hardware, enabling or disabling features such as filesystems, or including kernel debugging options for development purposes. The interface allows users to choose options intuitively, limiting complexities often associated with manual configuration.

Once the configuration is set, users can proceed to compile the kernel. Compiling transforms the source code into a binary that can be executed by the operating system. This process involves executing commands such as `make` and `make modules_install`. Depending on the system's resources, kernel compilation can be time-consuming. After compilation, users will typically next install the new kernel alongside the existing one, allowing for safe testing without disrupting the current system's stability.

Upon installation, it's essential to update the bootloader configuration —an important step in the customization process. This involves modifying the GRUB configuration file (usually located in `/boot/grub/grub.cfg`) to include the new kernel. After making the necessary modifications, regenerating the GRUB configuration with commands like `update-grub` ensures that the bootloader knows about the new kernel version and allows users to select it during the boot process.

Once the new kernel is installed and the bootloader configured, users can reboot their machines to start using the customized kernel. Testing its performance and functionality is critical to ensure that all hardware components and applications work as expected. If issues arise, users can troubleshoot by revisiting the configuration settings, consulting community forums, or referring to documentation related to their specific distribution or kernel version.

The process of customizing the kernel also fosters a deeper understanding of the underlying architecture of Linux. By engaging with the source code, users become more acquainted with system behavior, interactions between software and hardware, and the intricacies of managing resources. This knowledge is especially valuable for system administrators and developers, who can use their experiences to implement optimized configurations in live environments or contribute improvements back to the broader community.

While customizing the kernel can yield fantastic benefits, certain considerations should always be kept in mind. First, it is imperative to recognize that kernel updates can affect custom settings. Each time a new version of the kernel is released, users will need to reapply custom configurations and compile the new kernel, which can be a time-consuming process. Therefore, keeping track of best practices in documentation may assist users in replicating successful configurations in future releases.

Also, thorough testing of a customized kernel is essential. Users should assess the performance of their systems in various scenarios, checking for stability and compatibility. Incorporating rollback strategies, such as retaining the previous kernel version or utilizing backup tools, ensures that users can recover quickly if any issues occur during testing.

Finally, community contributions can significantly enhance the customization experience. Engaging with online forums, mailing lists, and knowledge bases can introduce users to best practices, tips, and new ideas from others who have successfully navigated the customization process. As Linux is a community-driven environment, sharing insights and learning from one another ensures that knowledge flows freely, empowering users to achieve their individual customization goals.

In summary, customizing the kernel is a powerful feature of Linux that enables users to optimize their systems for specific needs, enhancing performance and functionality. The process begins with obtaining the source code, configuring settings, compiling the kernel, and updating the bootloader. Users must engage thoughtfully with each step, ensuring thorough testing while remaining aware of the need to adapt custom configurations for future kernel updates. Ultimately, customizing the Linux kernel provides users with an engaging journey of discovery, allowing them to gain profound insights into the workings of their operating system while fostering a sense of ownership and empowerment within the Linux community.

19.4. Kernel Updates and Upgrades

Kernel Updates and Upgrades are pivotal within the Linux operating system, playing a crucial role in maintaining performance, stability, and security. These processes ensure that systems remain robust and are equipped with the latest features and fixes, allowing both developers and users to optimize their experiences without interruption. Understanding the importance of kernel management, users can streamline their workflows while maximizing their system's capabilities.

At the heart of kernel updates is the Linux kernel's role as the core component of the operating system, responsible for managing hardware resources, executing processes, and facilitating communication between software and hardware components. As technology progresses, new hardware and software capabilities emerge, necessitating regular kernel updates to ensure compatibility. Updates help introduce essential drivers for newly released hardware, optimize performance, and accommodate improvements in existing features.

Moreover, kernel updates serve as a vital line of defense against security vulnerabilities. Cyber threats evolve constantly, and with the growing reliance on digital systems, any security loophole can leave a system exposed to potential attacks. Linux's community-driven approach to security contributions means that vulnerabilities are often identified and patched rapidly. By regularly applying kernel updates, users can protect their systems from known exploits, enhancing overall security and data integrity.

Importantly, kernel updates typically follow a structured release schedule, allowing users to stay informed about new enhancements and fixes. Each kernel version is accompanied by release notes that outline changes, improvement areas, and known issues. This transparency fosters confidence among users and organizations and allows them to plan their update strategies accordingly.

Upgrading the kernel can be approached through various methods, depending on user needs and preferences. Many Linux distributions provide package management systems that simplify kernel upgrades. For example, on a Debian-based system, users can run commands like `sudo apt update` followed by `sudo apt upgrade` to ensure that they are working with the most recent kernel version. Similarly, on Red Hat-based distributions, users can utilize `yum` or `dnf` commands to execute upgrades seamlessly.

While updating and upgrading the kernel can often be straightforward, users may face unique challenges that require careful consideration. Depending on the kernel version and the specific features of the underlying distribution, compatibility issues may arise during upgrades. To mitigate potential risks, it is prudent to back up existing kernel configurations and data before proceeding with the update. This precautionary measure allows users to revert to a previous kernel or restore settings in case any problems arise during the upgrade.

Upon successfully upgrading the kernel, users should also evaluate the system's performance and functionality. Monitoring how applications interact with the new kernel version ensures that everything operates smoothly. It is vital for users to be aware of any deprecated features or functionalities that may alter their workflows, providing them with insights into how the updated kernel impacts their systems.

Beyond the technical facets of kernel management, it is essential to recognize the community contributions to kernel updates and upgrades. Developers, system administrators, and users alike actively engage in discussions regarding kernel enhancements, security patches, and best practices for maintaining system integrity. This engagement fosters a collaborative atmosphere that not only empowers individuals but also strengthens the Linux ecosystem as a whole.

In conclusion, Kernel Updates and Upgrades are foundational processes in ensuring the Linux operating system's performance, security, and overall usability. The community-driven model supports continuous innovation and collaboration, facilitating smooth transitions into new kernel versions. By embracing a proactive approach to kernel management, users can navigate their Linux experience with confidence, effectively harnessing the power of this versatile and dynamic operating system. As Linux continues to evolve, the commitment to regular updates and upgrades will remain essential, ultimately shaping the future of technology and ensuring robust, secure environments for users around the globe.

19.5. Beyond the Kernel: Community Contributions for Future Growth

In the ever-evolving technological landscape, Linux stands as a bastion of community contributions that fuels its growth and transformation. Beyond the kernel lies a vibrant tapestry woven by the hands of developers, educators, enthusiasts, and everyday users who continually enhance, adapt, and champion the operating system. This collective effort not only impacts the Linux experience but also shapes its roadmap for the future, reaffirming the importance of collaboration in open-source software development.

Community contributions take myriad forms, from coding and bug fixes to software documentation and user support. The Linux kernel itself is a living entity, with thousands of developers actively participating in its evolution. They respond to user feedback, embrace emerging technologies, and identify vulnerabilities—all while adhering to the open-source principles that govern Linux. Each contribution reinforces a culture of innovation, empowering individuals to experiment, share ideas, and refine features collectively.

One vital aspect of fostering these contributions is the establishment of user-friendly communication channels. Platforms like GitHub, GitLab, and mailing lists enable developers to collaborate seamlessly, share proposals, and engage in discussions around code development. This collaborative spirit echoes the foundational ethos of Linux, where knowledge sharing and collective problem-solving drive advancements in the operating system.

Moreover, educational initiatives within the community encourage new contributors to engage with Linux, instilling a sense of belonging

253

and purpose. Programming workshops, mentorship programs, and hackathons aim to expand the pool of contributors, ensuring that the Linux community remains dynamic and relevant. These educational endeavors open doors for aspiring developers, allowing them to form connections with seasoned professionals and learn the intricacies of the Linux environment. This nurturing of talent translates into continued growth for Linux, as fresh perspectives and skills are infused into the ecosystem.

Linux's impact extends far beyond technical contributions; it flourishes in the algorithmic diversity and ingenuity that arise from community-driven projects. Collaborations lead to the creation of innovative solutions that address specific user needs, resulting in tools tailored to various industries—be it scientific research, graphic design, or education. Open-source projects incentivize developers to rethink traditional paradigms of software development, prioritizing user agency and customization in a way that proprietary software often cannot.

Looking ahead, the commitment to community contributions will remain crucial as users and organizations navigate the complexities of a rapidly changing technological landscape. As emerging technologies —such as artificial intelligence, blockchain, and quantum computing —continue to reshape various industries, the flexibility and adaptability of Linux will serve as critical advantages. The open-source nature of the community invites interdisciplinary collaboration across fields, fostering the cross-pollination of ideas and innovations beneficial to all.

Yet, while the future appears promising, potential challenges loom on the horizon. The continued fragmentation of distributions may pose hurdles for users, as consistency and compatibility among varying versions become increasingly critical. However, by championing collaboration, streamlining communication channels, and prioritizing a unified vision, the Linux community can mitigate such risks and remain resilient in the face of emerging obstacles.

In summary, the community contributions that extend beyond the kernel are the lifeblood of Linux's future growth and sustainability. By creating an infrastructure that supports collaboration, education, and inclusivity, the Linux community ensures that it continues to thrive as a symbol of innovation and empowerment. The legacy of Linux is inherently tied to the ongoing dedication of individuals to protect its ideals of openness, collaboration, and shared ownership. Their collective contributions reflect the spirit of open-source software—one where every voice matters, and the shared pursuit of knowledge unites individuals in shaping an exciting technological future. As we reflect on the journey thus far, the promise of Linux's evolution remains steadfast, bolstered by the unwavering commitment of its community to foster growth, secure innovation, and explore the ever-expanding possibilities of technology.

20. The Legacy of Linux: A Reflection on Impact and Influence

20.1. A Global Movement

In the realm of technology, the evolution of Linux has ignited a global movement characterized by collaboration, innovation, and accessibility. This movement transcends geographical, cultural, and economic boundaries, allowing individuals and organizations from diverse backgrounds to engage with the operating system, share knowledge, and contribute to its development. As we reflect on the impact of this movement, it becomes evident that Linux has not only transformed the way we interact with technology but has also empowered communities across the globe to harness its potential for social change and economic growth.

The journey of Linux began as a personal project by Linus Torvalds in 1991 and quickly evolved into a community-driven initiative that resonated with users dissatisfied with proprietary systems. The ethos of open source—where users have the freedom to view, modify, and distribute software—became a driving force that ignited interest in Linux worldwide. This movement cultivated a culture of collaboration and shared knowledge, attracting developers, enthusiasts, and ordinary users who recognized that they could collectively shape the future of an operating system that embraced their diverse needs.

As Linux gained traction, its adoption by governments, educational institutions, and enterprises solidified its position as a reliable and versatile platform. Countries in the Global South, in particular, have capitalized on Linux to promote technology access and digital literacy. This phenomenon is evident in initiatives that leverage Linux to establish computer labs in schools, enabling students to gain hands-on experience with computing resources that may otherwise be inaccessible due to financial constraints. By providing free and powerful tools, Linux empowers individuals to learn, innovate, and explore career paths within technology.

The economic contributions of Linux are notable, as well. By reducing the costs associated with licensing fees for software, organizations can allocate their resources to research and development, training, and other critical areas that drive innovation. Furthermore, Linux fosters the growth of local tech ecosystems through the establishment of startups and entrepreneurship initiatives in developing regions. The availability of open-source resources encourages creativity and problem-solving, enabling entrepreneurs to harness technology to address local challenges and contribute to sustainable economic growth.

Additionally, Linux's influence spans various industries, impacting technological advancements across sectors ranging from healthcare and finance to education and telecommunications. In these fields, Linux serves as the backbone for software solutions, driving efficiencies and improving performance. This pervasive integration contributes to the overall economic growth of industries reliant on advanced technologies to deliver services and products, reinforcing the global movement toward a knowledge-based economy.

As the narrative of Linux continues to unfold, its presence in pop culture reflects the broader societal shifts it embodies. Movies, television shows, and books have increasingly referenced or portrayed Linux as a symbol of rebellion against corporate control and a champion of freedom. The Tux penguin mascot has become an emblem of the open-source spirit, embodying fun, creativity, and the collaborative ethos of the Linux community. This cultural resonance serves as a reminder of Linux's influence beyond technical circles, inspiring individuals and communities to embrace its ideals.

The ongoing role of Linux in education further exemplifies its impact and contribution to societal development. As educational institutions integrate Linux-based tools into curricula, students gain access to practical skills that empower them to engage meaningfully with technology. The open-source approach nurtures a culture of exploration and collaboration, where students are encouraged to take ownership of their learning experiences. Through projects, coding competitions, and contributions to open-source initiatives, learners can enhance their capabilities and prepare for careers in technology.

Moreover, the ripple effect of Linux's influence extends to future generations of innovators. As the movement continues to grow, new users are inspired to contribute back to the community, engaging in projects that drive technological advancements while upholding the principles of open-source collaboration. This cycle perpetuates a culture of continuous learning and adaptation, positioning Linux as not only an operating system but a conduit for social change and empowerment in the digital age.

In conclusion, the global movement surrounding Linux has profoundly impacted the technological landscape, economic development, and cultural narratives. By fostering collaboration, innovation, and access to technology, Linux has empowered individuals and communities across diverse contexts to participate actively in shaping their digital futures. As we reflect on this transformative journey, it is clear that the legacy of Linux will continue to inspire future generations of creators and innovators, cementing its place as a cornerstone of the open-source movement and an agent of positive change in the world. The ongoing commitment to promoting the ideals of collaboration and accessibility will ensure that the Linux story remains dynamic, inclusive, and rich with possibilities for years to come.

20.2. Economic and Technological Contributions

In the realm of technology, Linux has had a profound impact on both economic growth and technological advancement. Its influence extends beyond mere hardware or software; it has fundamentally altered how businesses operate, how technology evolves, and how communities engage with digital resources. Understanding the economic and technological contributions of Linux is essential to appreciate its role in shaping modern ecosystems and workflows.

One of the most significant economic contributions of Linux can be traced to its cost-effectiveness. By offering an open-source alternative to expensive proprietary systems, Linux has enabled businesses of all sizes to reduce their operating costs. Startups and small businesses, in particular, benefit immensely from the zero licensing fees that come with Linux distributions. This financial flexibility allows organizations to allocate their resources more strategically toward areas such as innovation, employee training, and customer service. As these companies grow, they foster local economies, creating jobs and stimulating community development, all while being powered by Linux-based infrastructure.

Moreover, the Linux ecosystem has become a breeding ground for entrepreneurship and technological innovation. The availability of robust open-source resources encourages developers and enthusiasts to innovate and create new applications tailored to specific market needs. Startups centered around Linux-powered solutions and services have emerged in various sectors, including cloud services, data analytics, and cybersecurity. As a result, Linux has catalyzed the growth of new industries and contributed to a knowledge-driven economy that prioritizes creativity, adaptability, and efficiency.

In terms of technological advancements, Linux has played a central role in driving innovation across various fields. Its flexibility and adaptability have led to widespread adoption in sectors such as cloud computing, artificial intelligence, big data, and the Internet of Things (IoT). For instance, cloud computing platforms built on Linux have become the standard for hosting applications, providing scalability and resource allocation that was once unattainable. With major players like Amazon Web Services and Google Cloud relying heavily on Linux, it has solidified its position as the go-to infrastructure for modern cloud applications, fundamentally changing how businesses engage with technology.

Linux's influence extends beyond the corporate world and into education and research, where it has fostered innovation in teaching methodologies and collaboration among academic institutions. The ability to leverage open-source software has democratized access to advanced computing resources, enabling students to learn essential technological skills without financial barriers. Many universities and research organizations have adopted Linux-based systems to support their operations and research projects, further facilitating collaboration among researchers worldwide. The shared ethos of open-source software allows academic institutions to engage in productive partnerships, exchange knowledge, and contribute to advancements in their respective fields.

Furthermore, Linux has become a catalyst for driving community-driven innovations. The vibrant community surrounding open-source projects has accelerated the pace of technological progress and improvement. Developers from diverse backgrounds collaborate across borders, contributing code, refining features, and developing new applications. This collaborative effort advances existing technologies and inspires new ideas and solutions, enriching the wider tech ecosystem. The continued growth and evolution of open-source projects demonstrate the potential for collective contributions to fuel creativity and innovation for a better future.

Linux has also made significant contributions to the cultural and social dimensions of technology. Its roots in the principles of collaboration and transparency have inspired communities to embrace these values actively. By promoting inclusive practices, Linux encourages diverse voices to engage in the development process, fostering a climate of creativity that reaches beyond technology alone. This cultural shift encourages organizations to prioritize community engagement, enabling positive changes that extend into society, such as advocating for digital rights and accessibility.

As we look toward the future, it is essential to acknowledge that the economic and technological contributions of Linux remain a dynamic narrative woven into the fabric of contemporary life. The ongoing excitement surrounding emerging technologies signals that Linux will continue to drive economic growth by empowering innovation and productivity across industries. By upholding the principles of collaboration, adaptability, and inclusivity, Linux can shape the evolution of technology while continuing to inspire future generations who will contribute to its rich legacy.

In conclusion, the economic and technological contributions of Linux are profound and far-reaching. By providing accessible alternatives to costly proprietary solutions, fostering entrepreneurship, and facilitating innovation, Linux emerges as a transformational force shaping the modern world. The collective momentum generated by the Linux community provides an exciting glimpse into a future where technology is not only about efficiency and profitability but also about collaboration, inclusivity, and social change. These contributions underscore the importance of Linux within the broader narrative of technological advancements and economic growth, reinforcing its status as an essential player in shaping the digital landscape.

20.3. Linux in Pop Culture

In the ever-evolving realm of technology, few subjects gleam with the innovation and intrigue akin to the Linux operating system. A beguiling labyrinth that has enchanted, and at times confounded, minds of tech enthusiasts, researchers, and developers alike, Linux is more than just software—it's a legacy. Whether discovered through its sprawling servers, dazzling desktops, or innovative device infrastructure, Linux is a tapestry of code, culture, and curiosity. Despite the cloak of technical jargon, at its core, Linux embodies a philosophy of collaboration and freedom that beckons the inquisitive spirit to explore deeper.

Join me, Diane B. Brown, as we embark on an explosive journey through the hidden alleys of Linux trivia, where each fragment of myth and fact intertwines to tell the grand tale of an operating system that changed the course of technology. We'll delve into the historical roots sprouting from Linus Torvalds' ambitious vision, traverse the technological evolutions that revolutionized the industry, and bash through the myths clouding Linux's true essence.

With each page, expect to dissolve misconceptions and illuminate the lesser-known facets of Linux. Whether you're a seasoned system administrator or a curious newcomer, there's a treasure trove of knowledge awaiting within these covers. Buckle up for an enthralling expedition where insight meets intrigue, as we traverse the nuances of this remarkable technology.

Throughout this exploration, we will uncover the global impact of Linux, leading us to understand its role as not just an operating system but also a significant cultural phenomenon. From its use as the backbone of high-performance computing to its embrace in educational institutions, Linux stands as an embodiment of collaborative effort, shining brightly in the rapidly changing technological landscape.

Linux's prominence in pop culture is indeed captivating. From references in films and television shows to its use as a rallying point for freelance developers, it has become a symbol of rebellion against corporate domination in tech. The adorable penguin mascot, Tux, embodies this spirit, serving as a whimsical yet impactful representation of the community behind Linux.

Linux is not just confined to the realm of programmers and tech-savvy individuals; it has permeated educational systems, helping foster the next generation of innovators. Schools and universities are increasingly adopting Linux to prepare students for non-proprietary thinking in an era of cloud computing and technological complexity. We will reflect upon the impact of this in shaping methodologies and tools that increasingly rely on collaboration and communal contributions.

In the backdrop of these developments, we are reminded that the legacy of Linux is a dynamic narrative firmly rooted in the ideals of accessibility and participation. The faces behind this movement—developers, educators, and everyday users—have played pivotal roles in fostering a culture of innovation that transcends geographical and cultural boundaries.

As we journey through the chapters, we will not only glean insights from the past but also explore the horizons of what is yet to come. Linux's integration into emerging technologies like AI and machine learning promises to usher in new realms of potential for connected devices, cloud computing, and data-driven decision-making.

The ultimate aim of this book is to inspire future generations to embrace the legacy of Linux, to engage with it, and contribute to its ever-evolving nature. With an eye toward frank discussions on sustainability, community engagement, and techniques for nurturing an inclusive technological ecosystem, this book seeks to serve as both a rich resource and a rallying cry for the continued exploration of Linux, open-source principles, and the remarkable journey that has ensued.

Let us dive into the pages ahead, unraveling the exciting tales of Linux and its monumental impact—on technology, culture, education, and our collective future.

20.4. Educational Endeavors and Innovations

In the ever-evolving landscape of technology and education, the impact of Linux has grown tremendously, fundamentally shaping tools and methodologies within academic institutions. With its open-source nature and commitment to accessibility, Linux not only democratizes technology but also provides an invaluable resource to educators and students alike. This subchapter will explore the various ways in which Linux is integrated into educational endeavors and how it sparks innovations that foster growth and learning opportunities.

Linux's flexibility and adaptability make it a fitting platform for educational settings. Institutions have embraced Linux not merely for its cost-effectiveness—eliminating licensing fees associated with proprietary operating systems—but also for its collaborative spirit, which aligns closely with the values of learning and knowledge sharing. As educational institutions face budget constraints, Linux allows them to provide robust computing resources without compromising on quality or functionality. Through customized Linux distributions, schools can tailor the operating experience to cater to different subjects, enhancing student engagement and facilitating a deeper understanding of technology.

The multitude of open-source educational applications available on Linux is a significant factor in its integration into the classroom. Tools like LibreOffice for document creation, GIMP for graphic design, and Blender for 3D modeling are only a fraction of the suite of applications that Linux offers, enhancing the curriculum across various subjects. Students learn to navigate rich, powerful tools that foster problem-solving and creativity, preparing them to engage effectively with technological challenges in the future.

Linux also fosters an innovative environment that inspires educators to experiment with teaching methodologies. The command line interface (CLI) and scripting of Linux provide teachers with opportunities to teach computer science and programming concepts in a practical manner. Students can delve into exciting projects using languages like Python or C, all promoted through a Linux-based environment. Coding competitions, workshops, and collaborative projects encourage a culture of exploration, increasing student participation and making learning fun.

Moreover, training students to engage in open-source projects creates an invaluable connection between education and real-world applications. Initiatives like Google Summer of Code or local hackathons offer students platforms where they can contribute to existing projects, sharpen their technical skills, and interact with established developers. Through participation in open-source projects, students gain insights into collaborative development processes and participate in a community that encourages knowledge sharing, mentorship, and cross-functional skills.

In addition to traditionally structured education, Linux emerges as a powerful avenue for informal learning. Approximately 90% of tech startups utilize open-source technologies, reinforcing the necessity for students to become familiar with Linux and its tools. By equipping students with the knowledge and skills to navigate Linux environments, educators prepare learners for careers in technology that increasingly prioritize open standards and platforms.

As we look toward the future, the role of Linux in education will likely expand and evolve, adapting to the demands of emerging technology trends. The integration of artificial intelligence, big data, and cloud computing into educational frameworks will accentuate the importance of Linux as a platform that facilitates learning and discovery in these critical areas. Providing students with access to cutting-edge technologies while using Linux-based tools inspires them to explore new concepts, experiment, and contribute to shaping the future.

In conclusion, Linux's integration into educational endeavors represents a transformative force, catalyzing growth, collaboration, and innovation among students and educators alike. By providing equitable access to technology, fostering creativity, and embracing open-source principles, Linux empowers individuals to explore their interests and develop critical skills necessary for success in today's digital landscape. As we continue to nurture the next generation of innovators, the legacy of Linux will remain intertwined with technology education, inspiring learners to harness creativity and collaborate toward meaningful solutions that address pressing challenges in society.

As we inspire future generations, it is essential to reiterate the values of collaboration, inclusivity, and adaptability that Linux embodies. By encouraging students to embrace the principles of open-source software, we empower them to become active participants in shaping their learning experiences and contributing to the evolving landscape of technology. The continued presence of Linux in education ensures its legacy lives on—inspiring future innovators to explore, create, and contribute to a diverse and interconnected world of technology.

20.5. Inspiring Future Generations

In the dynamic realm of technology, motivating future generations to engage with the principles, practices, and potential of Linux presents a vital opportunity to ensure the continued growth and success of the open-source movement. As we reflect on the remarkable journey of

Linux, which began as a collaborative project and has since escalated into a robust ecosystem that empowers individuals and organizations around the globe, it becomes evident that the involvement of passionate, innovative thinkers is crucial for fostering a brighter future.

Inspiring future generations starts with education and awareness about the vast possibilities that Linux presents. Educational institutions play a pivotal role in this endeavor by incorporating Linux-centric curricula that emphasize hands-on experience, critical thinking, and problem-solving. By teaching students not only how to use Linux but also how to contribute to its development, these programs cultivate a mindset where learners feel empowered to shape the technology that surrounds them. For instance, computer science courses that focus on collaborative open-source projects instill a sense of ownership and responsibility, encouraging students to actively participate in the Linux community.

Beyond formal education, grassroots initiatives that promote Linux among youth are gaining momentum. Clubs, summer coding camps, and community workshops provide supportive environments where students can explore Linux-based technologies together. By fostering peer-to-peer networks, these initiatives promote collaboration and establish mentorship relationships where experienced users guide newcomers. Hands-on projects, such as developing applications or participating in hackathons, provide exhilarating experiences that spark enthusiasm and creativity in young minds.

The stories of individuals who have transformed their careers and lives through Linux serve as inspiration for those coming behind them. Featuring successful Linux advocates and contributors from diverse backgrounds can motivate students and newcomers to consider pursuing their own pathways in technology. By showcasing inclusive role models who have made an impact within the Linux ecosystem, we can foster a sense of belonging and representation in this community—an essential element for nurturing talent from all walks of life.

Central to inspiring future generations is the principle of engagement in the growth of collaborative organizations and open-source projects. Encouraging young individuals to take part in initiatives such as Google Summer of Code or outreach programs—where participants can connect directly with existing projects—heightens their understanding of real-world software development processes. By diving into projects that resonate with their interests and passions, students can gain hands-on experience while simultaneously contributing to the communities they admire.

Emphasizing the significance of ethical technology practices also broadens the narrative surrounding Linux for young innovators. As discussions around data privacy, security, and ethical software design continue to intensify, instilling a sense of responsibility within future generations becomes indispensable. Linux's commitment to open-source principles inherently aligns with ethical considerations, emphasizing values such as transparency and user agency. By cultivating a philosophy that prioritizes ethical technology and community engagement, we can empower young innovators to navigate the complexities of the digital age with confidence and integrity.

Moreover, as technology advances, emerging fields such as artificial intelligence, machine learning, and Internet of Things (IoT) present ample opportunities for the Linux community to continue to flourish. Engaging students with projects that leverage these technologies within Linux environments fosters an understanding of their implications for society. As young technologists explore these domains, they will be better equipped to address the challenges posed by rapid advancements while harnessing their potential for societal benefit.

The legacy of Linux thrives on contributions from passionate and engaged individuals, reinforcing the notion that every voice matters. By encouraging future generations to embrace their creativity, curiosity, and collaborative spirit, we set the stage for a vibrant open-source community that continues to adapt and evolve. Engaging with Linux is not merely an individual journey; it is a collective adventure that holds the promise of shaping the technological landscape for future generations.

In conclusion, inspiring future generations to engage with Linux and empower them to become active contributors to the open-source movement is essential for perpetuating the legacy of innovation and collaboration. By providing robust educational frameworks, fostering inclusive communities, and instilling a sense of responsibility in ethical technology practices, we can cultivate an environment where creativity thrives. As we reflect on Linux's remarkable journey and the impact it has made on computing, we must recognize that our collective future hinges on the ideas, efforts, and passions of the next wave of innovators eager to explore the boundless potential that Linux offers. Together, we can continue to sew the fabric of collaboration and creativity, ensuring that Linux remains a beacon of opportunity and empowerment for all.

www.ingramcontent.com/pod-product-compliance
Lightning Source LLC
LaVergne TN
LVHW051439050326
832903LV00030BD/3162